CROSS LAMINATED TIMBER

A DESIGN-STAGE PRIMER
NIC CRAWLEY

RIBA Publishing

© RIBA Publishing, 2021

Published by RIBA Publishing, 66 Portland Place, London, W1B 1AD

ISBN 978 1 85946 922 4

The right of Nic Crawley to be identified as the Author of this Work has been asserted in accordance with the Copyright, Designs and Patents Act 1988 sections 77 and 78.

All rights reserved. No part of this publication may be reproduced, stored in a retrieval system, or transmitted, in any form or by any means, electronic, mechanical, photocopying, recording or otherwise, without prior permission of the copyright owner.

British Library Cataloguing-in-Publication Data
A catalogue record for this book is available from the British Library.

Commissioning Editor: Ginny Mills
Assistant Editor: Clare Holloway
Production: Sarah-Louise Deazley
Designed by Kneath Associates
Typeset by Fakenham Prepress Solutions
Printed and bound by Short Run Press Ltd, Exeter
Cover image: Rob Parrish
Endpaper image: Rosie Ashbourne

While every effort has been made to check the accuracy and quality of the information given in this publication, neither the Author nor the Publisher accept any responsibility for the subsequent use of this information, for any errors or omissions that it may contain, or for any misunderstandings arising from it.

www.ribapublishing.com

CONTENTS

About the author · IV
Acknowledgements · V
Introduction · 1

1 Manufacturing and processing · 7
2 Applications and use · 17
3 Context · 29
4 Feasibility and initial considerations · 35
5 Visual aspects · 43
6 Cost and value · 53
7 Planning and social issues · 63
8 Design and procurement · 69
9 Engineering aspects · 83
10 Refurbished structures · 93
11 Safety · 101
12 Buildability and assembly · 111
13 The international outlook · 121
14 Flexibility, use and life cycle issues · 129
15 Client issues · 141

CASE STUDIES:

Haus Gables, Atlanta, USA · 149
The Fitzroy, Falmouth, UK · 159
Fenner Hall, Student Residences, Canberra, Australia · 167
Ermine Street Church Academy, Huntingdon, UK · 173
Triodos Bank Office Building, Driebergen-Rijsenburg,
    The Netherlands · 179
6 Orsman Road, London, UK · 185

Conclusion: The way ahead · 191

APPENDICES:

CLT panel characteristics · 196
CLT panel surface quality · 197

Notes · 198
Index · 203
Image credits · 206

ABOUT THE AUTHOR

Nic Crawley is an architect with over 20 years' diverse cross-sector project experience. As the former Head of Sustainability at Allford Hall Monaghan Morris (AHMM), Nic helped establish the practice's award-winning sustainability agenda. He now works within the technical design group at AHMM, researching innovative architecture and promoting better ways of working and building.

ACKNOWLEDGEMENTS

It has been an absolute pleasure engaging with the many specialists, engineers, suppliers, contractors and other collaborators who have helped evolve our understanding of CLT's potential by generously sharing their time, knowledge and invaluable experience (and answering my many questions). These include all those from the UK, Europe and beyond who have provided insight into the many inspiring case studies and information included. There's insufficient space to credit each fully in turn but readers should understand that there is a wealth of experience available to help better consider and deliver CLT buildings. Each of these projects has been supported by a diverse team, with their own expertise.

The chapter author contributors are innovators and leaders in their fields and I would have liked to provide more space for them to share their experience. Do look them up, as they may be able to help support your ambitions.

I would also like to thank the project teams, both external and internal, as well as clients and collaborators, who have helped Allford Hall Monaghan Morris (AHMM) to deliver some great CLT buildings, as well as those who continue to explore better ways of building (there are plenty more brilliant buildings on the drawing board). Such work is one of the great joys of being part of such a future-facing practice.

Colleagues from across AHMM have supported the evolution and production of this book, from the outset to completion. Particular thanks are due to Rosie Ashbourne for ensuring that the images came together, as well as making a few.

Many photographers have generously allowed the use of their insightful and beautiful images, in particular Rob Parrish. Do seek out their credits, which are included at the back of this book.

The editing and production staff at RIBA Publishing and their supporting team have provided guidance and encouragement throughout.

This book is dedicated to my mother, and to her mother, both of whom understood the vital need for better thinking and doing.

INTRODUCTION

Cross laminated timber (CLT) is a relatively new material developed in the 1990s in central Europe where it is now well established in use. Referred to beyond the UK as crosslam, x-lam, jumbo ply or tilt-up timber, CLT is an engineered mass timber product manufactured from alternating direction layers (lamella) of small section timber, adhesive bonded and pressed to form large format, solid panels that are factory CNC machined with extremely high precision.

CROSS LAMINATED TIMBER

FIG 0.0 (chapter opener)

Standardised CLT residential modules, manufactured remotely and finished in a near-site facility, are tiered and cantilevered to make use of the material's inherent strengths at Dyson's Institute of Engineering and Technology, by WilkinsonEyre (2019-20).

CLT use is not widely understood in English-speaking markets although interest and application is growing rapidly. CLT structures in the UK, nearly all of which have been built in the last decade, represent around 1 in 40,000 of total UK dwellings and non-residential buildings – as such, very few professionals have experience in their design, procurement and construction. This differential is even greater in North America and Australia where fewer CLT structures have been developed to date.

We face significant present-day and future challenges, whatever our project roles, wherever they may be in the world and future material choices will involve greater consideration and scrutiny than ever before. Step-change solutions are required; we cannot be satisfied with making things just a bit better. We need to reconsider our approach to big ticket issues: reconsidering what we put in the ground, how and what we build above the ground, increasing urban densities, improving the quality and speed of construction, better addressing safety and wellbeing, slashing embodied carbon and energy impacts all while anticipating the expectations of future users of buildings, and absolutely critically, the future valuation of built assets.

This exciting and versatile material offers huge potential to make a positive contribution to our architecture, buildings and cities, creating additional options for developers, designers and teams with the potential to add value on many fronts, reducing risks and increasing design flexibility for those interested in building smarter.

BACKGROUND TO THIS BOOK

This publication began as an internal research project undertaken at Allford Hall Monaghan Morris (AHMM) into the use and application of CLT following very positive cross-sector experiences using the material. Being readily available, affordable, lightweight, easy to work and the only mainstream building material that grows naturally, timber has been used throughout history. It is generally considered a traditional building material rather than a modern one, but not as permanent as stone, steel or concrete or as flexible in its application.

Over the course of our work and research, we have investigated a range of historic and contemporary timber precedents. Three buildings stand out in contrast to mainstream assumptions about the apparent impermanence, inflexibility or performance limitations of building with wood.

Durability: Visiting Todaiji (the Great Eastern Temple complex) at Nara, Japan, visitors are struck by not only the scale of the Daibutsuden (Great Buddha Hall), it remains one of the world's largest timber buildings, but also the age of it – well over 300 years old **(Figure 0.1)**. Nearby, the western precinct of the Horyuji temple is home to the world's oldest timber structures that includes a pagoda with a central column protected by the built form, from a single tree felled around 600AD – over 1,400 years ago.

FIG 0.1

Reconstructed around 1692, the gargantuan Daibutsuden hall of Todaiji has survived well over 300 years in a zone of seismic activity.

INTRODUCTION

FIG 0.2
MIT Building 20, perhaps the most successful post-war 'temporary' building, being reduced to firewood during demolition in 1988 after 55 years of use.

Flexibility: Building 20 at Massachusetts Institute of Technology (MIT), Cambridge, Massachusetts, USA **(Figure 0.2)** was a temporary post-war wooden structure that became a phenomenon, home to some of the most important scientific minds and work of the 20th century, earning the nickname the 'Magical Incubator'. This was due in no small part to the building's inherent flexibility and ability to endure as a truly hackable space – a structure that occupants were able to modify to suit their particular, different and changing needs and even individual projects or experiments.[1]

Performance: Research visits to high performance buildings in Austria uncovered a new breed of structures: exotic forms of contemporary engineered timber of which the Messe Wels by PAUAT Architekten (2007) is typical **(Figure 0.3)**. This exhibition centre displays bold use of predominantly timber construction with suspended CLT slabs and unprecedented open plan circulation and exhibition areas, creating a large commercial building truly fit for the future.

Whether illustrating durability, flexibility or high performance in operation, the use of timber in each of these buildings also delights, whether intellectually or visually (or both), creating quite extraordinary spaces from an ordinary material.

3

FIG 0.3

Entrance foyer of Messe Wels, suspended CLT slabs and long span timber hybrid structures form high impact open plan commercial spaces.

Through project work and numerous discussions across internal and external teams, it became obvious that CLT use is not widely understood and that important and high consequence decisions are frequently made based upon incomplete information or incorrect assumptions. With many precedents and much of the literature published to date being beyond the reach of English-speaking teams, this book is an attempt to share experience and knowledge to better inform future decision making. In doing so, it will build upon recent UK experience in particular which is deemed to be exemplary with Hermann Kaufmann (an Austrian architect pioneering the contemporary application of timber and one of the best known advocates and champions of CLT use) recently declaring that 'London is the global capital of CLT building'.[2]

FORM OF THIS BOOK

This book introduces key themes and design considerations, supported by illustrated case studies, either short snapshots highlighting specific issues or longer descriptions expanding upon multiple points of interest. Contributions from other project team members are included to explain

INTRODUCTION

specialist areas of importance such as costs and value or the potential for engineering solutions and existing structures.

- The first part of the book introduces CLT, describing the production from forest to finished building, as well as how the material may be used, emerging patterns of adoption and some further context.
- The second part outlines the key aspects design teams should consider when thinking about using the material, exploring relevant issues from feasibility to early design and procurement.
- The third part considers more detailed issues including safety and fire issues, refurbishment potential and buildability, as well as views and examples from North America and Australia.
- The fourth part addresses issues around CLT and perception, life cycle issues and possible directions for the development and use of the material.
- In the final part of the book, extended illustrated case studies consider a number of the key issues surrounding building with CLT, and the concluding chapter looks ahead to consider the future of CLT and its applications.

As designers, decision makers and constructors, we are faced with a once-in-a-lifetime opportunity to better understand and apply an exciting new material that offers much potential to address contemporary issues. There are however important differences and significant challenges around the use of CLT that demand different approaches and application to that of other more familiar forms of construction. These diverse opportunities and challenges are not always widely acknowledged or understood and it is hoped that this book will both inspire and inform readers, whatever their project roles or experience, as we continue to explore better ways of building.

CHAPTER 1
MANUFACTURING AND PROCESSING

CLT was developed to add value to a plentiful supply of relatively low grade, fast-growing commercially farmed whitewood in Central Europe, predominantly Norway Spruce (*Picea abies*) as **Figure 1.1**. Other coniferous softwoods are utilised as available. North American species include the more durable Douglas Fir/Oregon Pine (*Pseudotsuga menziesii*) and in Australia, Radiata (or Monterey) Pine (*Pinus radiata*).

CROSS LAMINATED TIMBER

FIG 1.0 (chapter opener)

Automated finger jointing machine processing lamella boards.

FIG 1.1

An Austrian spruce forest. Large, medium-to-fast-growing trees reach 35–60m in height over 20–50 years.

FIG 1.2

Harvesting is heavily mechanised with trunks stripped and cut to length before being transported to a mill as 'roundwood'.

FIG 1.3

Dimensioned boards sorted by grade.

CLT factories are typically located close to sawmills. Turning trees into dimensioned and usable boards results in some fibre loss c. 40%, as sawdust and chippings, most of which is used locally for other processes. Timber used is typically PEFC or FSC certified so specifiers may be assured that sources and the supply chain are well managed (**Figure 1.2**).

Boards are sawn, graded and selected depending upon their position within the log section, for resultant strength, stability and surface quality. **Figure 1.3** illustrates sawn boards being presented for grading.

Timber is hygroscopic so the reduction and control of bound moisture to around 12% moisture content (MC)[1] is critical to ensure dimensional stability and tight tolerances **(see Figure 1.4)**. Fungal growth and degradation is a risk in use above 20% MC but not below.[2] Dry timber is also stronger, lighter,

FIG 1.4

A commercial convective kiln for artificially drying timber boards.

easier to handle, transport and work, a better substrate for adhesives and at lower risk from pest or insect degradation.

PANEL MANUFACTURING

Controlled factory environments

Off-site manufacturing can often be a little underwhelming, with workers in wellington boots using old fashioned processes in draughty sheds. CLT production is more akin to modern vehicle assembly with the flow of materials along a high-speed production line finely tuned with tightly integrated processes **(Figure 1.5)**. Factories are typically described in terms of annual output (m^3 per annum) and manufacturers typically offer tours with videos online showing various processes in further detail.

Finger jointing, cutting and planing

Defects such as splits or larger knots are cut from sorted boards. The resultant cut ends are finger jointed: spliced, adhered and cured. Such sawtoothed joints may be visible on a finished panel. Boards are then finely planed to ensure dimensional tolerances are acceptable and to optimise surface bonding potential.

Layup: outer layer

This first layer (lamella) will form the outer surface of any panel. Board orientation may be longitudinal (for longer spanning floor slabs or vertical

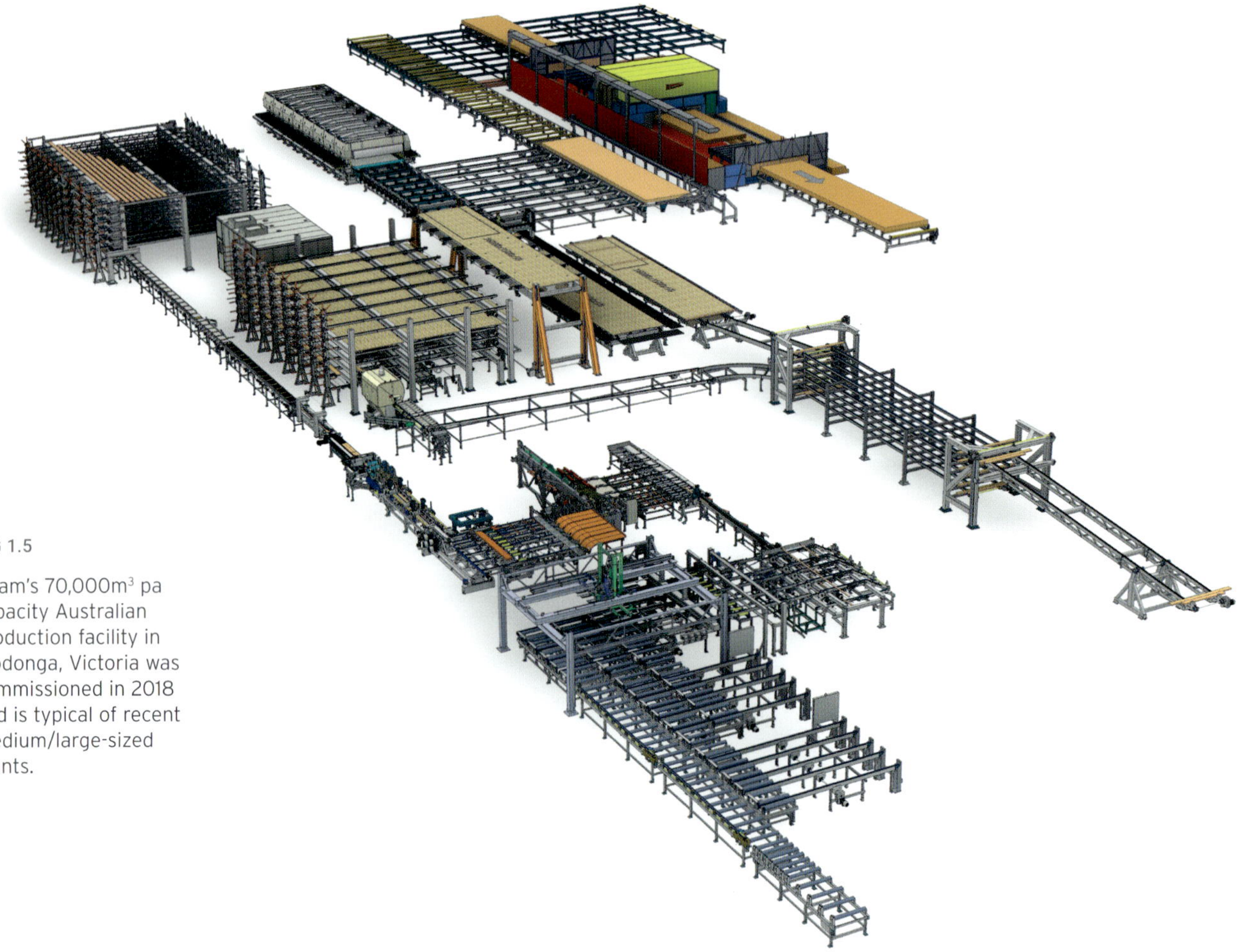

CROSS LAMINATED TIMBER

FIG 1.5

XLam's 70,000m³ pa capacity Australian production facility in Wodonga, Victoria was commissioned in 2018 and is typical of recent medium/large-sized plants.

FIG 1.6

Billet layup (the billet is the CLT 'blank', pressed and cured before processing).

CHAPTER 1 MANUFACTURING AND PROCESSING

shafts, as **Figure 1.6**) or latitudinal (for shorter or cross-direction storey height wall panels). Cut boards are positioned on a movable flatbed by automated chain belts or vacuum lifts.

Layup: adhesive application

Adhesive is applied over the entire surface at approx. 0.1mm thick (typically comprising around 0.6% of panel weight) as **Figure 1.7**. The most common adhesive is an environmentally friendly single component polyurethane (PUR) adhesive that is free of solvents, VOCs and formaldehyde (no off-gassing) that cures quickly in air when activated by the moisture in dried timber (termed cold setting).[3] Alternatives such as melamine urea formaldehyde (MUF) offer differing fire performance and may be set using microwaves when pressing.

Layup: subsequent layers

Subsequent layers are positioned promptly using vacuum lifting devices, as **Figure 1.8**. Board direction alternates 90 degrees so the timber grain direction above and below is always perpendicular. This transverse

FIG 1.7

CNC controlled adhesive application to lamella surface. Some manufacturers may side bond boards for additional stability.

FIG 1.8

Subsequent layers being placed. Panels are typically comprised of odd numbers of lamella for optimum stability.

CROSS LAMINATED TIMBER

FIG 1.9

Hydraulic press providing front and side pressure. Panels may be pressed for up to 30 minutes before adhesive is sufficiently cured.

arrangement of adjacent lamella increases panel stability and load-bearing capability considerably and minimises swelling and shrinkage to negligible levels by distributing the along-the-grain strength in both directions.[4]

Pressing and curing

The layered billet and bed is moved into a press. Mechanical presses impose high pressure loads (up to $0.8N/mm^2$) and some allow control over side and front/back pressure to ensure that boards are closely packed, minimising gaps (as **Figure 1.9**). Vacuum presses are available and can offer greater flexibility, including the potential for forming curved panels, but are less well suited to high capacity production.

Pressed panels

Pressed panels are trimmed to size by removing irregular edges (**Figure 1.10**) and may then be processed further or, infrequently, shipped directly to a customer. Composite spruce panels have a density of around $480kg/m^3$ and can be readily worked using traditional tools.[5] Further details of typical panel characteristics can be found in the appendix.

PANEL PROCESSING

Whereas panel production is an additive process (built up from boards, in layers), the processing aspect is subtractive (machining away material) so efficiencies in the first process – careful planning, optimum setting out – lead to savings in the second in terms of time, material wastage and handling efficiencies.

FIG 1.10

Billets are sized slightly larger than required panels to enable edge trimming once adhesives have cured.

CHAPTER 1 **MANUFACTURING AND PROCESSING**

CNC cutting

Processing is typically undertaken in the source factory using a CNC router moving over the panel as **Figure 1.11**.[6] Multi-axis machines allow more complex shape-forming with moving tools to cut, drill, trim or rout in different directions simultaneously.

Smaller apertures are cut out from panels (as **Figure 1.12**). Elements may be partially cut and temporarily left in place to provide stability during transport and erection or to provide cost-effective and simple temporary balustrade protection until they are removed as windows are installed on site.

Processing capabilities can vary. The following types of tools and cuts are common to many manufacturers:

FIG 1.11

CNC cutting machine. Each panel is processed in a single session, typically from one side (the upper surface).

Rebated panel edges (**Figure 1.13**) allow lapped or staggered panel joints, potentially improving fire and acoustic performance, air tightness and stability over butt joints.

FIG 1.12

Window or door aperture – internal corners can be routed square if required.

FIG 1.13

Rebate or stepped panel joints or apertures.

13

CROSS LAMINATED TIMBER

Slots (by circular tools or chainsaw as **Figure 1.14**) may be used for biscuit joints between panels, service runs or accommodating secondary elements such as brackets or lintels.

FIG 1.14
Cutting channels/slots.

FIG 1.15
Circular apertures.

FIG 1.16
Inclined circular saw.

Circular cuts (as **Figure 1.15**) are typically used for service penetrations (with sufficient tolerance for fire stopping, insulation etc).

Angle cuts may be required to accommodate irregular geometry and are likely made by circular saws (as **Figure 1.16**).

14

Drilling into panel edges (along the lamella planes) may be utilised for concealed service routing for small services, wiring etc. Surface routing to accommodate service elements flush with the panel outer face is dependent upon outer layer direction and performance to avoid compromising load-bearing/spanning capacity. Limiting all cutting/routing to a single side of a panel avoids the need to turn panels over which would reduce production efficiencies.

Labelling and quality assurance

Visual grade panels will be machine sanded; others may not be. Finished panels are QA labelled individually, as the example in **Figure 1.17**. Information varies by jurisdiction. In Europe, conformity requirements are defined by the harmonised standard BS EN 13017-1[7] and this is reflected in the CE marking applied.

FIG 1.17

Panel identification and QA labelling.

Panel transport from factory

If sites are remote, panels will be protected to maintain the necessary moisture content, either covered or wrapped on the truck bed or shrink wrapped, with factory offcuts used as dunnage to ensure stability.

Transport typically limits panel size. Many manufacturers offer larger panel sizes than can be readily transported by road, possibly up to 16-20m (maximum widths are usually around 3m). For the UK, panels longer than 13.5m may require non-standard vehicles or escorts and are therefore typically avoided.

Production and delivery is typically 'as required' (i.e. just-in-time), and installation sequencing is typically considered in advance to minimise site handling, whether panels are off-loaded to a storage area or installed directly from the trailer. BIM may assist planning this process, helping avoid the time and risk of double handling.

CHAPTER 2
APPLICATIONS AND USE

CLT is a material to be explored creatively, rather than a product that must be used or applied in a specific manner or as other materials. This chapter illustrates applications of the material to date, including notable milestone projects, but the potential for future use is exciting and wide open.

Rather than focusing on specific typologies, case studies (whether longer or shorter snapshots) range from community buildings to blue-chip HQs, schools to university buildings and single-family dwellings to multi-storey housing illustrating how a smarter way of building may be applied with a diverse (and expanding) range of structural approaches.

FIG 2.0 (chapter opener)

Alconbury Weald Club Building, Huntingdon, UK by AHMM (2015). CLT panels were used for floors and internal and external walls, including lift shafts and stairs (as the cover illustration to this book), utilised in conjunction with downstand glulam beams and columns to achieve longer spans and generous internal volumes as well as protective external cantilevers. (CLT was also used for elements such as reception desks).

PURE CLT

Pure (or full) CLT forms involves using the material as the principal superstructure element, including cores, walls and floors. Beyond single-storey and very low-rise structures where load paths and transfers are readily resolved, multi-storey CLT structures may take various forms. Common to most is the raising of panels above ground level, usually with reinforced concrete plinths or basement boxes that typically accommodate alternative functions to the lowest levels as well as efficiently accommodating any load transfers required. In lifting timber elements away from moisture, connection details to concrete elements become significant, having to resist other forces than just timber to timber connections and presenting interface issues in terms of differing tolerances and accuracy in setting out.

Cellular forms

Cellular, or honeycomb, structural forms suit smaller spans and domestic scale spaces and are common for residential uses. Storey height walls typically support floor panels running over with subsequent storeys built off these slabs (termed 'platform construction'). Such arrangements may use more timber than strictly necessary but can provide redundancy and safety because of the cellular nature of the structural system, and can enable a single contractor to rapidly complete much of the above ground construction, including most of an envelope.

Crosswall forms

Typically suited to larger spaces where CLT may span in a single direction between vertical bearing elements, this form enables room widths of up to 7m (although slabs become less efficient for spans above around 5.5–6.0m).

Examine the case studies for The Fitzroy or for Ermine Street Church Academy as examples of crosswall use where CLT walls are arranged perpendicularly to linear corridors allowing an open perimeter facade without structural interruption.

HYBRID FORMS

CLT is increasingly used in combination with other structural materials. To overcome the span limitations of panels, hybrid forms are well suited to larger spaces such as commercial buildings and may utilise engineered timber, such as glue-laminated (glulam) beams or columns throughout or incorporate non-timber elements such as steel or concrete.

The advantages of such an approach are clear: leveraging the best qualities of different materials to realise structures (and advantages) that would otherwise not be possible as well as introducing CLT elements such

CHAPTER 2 **APPLICATIONS AND USE**

CASE STUDY EXAMPLES

FIG 2.1 & 2.2

Murray Grove, Hackney, London, UK by Waugh Thistleton Architects (2008) was a British, European and global first: the first tall residential building built from CLT. The cellular form including walls, floors, cores and shafts was erected without a tower crane by a team of four in 27 days (over a nine-week period). Despite all CLT being ultimately concealed, this building was hugely influential globally, not least as a demonstration that CLT could deliver a high-density block of dwellings for a cost that was viable for a commercially minded private house builder client.

as floor panels into schemes where an entirely timber structure might be felt to be too unusual or challenging for some members of the project team.

Timber hybrids

CLT and glulam beams and/or columns result in structures that behave in consistent ways and present a unified aesthetic. Connection design and protection can become a significant issue for larger buildings but there are increasing numbers of large-scale projects utilising this approach.

Downstand beams can however pose challenges, not least in restricting internal heights and servicing arrangements. Post-and-slab arrangements may avoid this through the provision of flat soffit – a composition that typically limits the structural grid.

CASE STUDY EXAMPLES

FIG 2.3

Sky's Believe in Better Building, London, UK by Arup Associates (2014) was a pioneering commercial timber hybrid taken to site within three months and completed within twelve months by engaging with the contractor from the outset. Maximum use was made of pre-manufactured elements and wet trades were eliminated with CLT floors slabs combined with glulam beams and columns. Much timber is exposed within the open plan interior of this flagship building while going beyond net zero embodied CO_2 emissions. Another precedent on the same campus is de Rijke Marsh Morgan Architects' Sky Health & Fitness Centre, completed in 2015 (with the glulam and CLT structure fully erected over 25 days in winter).

Other hybrid forms

Combining CLT and other (non-timber) materials is becoming increasingly common. The earliest hybrid proposals may have incorporated a concrete stability core or steel elements for load transfers and the use of concrete or screed toppings to add mass to floor slabs is not uncommon in Europe (aiding acoustic and fire performance and limiting 'bounce'). More recently,

CHAPTER 2 **APPLICATIONS AND USE**

a broader range of solutions are being considered, using timber and/or steel and concrete in diverse combinations (typically with CLT floorplates at least, which may represent around 85% of a buildings superstructure material by volume). Such hybrids generally offer the best opportunities for building taller than pure CLT or timber hybrids and for achieving longer internal structural spans, better suited to the expectations of commercial building occupants.

CASE STUDY EXAMPLES

FIG 2.4 & 2.5

Brock Commons Tallwood House, University of British Columbia, Vancouver, Canada by Acton Ostry Architects (2017). This 400+ bed student residential project, the tallest use of CLT when built, demonstrated a game-changing construction methodology that was viable in North America and comparable in cost to a concrete alternative. Flat CLT slabs forming 17 floors above a ground/first floor concrete plinth were combined with glulam columns with vertical loads transferred through floors via steel connectors (with a concrete stability core). A steel framed pre-manufactured facade was installed externally – a model that could satisfy current UK regulation for so-called 'relevant' buildings. Built at a rate of two floors per week, this project also proved a milestone for speed and safety of assembly.

CLT/steel hybrids

At the time of writing, few CLT/ steel hybrids have been delivered in English-speaking countries. 6 Orsman Road, London by Waugh Thistleton (see case study) is likely the largest example completed to date, representing an efficient and legible form of construction with continuous CLT floors running over cellular steel beams. To many, this represents the most buildable and efficient hybrid form of application of CLT to commercial buildings and has the advantage of being based upon widely understood and accepted steel framing.

OTHER FORMS OF APPLICATION

Modular

Modular manufacturers may incorporate CLT as a substrate for robust single panels or for volumetric solutions (as **Figure 2.6**). Doing so provides a high degree of workability and flexibility in fabrication (panels may be processed/cut in-house by larger manufacturers or by the CLT manufacturer for smaller operations) whilst maintaining sufficient rigidity to survive being moved and transported long distances without the risk of damage to internal linings or fittings (as the Dyson Institute of Technology in Chapter 5 and Chapter 12 shows).

Planar forms

Applications exploiting the planar characteristics of the material are particularly interesting and offer the potential for maximising enclosure of larger volumes with a minimal amount of material. Shell forms may also be 'folded' by fixing angled panels (as the Haus Gables case study) for additional strength or rigidity.

FIG 2.6

Modular volumetric housing as developed by Swan Housing/ NuBuild, Basildon, UK (2018). This housing provider developed an off-site factory partly to overcome site quality issues and processes CLT panels in-house to build modules on a production line, fully fitted out before transport to site and assembly and cladding works.

CHAPTER 2 **APPLICATIONS AND USE**

FIG 2.7

Elephant House, Zurich Zoo, Switzerland by Markus Schietsch Architekten (2014). The CLT shell form of this enormous enclosure is held in place by steel ties providing a highly efficient form of long span enclosure. Covered openings allow daylighting without compromising the shell form.

Building elements or components

CLT can of course be used to manufacture elements of buildings off-site, allowing the installation of prefabricated parts or components regardless of the structural frame form. These may be particularly attractive for additions to existing structures where load-bearing capacity may be limited by the bearing constraints (as the Republic case study in Chapter 10 shows). Potential elements include staircases (linear or spiral as shown in **Figure 2.9**), rooftop pop-ups for skylights or furniture such as reception desks. CLT may also be used to create durable formwork for complex concrete elements.

Sculptural forms

Panels can be readily worked, shaped and combined and a number of installations have used CLT as the basis for highly sculptural installations, either exploiting planar strengths or as a material sculpted into flowing forms providing a backdrop for other activities. Such installations might be demountable and have been used in multiple locations.

23

CROSS LAMINATED TIMBER

FIG 2.8

The Hedberg, Hobart, Tasmania, Australia, by Liminal Studio with WOHA (2020). In order to achieve acoustic separation in this cutting-edge university performing arts building, three auditoria were formed from structurally isolated CLT structures within the steel and concrete framed building resulting in 12 weeks of programme savings. The image shows 105mm thick panels being installed with pre-cut apertures for connecting doorways and intermediate balcony structures.

FIG 2.9

Example of CLT sculptural use within the Omicron campus building, Klaus, Austria by Dietrich Untertrifaller Architekten (2014). Bonded, layered panels were shaped and sanded to create a fixed, flowing feature space within a commercial office campus.

CHAPTER 2 **APPLICATIONS AND USE**

25

CROSS LAMINATED TIMBER

FIG 2.10
Feature spiral stair of CLT treads between timber floor slabs with a tapered underside to each tread element reinforcing the sense of fluidity and movement (includes a concealed central steel section). Seed House, by fitzpatrick + partners, Castlecrag, Sydney (2019).

CHAPTER 2 **APPLICATIONS AND USE**

Tall buildings

The greatest potential, interest and application for CLT remains low- to mid-rise structures – up to 10/12 storeys. There are however plenty of dramatic headlines written around high-rise application and much associated research undertaken, often based around sketch proposals that stand little or no chance of being built. Beyond building codes being reconsidered to allow taller timber structures in many jurisdictions, the Council on Tall Buildings and Urban Habitat (CTBUH) amended their official height criteria in 2019 to include timber as a recognised structural material. There is no doubt that technological advances will allow more economical and taller timber structures and that they will likely involve some form of CLT that will help inform other applications. Where built to date, such forms are typically highly bespoke solutions and rather complex and as such, are not considered in great detail here.[1]

CASE STUDY EXAMPLES

FIG 2.11

At 24 storeys (84m tall, 25,000m^2 gross area) HoHo Wien, Austria, by Rüdiger Lainer + Partner Architekten (2020) is the world's tallest hybrid tower at the time of writing. Three-quarters of the structure is timber, including prefabricated CLT walls, CLT or precast concrete floor slabs to part and glulam beams. Housing a hotel, wellness centre and offices, all topped by six floors of apartments, this is a true 'city sandwich' and a fire engineering approach was used to demonstrate the safety of such a range of uses at height.

Assembly of each floor's timber components was completed in four days with pre-manufactured CLT walls partially exposed and internally protected with a UV and water repellent finish supplied with pre-installed windows (as illustrated elsewhere).

'We wanted to show that wood has the same possibilities [as] concrete or steel. And if we can build a high rise building using CLT then it should be easy to build normal housing projects of four to ten floors.'[2]

– *HoHo Wien architect, Rüdiger Lainer*

CHAPTER 3
CONTEXT

Having considered how CLT is manufactured and how it may be used, this chapter provides further context – outlining its development, milestone projects and drivers for future change to illustrate how the wider consideration of CLT may help address present day challenges.

FIG 3.0 (chapter opener)

Ermine Street Church Academy by AHMM, under construction with pre-cut notches for glulam roof beams to upper levels (see subsequent case study for details).

THE GROWTH OF A NEW WAY OF BUILDING

CLT was developed in Switzerland and central Europe, in part to address a glut of good value whitewood, making better use of non-premium timber. These regions have an unbroken tradition of building with timber and plentiful supply and the resultant material is widely adopted.[1] The first CLT building in the UK was completed in 2004, as the use of the material spread across the world initially using European supplied products and increasingly, regionally or locally manufactured panels.

Demand and supply issues

At the time of publication, there were around 650 completed CLT buildings in the UK, of a total building stock of around 24.2 million dwellings (of various forms) and c.1.8 million commercial buildings.[2] Annual CLT demand is estimated to be around 60,000m^3 per year (2020), the capacity of a single medium/large-sized production facility. There is no domestic production in the UK and a limited number of processors working panels, typically for their own use.[3]

Globally, demand is rising sharply and is projected to rise much further. Supply capacity is increasing with established producers significantly increasing production and new manufacturers establishing operations around the world using diverse species to suit local availability.

In general, only a handful of the larger manufacturers and suppliers make the headlines (the largest being Binderholz, KLH and Stora Enso) but across Europe there are many more suppliers, most being modest in scale but offering a variety of products, services and potential.

A very modern method of construction

CLT is best considered a material, rather than a system, despite the efforts of manufacturers who are understandably keen to differentiate their product. Each maintains slight variations in format, layup, processing capabilities and so on, and this lack of general standardisation does little to help those specifying or pricing projects who may need to consider alternative specifications/sizing to avoid limiting tender or supply options.

CLT is produced and processed to order and typically fabricated in a unique manner for each project. Design for Manufacture and Assembly (DfMA) principles are applicable (such as design rationalisation, better materials use, on-demand production and just-in-time delivery) but there is usually little, if any, repetition, a key precept of a true DfMA approach. CLT is typically considered a mass customised pre-manufactured product and may be more appropriately described as a form of MMC (modern method of construction).

FIG 3.1

CLT faced wall units being installed with windows and exposed internal face pre-finished (to lower building)

Regulatory agenda

UK application has to date been lightly regulated, with performance-based fire safety criteria enabling milestone projects. Limitations on combustible wall elements following the Grenfell Tower fire of 2017 have since severely restricted the application of CLT: a casualty of a poorly considered response, prescriptively banning certain materials in residential external walls at height. Suppliers, for which the UK represents only modest opportunities (typically single digit percentages of their overall market), were slow to respond to the new regulatory environment and outmanoeuvred by lobbying from those promoting the use of concrete.[4] Extensive study and evidence gathering, supported by large-scale testing, is now underway to address routes to compliance for fire safety reflecting the approach adopted in North America to support related changes to building codes.

Other countries previously limited the height of timber buildings to six floors, such as in Austria. As the potential (and the necessity) for mass timber use is increasingly well understood and the market matures, regulations and standards are generally being revisited globally, to ensure safety whilst recognising the potential use of CLT at scale. HoHo Wien (Vienna), as previously described, was the tallest timber building in the world (by some margin, when completed). In this context, the UK is a notable exception in restricting wider adoption for the time being.

OPPORTUNITIES FOR CLT AND BETTER WAYS OF BUILDING

Housing, workplace and refurbishment

There are significant housing crises the world over, as demand outstrips affordable supply in many countries and cities. Global population is expected to increase by 2.5bn by 2050 with increasingly higher density urban settlements. The UK requires 300,000 new homes a year (a significant increase on current provision) and much construction is frequently poor quality: alternative supply chains need to be developed to supplement existing methods and forms of construction.

The changing demands and priorities of workspace owners and tenants has shifted. Better performance is expected with a focus on issues of wellness and higher internal environmental quality that extends from visible issues to unseen aspects. Buildings are increasingly seen as a manifestation of a company's brand and principles and environmental costs of operations are increasingly frequently disclosed and reported upon (for operators as well as investors) in a market typically led by progressive early adopters and innovators, and attention is now shifting to include embodied/material impacts.

Building stock is however renewed slowly: 80% of UK buildings expected to be in use in 2050 already exist. As such, beyond considering new buildings, the need to reimagine and modify existing structures in an intelligent manner is also significant but not without challenges.

Construction industry issues

The increasingly fragile UK construction industry is seemingly engaged in a downward spiral with flatlining productivity lagging far behind other industries.[5] An aging, diminishing construction labour force is becoming increasingly deskilled. Poor perception of the industry and associated working conditions does little to encourage renewal of a workforce that accounts for 10% of total UK employment, 'Nobody wants to work in the rain and mud anymore'.[6]

Beyond significant and sustained pressures on costs, project programmes and risk transfer (due in part to the continued transformation, 'financialisation', of real estate from a resource to an asset class) there is insufficient investment in better ways of building. On-site construction quality is highly variable, unreliable and frequently very poor, wasting time and resources and resulting in poor performance in use.[7]

Consequently, the industry faces a 'lethal cocktail of low margins and high risks',[8] increasing pressures on quality, value and future flexibility, with design-for-compliance to absolute minimum legal standards too frequently becoming the baseline, allowing little room for innovation or improvement.

Materials use and impacts

Global materials use has tripled over 40 years. In 2017, 92.1 billion tons of material was extracted globally, a figure that may double by 2050. In a market of increasing scale and complexity, with ever more constrained resources, the linear model of extraction, use and disposal is no longer fit for purpose.

There is increasing recognition that off-site methods, dry construction and smarter assembly can help ensure minimal waste,[9] and maximum end-of-life value achieved for materials with the concept of the circular economy now widely understood and ever more widely addressed.[10]

Construction is responsible for around 45% of greenhouse gas emissions; 10% relating to new buildings and like other countries, the UK has announced legislation to decarbonise the economy by 2050. Carbon emissions to completion represent a huge proportion of total whole life carbon impacts from around a third (for office buildings) to a half (for residential). The UK Green Building Council estimates 65% of greenhouse gas impacts for new construction are generated by products and materials (embodied impacts) and their transportation and a further 20% by inefficient construction processes.[11]

Changes to UK Building Regulations have resulted in a significant reduction in the operational energy but do not address embodied carbon or energy in construction. Beyond reducing the negative impacts of alternatives, industry has realised that CLT buildings can act as carbon vaults, locking away significant carbon instead of creating significant greenhouse gas impacts from the use of steel and concrete.[12]

Tree planting is a popular means to offset residual carbon impacts for those unable or unwilling to reduce emissions at source. Trees absorb most carbon during their juvenile growing phase and when harvested, processed and used, store biogenic carbon allowing further planting to repeat this carbon-sinking process.[13] Plant-based buildings can help facilitate such a circular process providing a use and market for existing and newly pledged planting.

A CONSTRUCTION TRANSITION

As we collectively largely neglect to address these market failures, likely consequences appear to be increasingly severe. The future that no one wanted to contemplate, and some would refuse to consider, is almost upon us. As such, the climate emergency and an increased awareness of untenable environmental impacts is informing both business practices and legislative direction at increasing pace.

The energy transition for the decarbonisation of global energy systems is well underway. An increased awareness and application of CLT as outlined over subsequent chapters could make a very significant positive contribution to the construction transition, the step change that is necessary to better address both present day and future challenges.

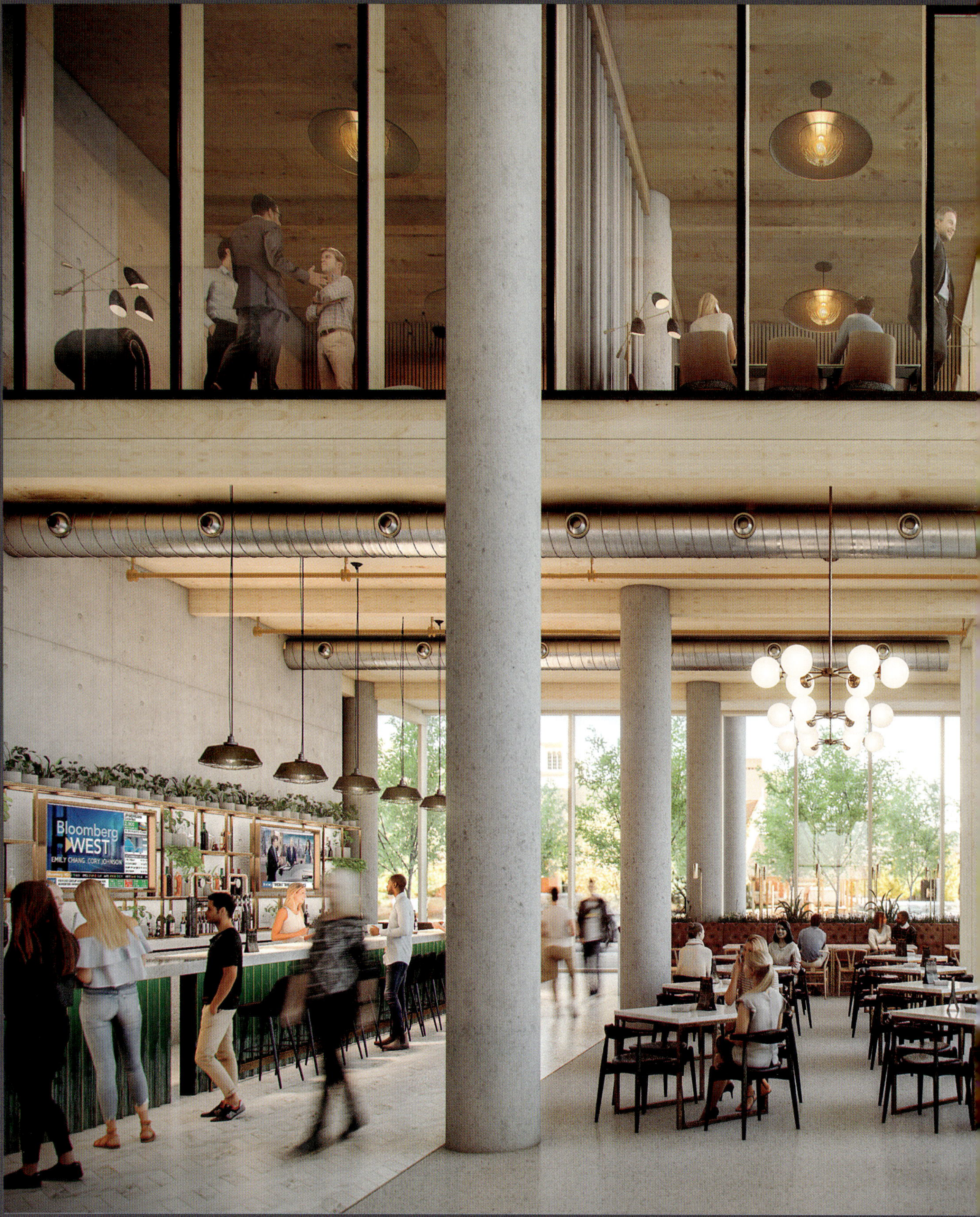
Bloomberg WEST
EMILY CHANG CORY JOHNSON

CHAPTER 4
FEASIBILITY AND INITIAL CONSIDERATIONS

It is unlikely that at feasibility stage a client or designer will be insistent upon a particular material choice. Time is well spent defining how various aspects of the project will be developed and assessed (leaving options open wherever possible) rather than making significant materials decisions. As such, this chapter is framed around a series of questions related to the consideration of materials that teams may consider at the earliest stages. It cannot be stressed enough that considering the use of CLT from the outset of any design, preferably involving specialist input, is by far the best way of realising the maximum potential benefits, including financial efficiencies, from the materials use.

FIG 4.0 (chapter opener)
Innovative early-stage proposal for tall office and residential building by AHMM, Central US (2019). Render of ground floor hospitality space illustrates CLT floor slabs and hybrid concrete and glulam structural frame.

STRATEGIC BRIEF AND CORE PROJECT REQUIREMENTS

Is a new building required?
The potential for CLT application to existing structures is illustrated elsewhere but lightweight additions to existing frames may be a meaningful way of adding value and meeting a brief without resorting to a new building.

When is project delivery anticipated?
Long-term projects may get caught out by future shifts in expectations so a forward-facing approach to construction should be adopted to anticipate likely trends and possible changes in expectations and legislation.

What is the client's attitude to innovation and sustainability?
Is there any appetite for building a better structure than the last one or would a contemporary form of construction reflect well on the business of the client or occupier? Understand sustainability aspirations and attitudes to life cycle issues, including how impacts may be monitored and assessed. Question whether a client appreciates the impacts of embodied carbon (as well as just operational) and how this may affect future investment decisions.

Does the client have views that would rule out the use of a particular material or way of building?
Understand whether a client body and their advisors or insurance providers (and those of potential occupiers) are open to modern methods of construction or have strong views about CLT construction.

OTHER ISSUES

How will decisions be made?
Beyond defining core requirements, a key issue is understanding or defining how options will be assessed – what information will be required to inform decision makers, what is important to the client (aspirations and objectives), how will issues be weighted in any assessment, what metrics will be required and who will be making decisions (or advising decision makers).

How are costs and tender prices being compared?
To enable meaningful comparisons and mitigate the likely higher build cost of CLT when viewed in isolation, a range of factors should be taken into account when assessing superstructure estimates and prices. Factors such as reduced programme, substructure savings, improved quality and higher certainty about outcomes (reduced risk), increased safety and benefits to follow-on trades and work are often overlooked when making side-by-side comparisons of structural systems.

Are there opportunities to realise benefits from a reduced build programme?
Understanding cash flow issues, funding milestones and letting or disposal strategies may help teams put a value to any programme savings that may be achievable from CLT use (this value is not always recognised but at the very least may serve to reduce project risks for various stakeholders).

What research may need to be undertaken for subsequent stages and concept design?
Better understand the material's potential and relevance and review precedents. This might include desktop studies, discussions with others (specialists or manufacturers) or building visits (there may be examples of CLT use closer to you than you might anticipate).

Who else will be involved in the project team?
The earliest stages represent an opportunity to influence or advise upon appointments, advocate for experienced specialist input or to better understand the attitude and experience of existing team members to new forms of construction and innovation.

Can appointments accommodate a DfMA approach if one is adopted?
Design for manufacture may require particular information to be finalised sooner than under traditional methods (for example, services coordination and builders' work holes for panels or specifications for finishes). Teams may seek to avoid the potential break in continuity between design, specialist design and contractor design: this disjointed approach is most typical of engineering appointments and may lead to duplicated work or changes to a design to suit reworked proposals unless specialists are engaged early.

Is there sufficient time to develop a design for off-site manufacture?
Design development is an iterative process and takes time. Harvest any lessons from previous team experience that may streamline this process. Overall programmes may be reduced but design time to produce sufficient information before manufacture may be extended beyond that required for a traditional start on site.

How would the team (including clients) react to particular proposals?
If proposing CLT use early on, ascertain the project team and decision makers' attitudes: their view of the material, their experience of using it, and any motivation for doing so. Give them a copy of this book or direct them to related resources.

As an initial brief develops, are there any targets for efficiencies or savings?
Scale and repetition can offer cost advantages to CLT use. Beyond time or programme, targets could be related to defects or safety, waste or material efficiency or carbon savings – all typically judged against traditional benchmarks. Ensure that any aspirations or metrics are clearly incorporated into the project brief.

SITE OPTIONS AND FEASIBILTY STUDIES

Are sites accessible or not?
A consideration of site logistics and approaches should be made at feasibility stage to understand access routes, any key limiting dimensions and potential constraints on construction, either deliveries, crane access or service and storage areas.

Are there any challenges below ground?
Poor ground conditions or below ground infrastructure can severely limit development options and are common in urban centres. Many potential development sites lie vacant for this reason. Lighter CLT structures may enable development to progress or improve viability by adding additional capacity to sites of limited bearing capability. Some sites do however require mass in some form, for example a high water table may pose challenges to a lighter structural solution and replacing existing structures over underground assets can be problematic if existing mass is not replaced.

Is there any support or assistance available for particular forms of construction?
Local legislation or policy may be applicable to the likely building form. There may be a local timber encouragement policy ('wood first'), officially adopted or informal, which might facilitate or ease the planning process (as discussed elsewhere) and in limited instances, financial incentives for building using timber.

Are there any social challenges anticipated?
Social issues are often overlooked but can help influence planning decisions. Check whether there are any issues with immediate neighbours, a particular concern in dense urban environments. Stakeholders may include existing tenants, local interest groups or those with influence over decision makers. Consider any likely restrictions on noise or working hours, any limits to vehicle movements or other neighbourly concerns that may be alleviated or negated by CLT use.

What would be acceptable ways of building this particular building?
Consider all options that might be appropriate for such a building type and likely form. The answer is not always CLT (or any other specific material); for example, CLT will not be the best choice for a 40-storey residential tower or an underground car park. Existing precedents can help inform this important consideration that will help direct future detailed studies.

How will BIM be used?
As with other forms of MMC and indeed all construction of scale, BIM use should be considered at the outset. Establishing protocols for project use and a consideration of appointments (and any design responsibility matrix)

CHAPTER 4 **FEASIBILITY AND INITIAL CONSIDERATIONS**

will lead to benefits in time and BIM may be used to test options and help inform the development of a brief. 3D modelling is well suited to mocking up approximate panel arrangements to understand initial potential.

PROJECT EXAMPLES HIGHLIGHTING VARIOUS FEASIBILITY STAGE CONSIDERATIONS

The following projects are included to highlight the diversity of key drivers, and challenges, at feasibility stage.[1]

Proposals for large-scale commercial workspace over existing underground station, London

Early optioneering led to a preference for a CLT/steel hybrid structure over existing underground structures to allow an additional two floors of lettable area (and therefore significant value) that would otherwise not be achievable using a conventional form of construction. A significant supporting factor was the appeal of a very significant reduction in construction-related heavy goods vehicle movements to the client, a metropolitan transport authority with responsibility for road safety (as **Figure 4.1**).

FIG 4.1

Proposal for tall, commercial office building over station development (2020).

New primary school for newly planned community, Cambridgeshire

AHMM joined an existing framework team where the (employer) contractor dictated from the outset that the low-rise school building would be constructed from CLT, based on past experience with the material and known benefits in terms of buildability and speed of construction (essential for meeting programme requirements tied to the academic calendar). The architects greatly benefitted from this practical experience and that of the associated consultants (see the extended Ermine Street Church Academy case study).

Proposals for mixed use multi-storey residential and commercial building, Central US

To reflect a client's ambitions for a novel form of construction to differentiate this speculative building in a generic market, a CLT/timber/concrete hybrid was proposed and developed with residential use over commercial office, taking advantage of recently revised building codes. Budgets were however reconsidered in light of revised economic forecasts and the capital expenditure of such a building in this part of the city led to the timber proposals being abandoned as it was deemed too expensive in comparison to alternative traditional forms (as **Figure 4.2**).

39

CROSS LAMINATED TIMBER

FIG 4.2

Proposals for exposed CLT with glulam to lower levels of tall mixed use building, Central US (2019).

Proposals for large-scale hybrid office floors for technology firm HQ, London

Key issues at early design stages included extremely high sustainability aspirations (including embodied carbon impacts) and priorities around buildability and performance in use. An important driver in developing hybrid CLT proposals with a steel structure (with panels bearing on the lower flange of beams to achieve a flush soffit) to tender stage was an aspiration to optimise internal environmental quality which included a consideration of biophilic aspects.

CHAPTER 4 **FEASIBILITY AND INITIAL CONSIDERATIONS**

FIG 4.3

Proposals for flush soffit hybrid solution to commercial office, London (2015).

41

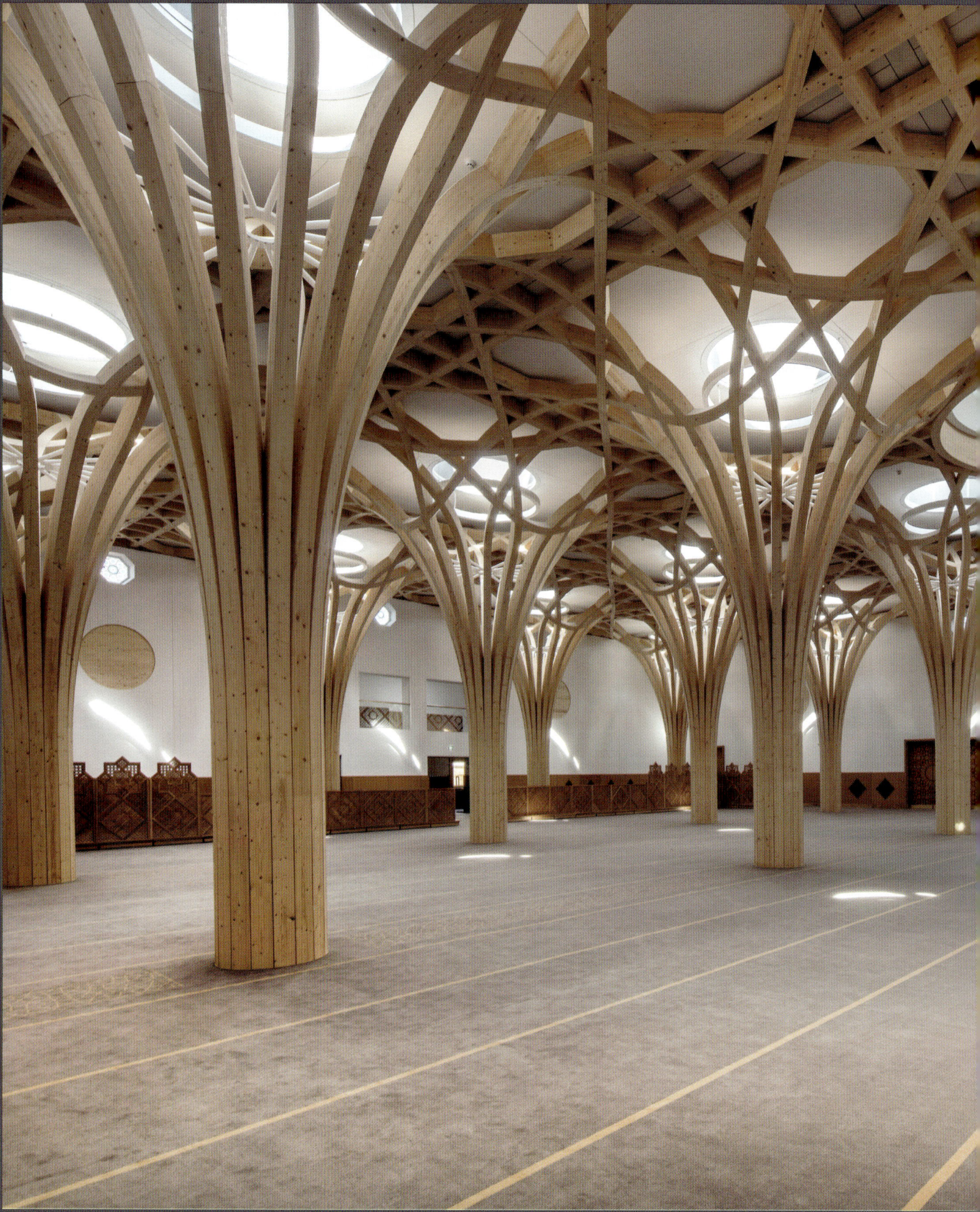

CHAPTER 5
VISUAL ASPECTS

Exposing CLT reflects the increased expression of pattern, texture and natural materials in architecture and interiors and an apparent awareness and acceptance, or even celebration, of what the Japanese term *wabi-sabi*.[1] However, CLT does not need to be visible to be advantageous in use. Limitations on expressing structural elements may be due to issues of perception, taste or important performance aspects, typically fire or acoustic issues. As such, typical CLT apartment buildings in the UK, including the highest profile examples, have nearly all (if not all) CLT panels concealed rather than exposed.

CROSS LAMINATED TIMBER

FIG 5.0 (chapter opener)

The main prayer hall of Cambridge Mosque by Marks Barfield (2019), with white painted CLT wall and roof enclosure beyond tree form glulam structures.

FIG 5.1

Typical interior view, full CLT structure concealed.

MANAGING EXPECTATIONS

As a composite formed from multiple sections of a natural material with inherent, sometimes significant variations, deviations in appearance must be expected. Some aspects can be controlled; others are less predictable or unavoidable. Other features may become apparent only over time, e.g. with changes to moisture content and resultant movement or exposure to light. Managing expectations from the outset is critical. Teams and clients should remember that all materials will move to some degree and even small cracks or tolerances may be noticeable when viewed across large panels and that structural elements (concrete, steel or timber) should not be assessed as one might a piece of furniture. Such detail is often overlooked leading to surprises on site and difficult conversations between teams and clients.

Figure 5.1 shows AHMM's Cobalt Place (102 apartments, completed 2015). CLT was reluctantly concealed to suit the sales agents' idea of what would suit the local market (that included wooden flooring). Doing so did however prove a cost-effective and easily understood and conventional means of providing fire protection and appropriate acoustic performance.

CHAPTER 5 **VISUAL ASPECTS**

CASE STUDY EXAMPLES

FIG 5.2

Accommodation pods for the Dyson Institute of Engineering and Technology by WilkinsonEyre (2019–20) use a factory manufactured 26m^2 CLT module, to form 67 bedrooms and associated support spaces. Internal quality was highly important to the client, and panels are exposed wherever possible within (including to bathrooms) with matching custom furniture, all tested and finalised using a full-scale mock-up.

Pods arrived fully completed externally and fitted out internally following finishing in a near-site facility. This allowed some leeway in terms of timing of site operations and was made possible by the rigid CLT 'chassis', sized around optimum transport dimensions and standardised to reduce complexity and manufacturing variation.

DESIGN STAGE ISSUES

Surface appearance

It is important to understand and communicate the material's character, behaviour and limitations and communicate these to stakeholders. Surface quality may be defined by local standards,[1] but manufacturers each use differing terms to describe various finishes, as **Table 5.1** shows.[2]

45

CROSS LAMINATED TIMBER

Table 5.1 Summary of defined surface grades and example manufacturer descriptions[3]

Manufacturer	Lowest grade	Medium grade	Highest grade
According to European standard[4]	Visible surface not covered by standard	Planed, may be lightly sanded to Class B/C	Planed and sanded to Class A/B
Binderholz	Non-visible (NSI)	Industrial areas (class BC)	Living areas (AB)
KLH	Non-visual Quality (Nsi)	Industrial Visual Quality (Isi)	Domestic Visual Quality (Wsi)
Stora Enso	Non-visible quality (NVI)	Industrial Visible Quality (IVI)	Visible quality (VI)

FIG 5.3

Timber species, availability and cost vary by region. Manufacturers typically offer a default (economic) option but may offer a range of timbers with differing characteristics and surface qualities. From left: Douglas Fir, Pine, UC3 pressure treated Pine, Spruce – as available from French manufacturer Piveteaubois.

FIG 5.4

Soffit heights and effective viewing distances.

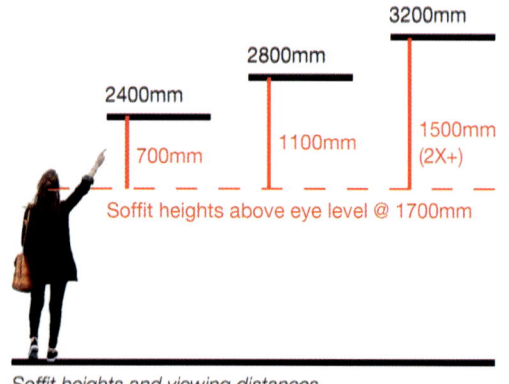

Soffit heights and viewing distances

Manufacturers typically provide benchmark samples or indicative images but the importance of mock-ups cannot be stressed enough given the potential variety in appearance. In some markets, there may be a choice of species used to form CLT, or decorative outer layers, with differing performance and visual characteristics, as **Figure 5.3**.

For a more detailed summary of the range of surface characteristics by grade, refer to 'CLT Panel Surface Quality' within the Appendix.

Viewing panels in-situ

The highest grade (often termed domestic visual quality) may be appropriate when exposed adjacent to occupied zones; however, other areas may suffice with more cost effective lower grade panel surfaces. Viewed from further away, a lower grade of panel may be sufficient visual quality and for overhead applications, only a modest increase in height, as **Figure 5.4**, can double the effective viewing distance.

Aging of exposed timber

Yellowing and aging, which may be referred to as 'suntanning', of spruce and other whitewoods (other timbers typically darken) is the visible sign of

CHAPTER 5 **VISUAL ASPECTS**

lignin degradation over time. This is caused by ultraviolet (UV) light from both natural and artificial sources although it will be most apparent in areas receiving direct sunlight.[5] This effect, often seen within the interiors of older alpine chalets, has been described as 'aging gracefully, mellowing to a rich honeyed tone over time'.[6] Some may view it less favourably, particularly when it results in contrasting light and dark 'shadows' being created by areas protected from exposure by furniture, fittings or picture frames. Owners and occupiers should be made aware of the issue and although affected areas can be re-sanded to expose paler wood this can be disruptive to occupants.

CLT surfaces and applied finishes

Some manufacturers offer factory-applied surface finishes such as clear or UV-protecting lacquers, UV stable silicate finishes, tinted or opaque finishes with or without fire retardant for limiting surface spread of flame

---

CASE STUDY EXAMPLES

FIG 5.5

At Cambridge Mosque by Marks Barfield Architects (2019), shadow gaps were included to CLT panel interfaces at wall/roof junctions with small chamfers to panel edges elsewhere to help mitigate the visual impact of any minor misalignment. Lower levels (adjacent to kneeling worshippers) are lined with a finely finished timber element to contrast with the CLT above, where likely minor changes to panel surfaces over time may result in some surface cracking (the effect of which could be amplified by the opaque white finish or fire retardant). Panel visual appearance was based upon large scale mock-ups and large circular apertures (visible below) were machined on site to accommodate a late instruction for flush mounted motifs internally.

CROSS LAMINATED TIMBER

FIG 5.6

Freshly sanded spruce sample.

FIG 5.7

Aged spruce panel.

FIG 5.8

Coatings on spruce, from top: Two coats of white wax oil; Two coats of black wax oil; Softwood lye treated.

but this is not typical. Most are reluctant to apply liquid coatings in their (dusty) factories to avoid slowing down production and taking up valuable space.[7] Such finishes are typically applied on site once panels are installed, for similar reasons and although generally not conspicuous, clear finishes may change the light reflectivity of the surface slightly.

Figure 5.6 illustrates a freshly sanded spruce panel edge. By way of contrast, **Figure 5.7** indicates a section of wall of untreated spruce, exposed to internal artificial light for around three years.

Decorative or protective waxes or oils may be applied to well-finished (domestic quality) panels to areas within reach of occupants (i.e. where most likely to show staining or dirt and oil build-up from occupant contact). Note that any stain or wax/oil treatment may highlight different parts of a panel depending upon whether the end grain is exposed or not (highlighting cut grain at panel edges). **Figure 5.8A** illustrates the effect of two coats of white wax/oil stain – the effect is marginal due to the pale colour of the stain and the timber but UV retardant additives ensure that this tone would be maintained. **Figure 5.8B** shows the effect of two coats of black wax/oil stain. The dramatic effect on the end grain (with radial rings seen) reflects the more absorbent nature of this section whereas the impact on the long grain sections is still limited.[8] Lye is a surface treatment that mitigates the yellowing of softwoods (**Figure 5.8C**), enhancing the natural grain of wood and creating a light whitewashed effect when applied to spruce.

Surface boards may move or shrink and small gaps will likely open up – this is likely within the first year after installation and possibly beyond. **Figure 5.9** illustrates gaps and cracking to vertical wall panels (as well as a visible finger joint to the outer board). Such cracks typically remain visible.

Consider allowing a heating season before painting if possible. **Figure 5.10** illustrates multiple fissures in the surface of a panel coated with two coats of white tinted fire-retardant finish shortly after the panels were installed. Despite each crack being only quite small, the colour contrast is quite marked. Such splits may be compounded above heat sources where the moisture content is reduced below that elsewhere in the building (**Figure 5.11**). Painting over knots, and surface deviations can be challenging; they will show through most light-coloured finishes being perceived as defects or marks. Consider a non-opaque colour tint to soften variations in the surface rather than trying to conceal them.

FIG 5.9

Vertical splits to outer lamella of vertical wall panel (beside finger joint in surface board).

FIG 5.10

Panel with two coats of opaque white finish, knots and splits clearly visible.

48

CHAPTER 5 **VISUAL ASPECTS**

FIG 5.11

Wall panel above radiator (with clear flame retardant finish) with disproportionate number of vertical splits due to localised heating and drying effects. NB: a vertical panel joint can be seen to the right of radiator.

Many common areas and commercial or larger buildings will require a liquid applied fire-retardant coating to limit surface spread of flame to exposed panels. Such coatings may be transparent, tinted or opaque and coloured as required, with varying degrees of gloss or reflectance. All will however modify the matt finish of timber and may appear worn over time in highly trafficked areas where occupants come into regular contact with the surface. All finishes used should be compatible with treatments such as fire retardants or edge sealants.

Panel connections and joint details

Panel connection design is frequently overlooked and can impact design time as well as cost. Exposed panels might be readily fixed with concealed fixings (fixings are typically long wood screws), screwed from back faces if access is readily available but will be more of a challenge when visible on both sides.

Panel connections may be considered as follows:

- Exposed, utility. The cheapest, most robust fixings are typically not attractive (lots of screws and/or galvanised brackets are used unless specified otherwise).

CASE STUDY EXAMPLES

FIG 5.12

When designing the Stapferhaus exhibition hall, Lenzburg, Switzerland (2018), the architects, pool Architekten, specified a blue-black stain to internal CLT wall and ceiling panels, glulam structural elements and timber floor. The overall effect is of a consistent, monolithic form whilst the texture and grain of timber elements is visible when viewed close up or in reflected light.

CROSS LAMINATED TIMBER

FIG 5.13

Weathered samples, from left: Top surface fully exposed to weather; Fully submerged (no air).

- Exposed, refined. May be more expensive and challenging to coordinate and deliver. These may include rebated, slotted or lapped joints.
- Concealed (e.g. plugged or covered afterwards, possibly with cover plates).
- Not visible (fully hidden connections and brackets).

Although factory finish and panel quality can be high with extremely tight tolerances, very large and cumbersome panels can be easily mishandled and edges to be exposed are not readily repaired. Panels need to be manoeuvred on site and edges and corners can be easily damaged. Placing structural panels is not like crafting furniture so consider 'aiming to miss' – avoiding unrealistic details and outcomes by staggering joints, offsetting datum lines from prominent features or introducing chamfers, rebates or shadow gaps to panel edges to help ensure that installations are not compromised by matters beyond your control. Coordinating exposed panel corners such as at the intersection of four panels at a single point, for example, may be a challenge due to cumulative tolerances, however small.

Surface board or grain direction should always be checked if it is being exposed to ensure it runs the intended direction and the visual quality of panel edges can be variable (they are typically not controlled), so it is important to discuss these with suppliers early.

Appearance after exposure and wetting

Panels are not intended to be exposed to moisture for significant periods. **Figure 5.13** illustrates the effects of medium term exposure (nine months) on panel samples of spruce. Colour effects aside (samples exposed turned a glorious silver colour), samples exposed to water and air typically cracked and began to delaminate in part. The sample fully submerged displayed deformation but no decay (which would likely require exposure to air).

Realistic rendering

Many visualisations deliver an unrealistic impression of how exposed panels will look. Given the importance of managing stakeholder expectations and the increasing reliance on digital models and rendered outputs to inform decision making and sign-off from early stages (as well as potentially sales), **Table 5.2** outlines what may be considered realistic when developing and presenting proposals.

Such details may seem minor but will help avoid surprises, disappointment or extra work, ensuring proposals are acceptable, realistic and affordable.[9] Consider reviewing outputs against images of any completed local precedents for comparison once these issues have been considered.

FIG 5.14

Example of a particularly convincing pre-construction render, of a proposed modular CLT scheme for developer Urban Splash.

CHAPTER 5 **VISUAL ASPECTS**

Table 5.2 Representing exposed CLT in renders and visualisations

Element	Aspect	Realistic representation	Not realistic
Soffit	Direction of boards on visible surface; Panel thickness where exposed	Boards aligned with primary direction of panel span i.e. to walls or between beams; panel thickness c.160-300mm depending on span	Misaligned with primary span; overly thick panels or lamella (see dimensions noted elsewhere)
Floor	Typically not used for flooring	Most softwoods are insufficiently durable for foot traffic. Show other flooring	Showing CLT panels exposed to form floors
Wall	Direction of visible boards (outer face); Panel thickness	Aligned vertically (typically), along lines of structural loading; panel thickness c.80-160mm depending on design	Horizontally aligned, i.e. perpendicular to loading; Very thick walls (>200mm)
Panels generally:	Panel size/joints	3m x 16m maximum (generally); narrow joints c.5mm; typically small chamfer to long edges (NB: outer layer direction typically defined by loading/span, as above, not panel orientation); Typically read as butt joint to visible surfaces	Seamless joints; panels not shown; Boards continuing across adjacent panels
	Lamella board length (each lamella [layer] formed of board)	Long boards - typically mixed lengths up to 3m. Differentiation between boards at panel joints	Endless lamella boards; Lamella continuing past panel joints
	Lamella board width	Typically consistent, c.130mm max width (high quality), c.200mm (regular grade)	Very wide boards; more than 300mm or varied width
	Timber species/colour	Reflect local availability; Use paler colours as fresh sanded finish, not aged or 'suntanned'	Unfamiliar or unrealistic timber species, grain or colour; Hardwoods (such as oak)
	Knots; Growth rings; Defects and surface variation	Typically includes knots, often very many, up to 40mm dia. See description of panel grade elsewhere. Growth rings will be varied and visible unless viewed from afar; Scale and contrast within boards will vary	No, or few, knots shown. Even panels with little or no colour or surface variation, no visible growth lines
	Exposed edges	Odd number of lamella (typically 3/5 for walls, 5/7 for slabs). Alternating parallel/perpendicular make-up for adjacent layers	Even number of lamella; unrealistic thickness; perfect appearance of cross layers (NB: controlling quality of layers exposed at board edges is not typical)
	Panel connections	Can be concealed/'not visible' if specified (may attract a premium to exposed panel joints or to glulam elements)	No fixings shown, particularly with hybrid forms e.g. glulam beam/wall interfaces
Other details	Services	Can be concealed (i.e. fed from rear or drilled into panel) if considered early, otherwise must be surface mounted (including distribution runs). Compartment penetrations may require fire stopping	Visible service penetrations with no tolerance/fire stopping

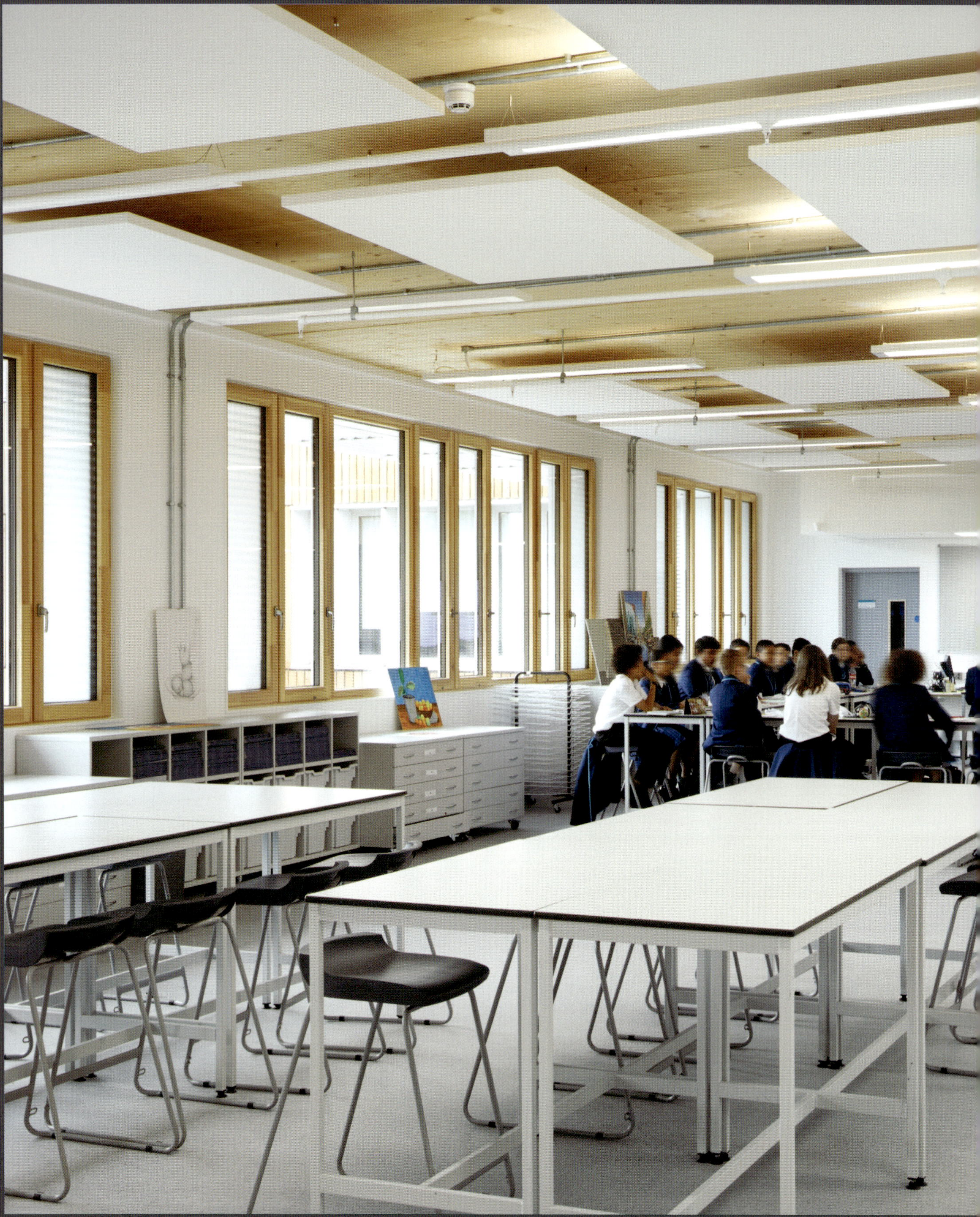

CHAPTER 6
COST AND VALUE

We cannot discuss cost and value without defining the terms. In this chapter we will talk about cost, not price, as these are totally different. Cost is generally defined as the amount of resource or opportunity (money) required to create something or deliver a service. There is then the value (and capital cost) at inception, whole life value throughout the life of the building and more recently, social value is considered increasingly important. CLT can create a less harsh environment within a building and wood is more aesthetically pleasing than other construction forms and it can be argued that the value to and wellbeing of a person in using the building is improved. It can be said that the value of something is subjective, but with assessment and benchmarking, increased objectivity can be created with less room for challenge.

CROSS LAMINATED TIMBER

> This chapter was contributed by *Ian Dacre*, quantity surveyor and partner at Rider Levett Bucknall (UK). Ian has a particular interest and experience in cost management of timber construction and off-site manufacturing.
> Case study examples by Nic Crawley.

FIG 6.0 (chapter opener)

Flexible teaching spaces are formed by extra long span CLT floors to Harris Academy, Sutton, by Architype (2019).

People are understanding more about the environmental impact of construction and carbon value benefits. Other structural materials are increasingly being recycled and reused, but once they are extracted from the ground in their raw forms, they are gone for ever whereas trees are renewable and therefore more sustainable.

CAPTURING THE DESIGN VALUE IN PROCUREMENT INTEGRATION

CLT can be used to form a whole building structural solution (external walls, floors, internal walls, roof) with a single point of responsibility for design, supply and installation. Designers have the flexibility to use CLT for only

CASE STUDY EXAMPLES

FIG 6.1 & 6.2

Piercy&Company's Drayton Green Church (2018) demonstrates the value of smart design and the elegant yet cost-effective use of materials within a limited budget.

A dynamic pleated roof form is achieved by exploiting the planar qualities of CLT with a steel frame carefully concealed beyond coordinated spruce panels, all beneath a light white surface finish. The highly expressive soffit, with soaring vaulted volumes celebrates a contemporary but unmistakably ecclesiastical function providing space for 200 worshippers alongside community and administration areas. Project time spent designing the roof form was offset by reduced time on site and an efficient build.

CHAPTER 6 **COST AND VALUE**

FIG 6.3

Unaligned objectives.[1] The current procurement model with many differing facets of project interfaces and stakeholders offers little incentive to align interests, leading to the repetition of errors, failure to innovate or adopt best practice and the delivery of inferior products.

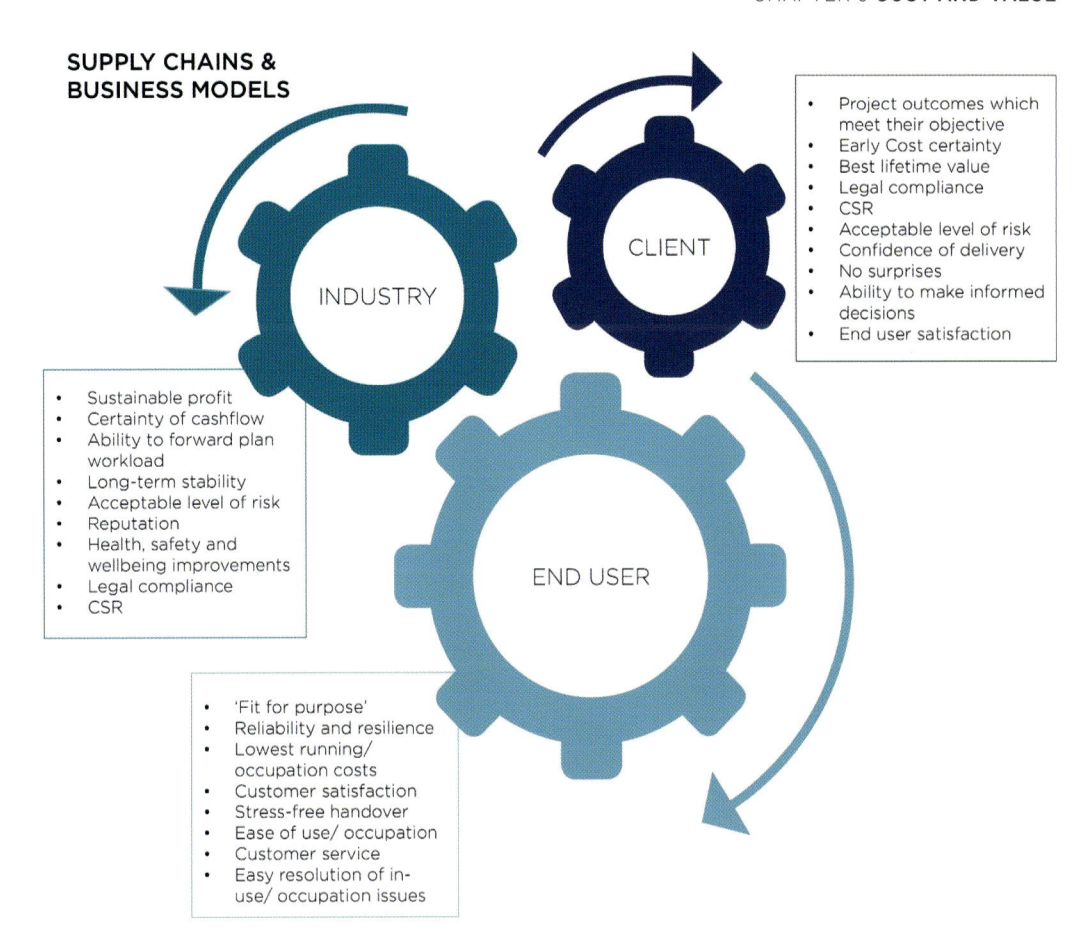

SUPPLY CHAINS & BUSINESS MODELS

INDUSTRY
- Sustainable profit
- Certainty of cashflow
- Ability to forward plan workload
- Long-term stability
- Acceptable level of risk
- Reputation
- Health, safety and wellbeing improvements
- Legal compliance
- CSR

CLIENT
- Project outcomes which meet their objective
- Early Cost certainty
- Best lifetime value
- Legal compliance
- CSR
- Acceptable level of risk
- Confidence of delivery
- No surprises
- Ability to make informed decisions
- End user satisfaction

END USER
- 'Fit for purpose'
- Reliability and resilience
- Lowest running/ occupation costs
- Customer satisfaction
- Stress-free handover
- Ease of use/ occupation
- Customer service
- Easy resolution of in-use/ occupation issues

one element, say internal walls, if required, whether purely structural or to create a finished surface.

Whatever the approach, delivering the best procurement strategy in any project is critical to overall success, realising the right cost and value balance and not just simply transferring the risk. The typical project has the usual design team members with advice sought as required from further down the supply chain. Let's instead capture the expertise and value from the CLT providers by inviting them to be part of the design team and work as an integrated team to deliver an efficient solution from the outset.

Bringing on board the provider or specialist contractor early allows some of the differing facets of project interfaces to be managed efficiently with the expertise of the supplier. This will ensure all parties are moving in the same direction to the ultimate benefit and increasing the value in the successful project delivery.

COST

Cost certainty can be improved earlier on projects if collaboration and involvement of the CLT provider is adopted. The project cost manager will

55

benefit from improved accuracy in estimating resulting in fewer challenges later in the procurement cycle when formal tenders are obtained.

The future environmental agenda will impact on planning with the process possibly affecting programme and costs of projects. We cannot just focus on capital cost – whole life cost considerations have far more impact than the initial capital outlay. Mark Farmer in his report on construction 'Modernise or Die' stated the cost plan has to move away from the capex fixation if the end pre-manufactured value to the client is improved.[2]

One issue that does require addressing is where we obtain benchmark cost data for CLT use. Where do we acquire estimated rates for budget cost planning? Could this be hindering the increase in CLT use? It is an emerging method of construction with limited market expertise. The costs and risks, benefits and opportunities, may therefore not be fully understood compared to more established forms. Rider Levett Bucknall (RLB) is addressing this with their suite of Timber Estimating Guides: Timber Frame, SIPS and CLT. This will hopefully break down the perceived barriers and answer more of the important cost questions.[3]

VALUE IN THE QUALITY

Producing the CLT structural solution combines the close integration of design and manufacturer from one organisation in a controlled factory environment allowing efficiencies to prevail. The supplier is able to design and get the best possible value out of the product and factory conditions ensure a degree of certainty can happen – getting it right first time, eliminating errors, reworking and waste.

Services integration is possible into a CLT panel removing the 'messy' on-site builders' works stages. This is a cost-effective solution, undertaken at design stage and in the factory, for later programme savings. It requires a coordinated design upfront, in the main, but it does not preclude adjustments later. Future-proofing to increase value may be possible by routing for ducts and conduits into panels.

MANAGING WASTE

Creating anything within a controlled environment will reduce waste. The off-site manufactured solution of CLT minimises waste in the factory as timber is cut precisely to the sizes required for the panel creation.

When panels are delivered to site they are, in most cases, offloaded, placed and fixed into position in one go. There is no further cutting and sourcing of other materials to assist in the erection process – it is one complete package that comes from the factory.

THE AESTHETIC VALUE?

CLT is available in three different grades. Non-visual grade is generally hidden behind other more traditional treatments and finishes (although it can be left exposed internally). Industrial and domestic visual is a finished product that may have a sealant or stain protection pre-applied. This results in a finished product as soon as it is installed with appropriate protection being required for remaining site works.

CLT can be a cost-effective structural solution with improved value being achieved through not having to apply further finishes or treatments. If this exposed finish is not required, it can easily be painted, fully or partially covered to change the look and feel of the environment in which it is situated (as outlined in Chapter 5, Visual aspects).

CASE STUDY EXAMPLES

FIG 6.4

Flexibility and value at Harris Academy Sutton, Surrey by Architype (2019). Floor slabs were sized to bear on external and central spine walls only, using continuous panels longer than the 8m span achieved. A screed topping added mass, limiting vibration and noise transfer, resulting in heavier slabs than typical for CLT structures but internal partitions can be added or taken away to reflect changing needs over time, adding to long-term value.

Post-planning, the team agreed a number of changes to better utilise the CLT superstructure including the omission of ceilings and the introduction of acoustic rafts below otherwise exposed soffits. This resulted in a significant cost saving as well as reduced time, materials and trades required on site.

ARE THERE BENEFICIAL PROGRAMME IMPLICATIONS?

In essence, yes. The overall speed of erection is one factor but there are others. The lightness of the frame can have an impact on the chosen foundation making it simpler to design and construct. Owing to the 'smaller' foundation solution there will be fewer transport movements for deliveries of concrete and excavated waste removal.

The frame itself is erected from the delivery vehicle meaning no storage on site required and it is placed in position straight away with no double handling. One thing to bear in mind due to the erection speed, it is advantageous for the CLT contractor to have their own crane or dedicated use of the site crane during installation. For the true benefit, the installation cannot be delayed by others using the crane.

Informing and educating follow-on trades in the use of CLT will help them better plan and deliver their elements, realising programme efficiencies as far as possible. They could commence their works earlier as once erected the CLT is complete: walls, floor and roof. Depending on the project requirements the CLT, internally, could be the finished product negating the need for the follow-on works – protection is vital.

It is far easier for the follow-on trades to screw into timber for a fixing rather than into masonry or concrete, and it is less messy. The programme value is achieving the building earlier. Lower finance costs and a quicker return on investment – these being crucial for most clients.

For some clients the programme is priority, for example, in the education sector where the facilities must be ready for the new term. Quality is essential for others with wood generating a warmth and a wellbeing value.

HOW IS HEALTH AND SAFETY AFFECTED?

Construction can be dangerous with very many separate individual trades used to create the building. CLT can have, and is having, a major impact on minimising construction health and safety risks with the panels created in carefully controlled factory conditions and lifted into position as required by mechanical means utilising pre-installed lifting points. Once secured, the next panel in the erection sequence is placed and so on. Panels may be up to 50m^2 in area so in a very short space of time the shell of the building can be erected.

This means that fewer people are on site, construction time is reduced overall and the panels can create a 'finished product', reducing the need for follow-on trades and subsequent snagging visits. Overall construction risk is reduced as fewer interfaces are required to other trades as the product is created off-site with mechanised erection.

A typical internal wall for a project is made up of structure, plasterboard and plaster, decoration and services – with CLT that may be cut down to the material itself plus services. The number of trades or procurement packages, to finish a wall, are reduced by two or three.

ENVIRONMENTAL VALUE

The present day 'green credentials' of building with CLT far exceed any other structural materials. In the future will more emphasis be placed on the green status or energy criteria of a building? Energy Performance Certificates (EPCs) are mandatory in public buildings today, but will the future be more focused on whole life values of the buildings we use and live in? How do we recycle our buildings? All materials can be recycled to some extent, but once the more traditional ones are mined, they are gone forever. CLT remains stable over its life and therefore can be demounted and used again. The panels can therefore be recycled whilst retaining maximum value at the end of their life on site.

Building owners and occupiers are ever more focused on the value the buildings have on the environment. The green status a building has may affect its future values when being sold or rented, this being both in the commercial arena and to the homeowner. One thing is certain, good quality buildings will be valued for a long time. When their original designed use is redundant, they are recycled (refurbished) into something else.

VALUE FROM THE OUTSET

To realise CLT's full value and potential, the industry needs to be consulted early in the design stages of the project. This is where true collaboration, improved value and efficiencies can be incorporated into the design at the earliest possible time. This is to engineer the *structural* value of many differing aspects into the project.

If the whole frame solution is adopted in a 'one stop shop' approach, the value of having a single point of responsibility for the structural frame can be of benefit to some sectors. The cost of a CLT framed solution may be, elementally, marginally more expensive than the more usual frame forms. As outlined above, there are other aspects that make CLT a truly cost-effective option.

The whole life cost effect has to be considered. If the capital cost increases but whole life reduces the increase in overall value is a benefit in considering a CLT solution. There are wins for all: building owner/user, environment, community and increased social value.

VALUE IN THE FUTURE

How will we assess the value of a CLT structure, or any other off-site manufactured building, in the future? Will a more environmentally and 'net

CROSS LAMINATED TIMBER

zero carbon' (or carbon negative) building be in demand and, as such, be valued accordingly?

We do not know the answer, but the future demand of built environment assets will have to be more considerate of 'whole life costs and value' covering all aspects, including social value and wellbeing of users. Feasibly, the more traditionally constructed buildings become redundant, and 'stranded assets', in the future. Will these buildings have a lower status or value therefore society will avoid them? Will they simply be demolished and removed, with as much of the construction materials recycled as possible?

The increased awareness of social value and wellbeing in society will support the future use of CLT which results in better quality buildings. Having a good quality building improves the *performance* of users and having the warmth and appearance of timber on display in a building adds to the wellbeing factor. **Figure 6.5** shows the benefits to the occupants or users of a good quality building in differing respects.[4]

The construction sector is increasingly aware of having to act on its environmental impact and is mindful of the conscience of society. CLT is one product that *ticks the boxes* in many areas in this regard. The

FIG 6.5

The potential benefits of high quality buildings.

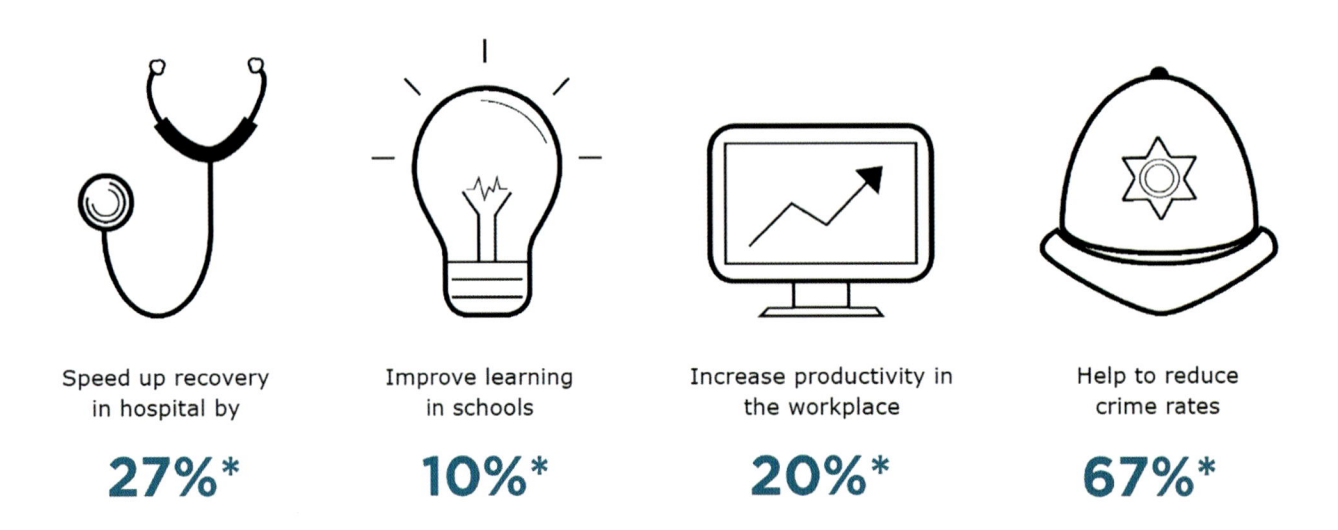

High quality buildings can:

Speed up recovery in hospital by	Improve learning in schools	Increase productivity in the workplace	Help to reduce crime rates
27%*	**10%***	**20%***	**67%***

*The value of good design: How buildings and spaces create economic and social value
Commission for Architecture & the Built Environment

points discussed in this chapter improve the programme for the return on investment for the client and funders for any project utilising CLT.

All the above issues discussed are intrinsically linked, making CLT a truly cost-effective and valued structural solution for many buildings. Even if not adopted as the whole frame there may be significant value benefits in using it, for example, as an internal floor solution.

The technical aspects of CLT throughout this book highlight the opportunities and issues to be overcome in using CLT. We need to dispel the myths and allow people to make an informed cost and value decision for their use of CLT, taking into account all the relevant factors.

The factors that create improved value to construction of utilising a CLT product can be summarised as follows:

Programme
- Erection of the overall frame – fewer labour hours required on site
- Programme on site is quicker

Site
- Tidier and cleaner site
- Follow-on trade benefits
- Service penetrations built in
- Minimal construction waste
- Savings on foundation loads and materials

Health and Safety
- Safe and controlled factory manufacturing
- Fewer people required on site

Procurement
- Single point responsibility
- Warranty/guarantee for entire superstructure

People
- Social value benefits
- Timber conveys warmth and is warm to the touch
- End user 'wellness' benefits

Environment
- Environmental and carbon considerations – both now and for the future
- Fewer transport movements during construction

Finish
- Factory produced accuracy
- Improved site tolerances
- Can be a finished product – protection essential

Key issues to consider
- Design freeze to benefit from off-site manufacture
- Protection essential if finished CLT used
- External weather-tight envelope required
- Financial exchange rates can affect capital affordability

CLT is marginally a more expensive product when compared in isolation to the other more traditional materials. Taking into account the above 'value factors' the cost reduces significantly, making it an economic and valuable building material now and in the future.

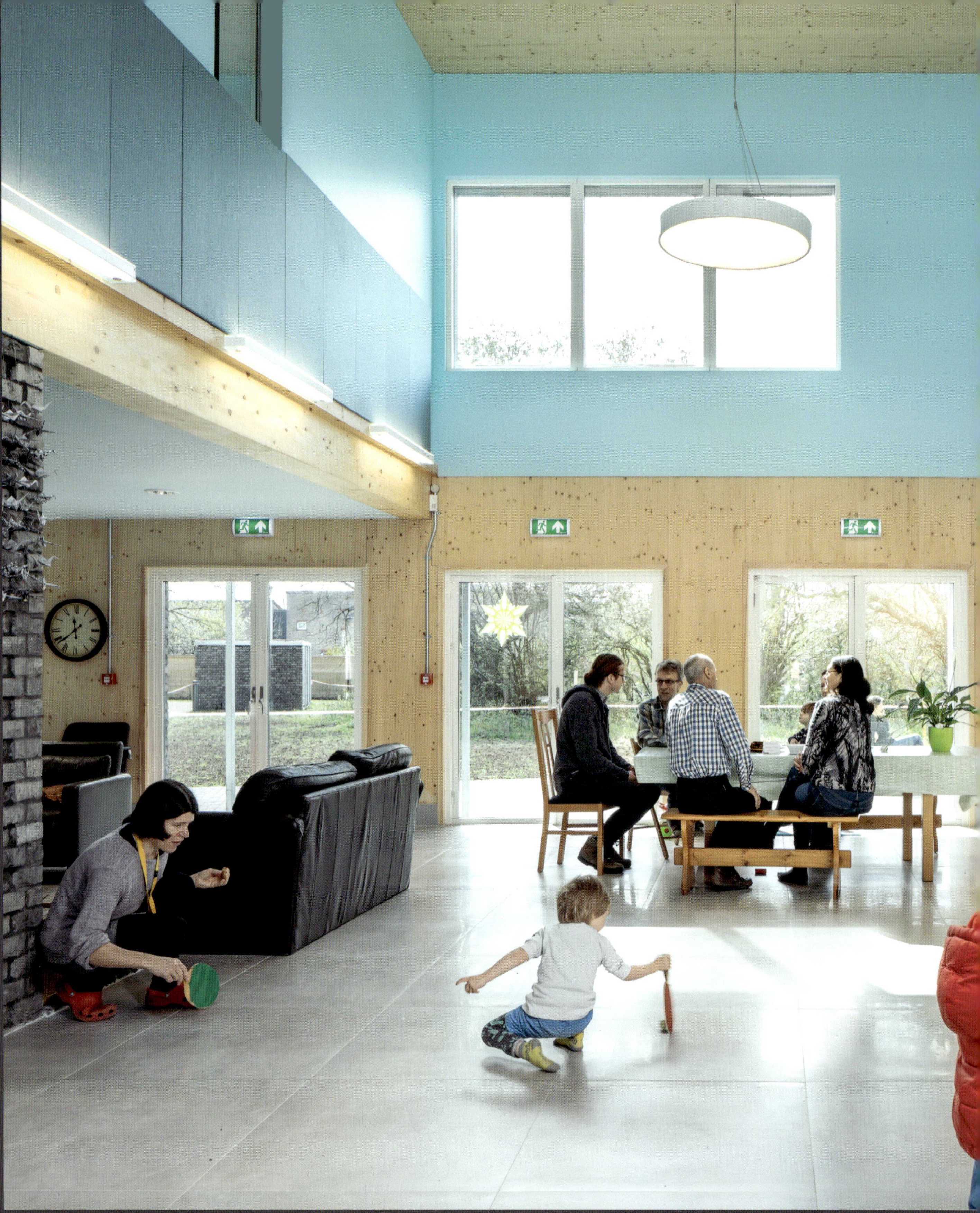

CHAPTER 7
PLANNING AND SOCIAL ISSUES

CLT use has significant social consequences at various levels and scales. Consequently, there are an increasing number of 'timber-first' policies being established globally, with policies introduced from Germany to Japan.[1] Interest from planners across the UK is significant and one UK local authority, the London Borough of Hackney (LBH), has done more to promote the use of CLT and timber building than any other.

CROSS LAMINATED TIMBER

FIG 7.0 (chapter opener)
Double height CLT formed community facilities serving new housing at Marmalade Lane, Cambridge by Mole Architects, 2018.

Following the completion of Waugh Thistleton Architects' milestone Murray Grove (2010), the London Borough of Hackney hosted a Wood First conference in May 2012. The council proposed a wood-first policy for new developments, recognising that building with timber would enable a reduction in the carbon content of new development to reflect sustainability policies. Trade associations representing other material suppliers quickly raised objections, threatening legal action challenging proposals for a formal policy, a move the borough lacked the resources to challenge.[2]

Much development in the borough over the decade since has been of medium scale, multi-storey up to 10-12 floors and relatively high density. This scale is often well suited to CLT use in terms of readily achievable performance, efficiency and good value and as such, an informal wood encouragement policy has resulted in a concentration of buildings exploring various forms of timber use, notably across all sectors, including some of the tallest and largest CLT buildings in the world (when completed).

THE INFLUENCE OF PLANNING POLICY AND DEVELOPMENT CONTROL

In the UK, development potential – the value of a site and resultant profit potential – is typically defined by planning permission (or the potential for such a consent). Easing the development process and obtaining a favourable reaction from planning authorities, whether officers or members, has huge value. This can unlock further funding and offer a degree of certainty by defining project direction and form. As such, an official policy prioritising timber use is one of the most powerful tools that might be used to encourage the take up of lower carbon forms of construction, and as seen in Hackney, an unofficial policy can still deliver surprising results.

National/provincial impacts

Countries rich in forest resources typically benefit from a heritage of building with timber and the associated established skill base. Promoting the increased use of timber for buildings in such regions not only promotes economic activity and employment but also can generate significant additional benefits through further investment and innovation.

One of the first regions to heavily promote timber use was British Columbia, two-thirds of which is forested. The Wood First Act 2009 was introduced aiming to 'facilitate a culture of wood by requiring the use of wood as the primary building material in all new provincially funded buildings'.[3] This has contributed to British Columbia reinforcing its position as a global centre of innovative timber industries, with globally important CLT precedents as well as manufacturing expertise.

The French government decreed that 50% of all new French public buildings be built from wood or other organic material by 2022 as part of ambitious sustainability aspirations.

CHAPTER 7 **PLANNING AND SOCIAL ISSUES**

Forest industries and rural areas

Manufacturing and processing CLT are typically undertaken adjacent to or near to sawmills, close to sources of timber. This may be deemed a positive consequence for rural communities, adding value to material locally and creating employment opportunities. Considerations of how forest resources are managed shouldn't be overlooked and are typically considered for timber sustainability certification purposes, albeit in particularly limited ways. However, an industrial scale, monoculture approach to plantation management can lead to significant biodiversity losses, particularly if land was previously mixed forest or under alternative use.

Increased timber use will also typically displace increasingly unpopular quarrying activities and extractive/industrial processes otherwise required to extract and process ore, limestone or aggregates.[4]

Regional/city scale

Mass timber use typically minimises vehicle movements, with far fewer vehicle movements for material deliveries and fewer workers on site (from 50 to 80% reductions, estimates vary). Concrete mixers may be required for foundations only and multiple panels are efficiently stacked in the factory on trailers to suit site access and logistics. Congestion, nuisance, pollution and risks to communities and neighbours as well road users, including pedestrians and cyclists, may therefore be reduced.

Recent discussions with a local government transport authority regarding an over-station development, potentially for their own occupation, highlighted such benefits. A huge increase in the popularity of cycling has led to an increase in cyclists' deaths on the roads, frequently involving heavy goods vehicles. Any likely reduction in HGV movements through the city centre because of CLT construction was deemed to be a positive, particularly one that might lead to a significant and quantifiable reduction in risk to citizens.

Promoting the use of lower embodied carbon materials in the near future may also maximise the potential for the long-term economic success and value of an area. If other buildings fall out of fashion because they are deemed to be too high impact or no longer attractive to incoming owners or tenants, demand will fall and prices will follow while the chances of disruptive redevelopment occurring sooner increase.

Neighbourhood aspects

A shorter superstructure programme may significantly reduce disruption to existing neighbours. Construction sites, during frame erection, and for follow-on trades, are typically quieter without very noisy activities such as formwork placement, whilst generating significantly less dust and enabling hot works that create risk or wet trades that slow down subsequent work to be reduced to a minimum or even eliminated entirely.

Comparatively little laydown space is required during construction whether panels are lifted directly from trailers or stacked on site. As such, neighbourhood impacts of site hoarding on pavements, highways and public spaces may be comparatively limited. Such aspects are of particular relevance to high-density urban environments where increased proximity to a site frequently amplifies neighbours' concerns, whether relating to perception or actual disturbance.

Social aspects for construction site labour

The installation of pre-manufactured components has a very significant social impact beyond the safety issues discussed in Chapter 11. The numbers of superstructure workers required for a CLT frame is typically a fraction of that required for alternatives and they are needed on site for less time since frame construction can be much faster (again, greater benefit may be felt on high-density, busy sites).

Follow-on trades have also reported significant improvements in their working environment with a resultant improvement in outlook from warmer, quieter and cleaner sites where trades are happier working. Providing easier work as well as a significantly better working environment is a very good way of encouraging safer and better quality outcomes whatever the work package. Anecdotal evidence of subcontractors completing work earlier than planned because of improved conditions is not uncommon (but this can also adversely affect site programming if not planned effectively).

Benefits for owners, occupiers and users

Benefits for occupants and users may include: high quality internal environments and efficient energy performance due to relatively high performance of CLT envelope construction with limited uncontrolled leakage potential; the hygroscopic action of exposed surfaces; long-term value or exposure to natural forms or biophilic elements. Some may appreciate the feel-good factor (or bragging rights) of being associated with cutting edge and low impact buildings, particularly when the impacts of more aspects of our lives are coming under ever increasing scrutiny. Custom build participants and those commissioning private homes may appreciate the speed of construction and certainty in installed quality.

CHAPTER 7 **PLANNING AND SOCIAL ISSUES**

CASE STUDY EXAMPLES

FIG 7.1 & 7.2

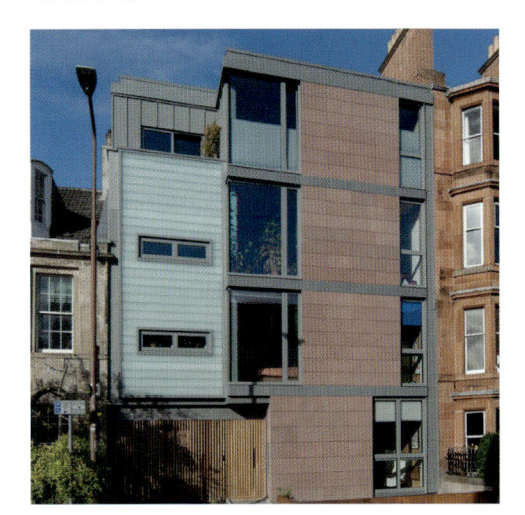

26BS (2017) is a collective custom build for four families near Edinburgh, initiated, designed and managed by architect John Kinsley. The building addresses the participant's requirements for flexible, high quality homes with exemplary sustainability and performance credentials. Procuring a predominantly CLT superstructure alongside limited other key packages avoided the need for a main contractor (or house builder's profit) delivering shell and core homes at cost price. Following the Scottish tenement approach over four floors, a central CLT core with glulam beams and CLT slabs spanning to perimeter supporting walls of the same allows participants flexibility with internal planning and fit-out.

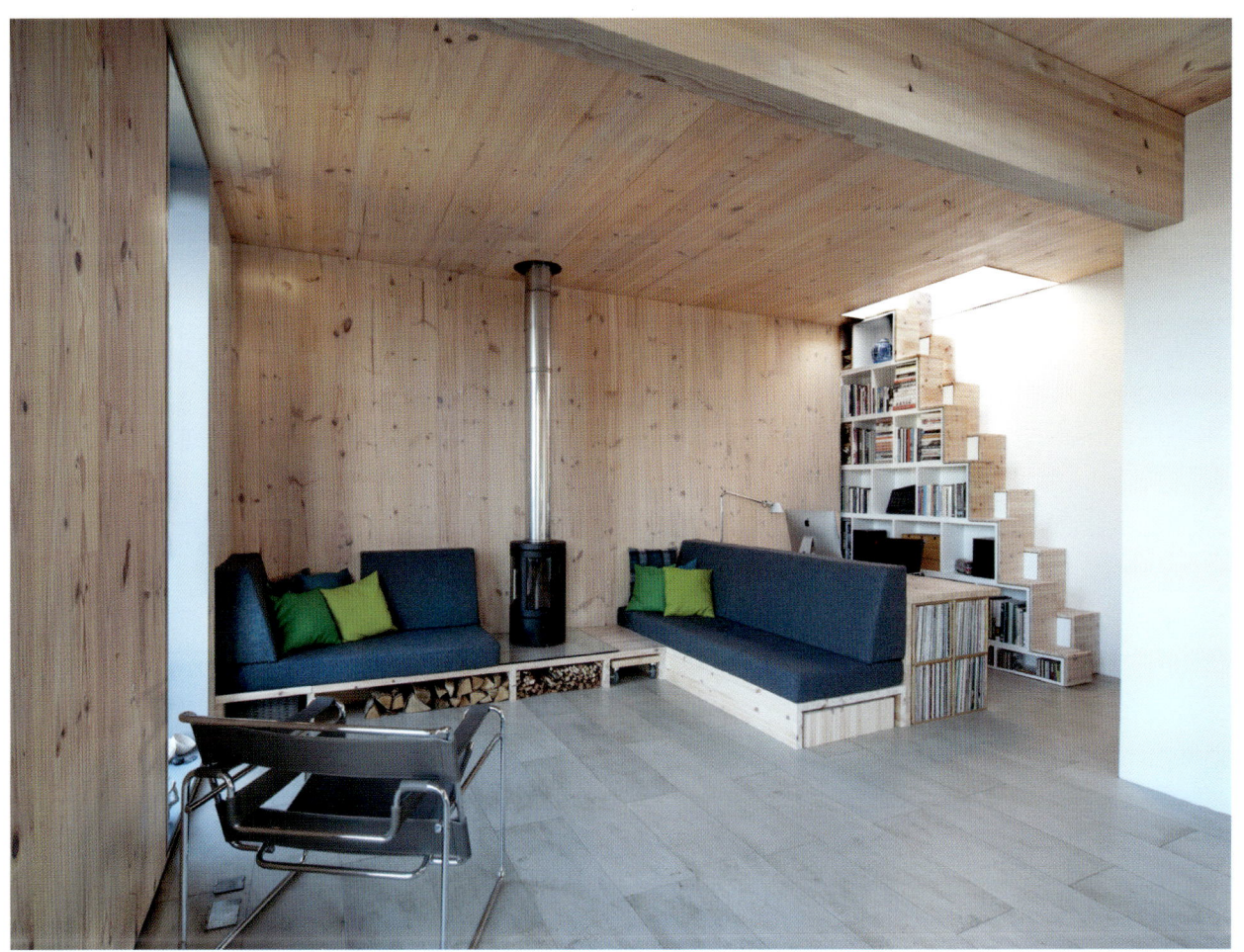

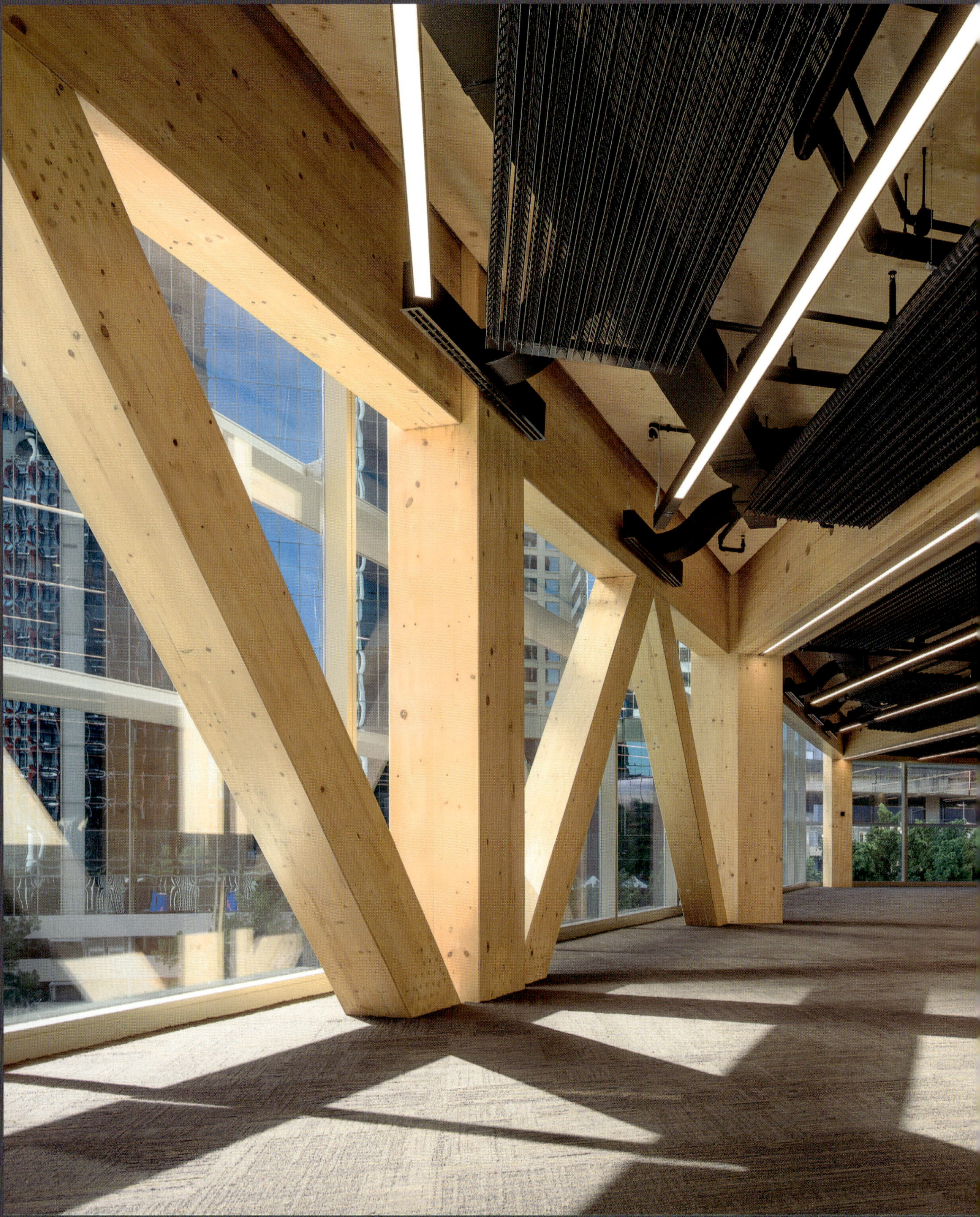

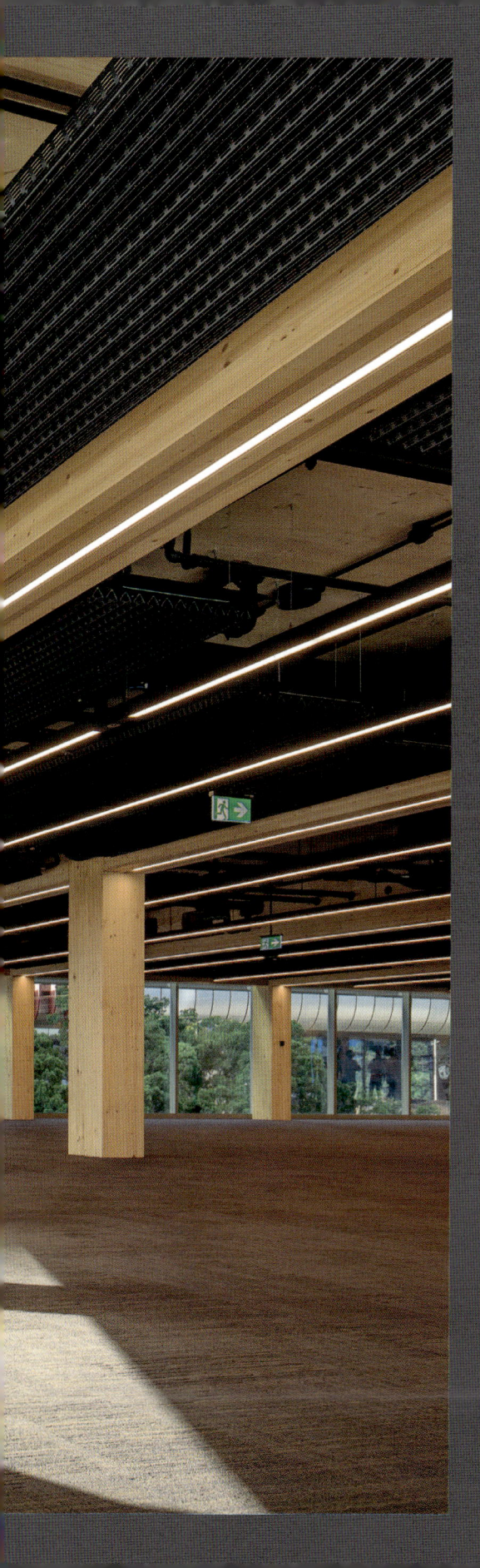

CHAPTER 8
DESIGN AND PROCUREMENT

More so than other forms of construction, the issues around design and procurement discussed here are closely interrelated with CLT use, due in part to the relative inexperience of the industry (in the UK and other English-speaking regions), from consultants to contractors, an expanding supply chain and associated issues of technical uncertainty and risk (whether potential or perceived).[1]

CROSS LAMINATED TIMBER

FIG 8.0 (chapter opener)

Expressed services coordinated with a timber hybrid glulam structure on a CLT soffit for International House, a trend-setting commercial office precedent in Sydney (by Tzannes Associates, 2017).

RIBA PLAN OF WORK STAGES

Stage 2: Concept design

Stage 2 is the time to agree, and importantly sign-off, the architectural concept and engineering strategies, recognising that subsequent changes may be disruptive and compromise efficiency. Changing to a CLT structure at later stages will fail to realise many of the advantages of having adopted such an approach earlier (but is not uncommon). This stage is a good time to review and communicate the benefits of CLT use to ensure they can be realised wherever appropriate. If not already in place, a detailed design responsibility matrix should considered with appropriate experience and inputs sought as required.

CASE STUDY EXAMPLES

FIG 8.1

Hands Building, Mansfield College, Oxford by Mica Architects (2017) demonstrates the early integration of architectural and structural strategies to benefit procurement. A deep concrete basement (housing the Bonavero Institute of Human Rights) was designed to counter non-standard buoyancy and heave effects. These were due to the lightweight nature of the CLT structure forming four floors of student accommodation over. (Foundations to CLT structures may typically be reduced in scale unless there is significant accommodation incorporated within basement areas.) The CLT superstructure was designed and fabricated during the relatively slow basement construction period, allowing a rapid build once the project emerged from the ground.[2]

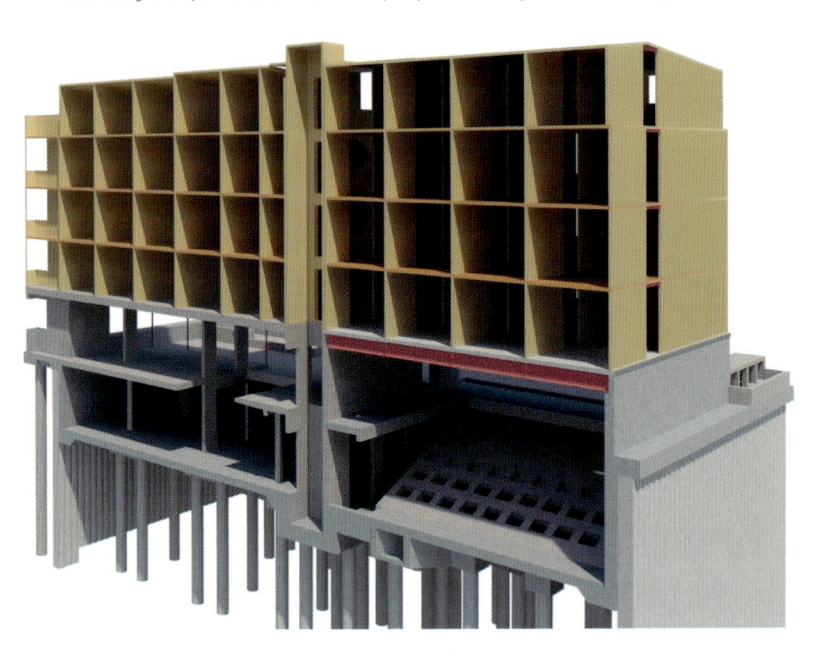

Stage 3: Spatial coordination

The coordination of detailed engineering strategies (structural, servicing, acoustics and fire being the most relevant) with the architectural model is fundamental, as is optimising the design for manufacture. This will inform the cost and reduce subsequent risks, particularly when design responsibilities for such elements may change to suit a building contract. For this reason, teams may also wish to record further detail as to why decisions are made or particular approaches are adopted to avoid ambiguity should others become involved. Doing so can help prevent value engineering becoming simply cost cutting when the full benefits of CLT use are not understood. Well-developed BIM models and the use of benchmarks and mock-ups can help. Key deliverables for CLT projects will include coordinated designs for services installations and penetrations, typically ahead of those required for conventional builds.

Stage 4: Technical design

The RIBA Plan of Work advocates completing all the design information for manufacturing and construction before the end of Stage 4. Accordingly, the impacts of differing procurement strategies on design intent, information production and coordination (frequently most obvious in terms of building services) should be clearly communicated and understood by the project team and client and this is where previous experience or early stage collaboration can have great impacts.

Design and coordination responsibilities for all pre-manufactured elements will need to be revisited, allowing sufficient time when working back from the information required for panel manufacturing. Any design responsibility matrix should be reviewed and all parties should agree that unless exceptions are defined, and then carefully managed, the scheme for construction is frozen at this stage. Where information is required before the full completion of a stage, teams should be very clear about tasks required (and outstanding) and the responsibility for all associated deliverables.

KEY ISSUES

The following considerations are not exhaustive and project priorities will no doubt vary depending upon location, team experience, sector, form of procurement etc.

Appropriate design

This may include ensuring that material choices are appropriate to the intended function and likely form, addressing brief requirements or site conditions and that where possible the benefits of the material use are realised fully, accounting for issues of delivery cost, programme

CASE STUDY EXAMPLES

FIG 8.2 & 8.3

The form of this new dwelling, Burwood House by Catja de Haas Architects (2019), demonstrates the need for clearly defined responsibilities in collaborative design. As well as areas of self-supporting CLT, some panels to perimeter elevations and a projecting upper floor are supported on a slender steel frame. These panels in turn support secondary elements such as glazing or cantilevered balconies that were not included with the CLT package. At early stage an outline structural design was prepared to give initial CLT loading for steelwork design that was then validated when a CLT designer contractor was appointed. They then integrated loadings from these secondary elements into the later stage CLT design.[3]

CHAPTER 8 **DESIGN AND PROCUREMENT**

and long-term value. Consider using CLT for its own strengths and characteristics rather than simply replacing another material and do not use it where it makes more sense to use other materials – it is certainly not appropriate for all circumstances or situations.

Avoiding significant spans (greater than 6.5m) and unnecessary materials use to areas where it may not be required (such as panels with large openings) will improve efficiency as will rationalising load paths, aligning functions and elements vertically and minimising transfer structures, typically more so than with other forms of construction.

Collaboration

The UK government's construction and industrial strategies emphasise the benefits of collaborative working with early contractor and specialist engagement. The input of experienced others pre-contract is typically of enormous value – a recurrent theme in case study projects. Specialist

---

CASE STUDY EXAMPLES

FIG 8.4 & 8.5

The Seed House, Castlecrag, New South Wales, Australia, by fitzpatrick + partners (2019) is clearly a passion project for a well-resourced architect with a lot of ideas. CLT forms lightly supported roofs, floors, stairs, external walls, internal partitions and even doors – exposed throughout and complemented by other more finely finished timbers. Complex spans, cantilevers and box elements leverage the material's bidirectional strength rather than simply acting as ordinary load-bearing elements. A significant investment in design and analysis time included 800 hours of finite element analysis alone, considering large panel spans and the bounce and vibration of cantilevered elements.

contractors and suppliers will likely be available to contribute and many manufacturers offer design and consultancy services.

Roles and design and coordination responsibilities for all pre-manufactured elements will need to be developed and defined, allowing sufficient time working back from the information required for panel manufacturing. In the case of CLT projects there will be likely related challenges due to differing specialist design responsibilities. A structural engineer may produce initial designs, for this role to be passed to a subcontractor (or their specialist timber engineer) and building services strategies may be insufficiently well advanced or detailed to provide appropriate information to manufacture panels. It is not uncommon for late inputs from a services subcontractor (not forgetting any necessary coordination) to delay the manufacturing of panels.

CLT specific roles and responsibilities to address on any pre-tender design responsibility matrix should consider design, detailed design and construction information responsibility, (including any checking requirements of subcontractor proposals) for fire stopping and protection – a fire safety specialist should be included and moisture management planned – both during superstructure erection and during subsequent site works to handover and the design of connections between structural elements, particularly if complex/non-standard or intended to be fully exposed.

Regarding design of interfaces between different elements – the detailing of hybrid forms (beyond full CLT) can increase requirements from designers very significantly and this should not be overlooked.

BIM benefits

The use of BIM throughout the design process promotes collaboration, allows the rapid design iteration and optimisation of CLT use and can improve costings. There is the potential to link to other tools such as finite element analysis software and it will assist the detailed cross-discipline design coordination necessary through to information for manufacturing. Looking ahead, BIM may also be used for 4D planning of logistics and works on site (with attendant efficiencies as well as time and safety benefits for follow-on trades) and ultimately provide a detailed record of CLT components used, ensuring a building remains a well-understood asset regarding future adaptation or the reuse of components rather than becoming a liability over time.

Insurers, risk managers, warranty providers and building control

All such bodies are inherently conservative and must be engaged well in advance of any final decision or sign-off required. All will have a view of CLT use and few will view it favourably unless specific conditions are met. The team may need to work together to understand and address concerns

CASE STUDY EXAMPLES

FIG 8.6

Cambridge Mosque (2019) is a community and faith building with adjoining residences, designed entirely as a timber hybrid with an expressed repeated tree form of central glulam structural elements with solid CLT walls and prefabricated insulated CLT wall and roof panels (painted white as recessive, enclosing elements).

Marks Barfield Architects engaged an engineer with exemplary timber experience directly to advise on initial design development and tender analysis, including moisture and movement issues, ensuring that architecture, engineering and materials use were fully integrated (and buildable). The client also employed the timber subcontractor before novation to best leverage their experience and design input.

raised and this is another area where early collaboration can pay dividends. Fire and safety issues are addressed elsewhere but prominent issues may include: durability and moisture management (see below); rigorous site management and the inspection of works; compartmentation; voids and the continuity of barriers and issues beyond life safety (such as repair after damage). Extra care should be taken where there is legislative ambiguity or uncertainty around particular aspects of a materials use.

Beyond addressing negative concerns and risks, consider positive impacts of CLT use that may appeal such as the need for better and earlier coordination of designs, additional measures that may reduce risks or improve safety, the benefits of improved quality and certainty of what is being installed (with CLT, you get what you draw) and the reduced need for on-site decision making and 'fitting'.

Moisture management

Durability risks due to moisture damage are a significant challenge, one of the key issues for CLT use, and are almost always underestimated. Beyond considerations of the planned construction sequence to allow sufficient drying of moisture before being sealed up, any areas of potential water or moisture ingress or collection in use pose a risk to CLT elements if undetected over time. If CLT gets wet and stays wet, it will likely decay. This issue has the potential to cause huge problems during the lifetime of a building and MUST be considered and addressed through design, construction and use.

Particularly vulnerable areas include ground floor/lower level CLT interfaces, end grain exposure to the edges of panels, envelope detailing and penetrations where unseen failures may compromise internal elements, flat roofs where failed membranes/waterproofing layers and subsequent leaks may go undetected and terraces, for similar reasons. Counter measures may include end grain sealant for temporary site protection of panel edges, using breathable elements and insulation where possible, considering other structural materials for flat roofs or incorporating shallow pitches to all slabs with drainage or ventilation zones above panels (especially for warm roofs). Consider partially open joints to 'flat' panels laid to shallow falls or incorporating multiple small perforations to panels forming roofs or below wet service installations (such as WC areas) so any water penetration beyond is made apparent to occupants below (soffits perforated in sensitive areas by 10mm weep holes may be preferable to unseen leaks above panels).

CLT has relatively low thermal conductivity (c.0.13W/mK) and given its potential to cantilever, it may be tempting to continue floor panels from internal to external areas, forming terraces or balconies while minimising cold bridging. Unless there is a well-managed, robust and continuous layer of protection, such as that to a continuous shallow pitch roof, possibly with weep holes, such arrangements are best avoided. This is because damage

CHAPTER 8 **DESIGN AND PROCUREMENT**

CASE STUDY EXAMPLES

FIG 8.7 & 8.8

Harris Academy Sutton, by Architype (2019) uses a CLT and glulam structure to upper floors, factory cut to accommodate a limited amount of steel structure.

Full Passive House performance standards resulted in many coordinated service penetrations through load-bearing elements, with some additional openings formed during construction but large format panels helped achieve excellent airtightness.

Thin floor finishes to concrete slabs resulted in bespoke timber to slab connections (that might otherwise have been concealed in a flooring zone) and building in falls to upper level panels with temporary and permanent drainage points in beams and upstands enabled water to be managed on site.

or failure of protection to external areas might compromise the integrity of internal CLT elements, particularly floor elements which are typically more difficult to protect, ventilate or inspect.[4]

Beyond manufacturers' guidance, the (UK) Structural Timber Association publish extensive guidance around issues of durability and moisture control and further discussion is included within Chapter 12.

Acoustic strategy

Alongside durability and fire issues, acoustic challenges are a critical issue when designing with CLT (typically due to the material's lightweight nature). The most successful projects consider and define such issues early on and integrate solutions though design development in collaboration with specialists. Test data from manufacturers or previous projects can be particularly useful when available.

Tolerances and interfaces

Values typically vary between producers but CLT generally offers much tighter general tolerances than other materials. Whereas dimensions of concrete elements may vary as much as +/- 25-30mm, geometric tolerances for CLT panels may be as low as +/- 1-2mm by default. Similarly, the size or positions of openings can be tightly controlled with similar comparative values for CLT products, compared to similar figures as above for large openings in concrete.[5]

Such unprecedented accuracy for setting out of panels and apertures provides less opportunity for error which is good for fire stopping, acoustics and air/weather tightness as well as better coordination with external elements such as cladding, reveal linings or service penetrations. These are however not dimensions most constructers would recognise on a building site and whilst they may seem almost magical, the tolerances and geometric variations of all other elements and materials at interfaces, connections etc will be much greater (i.e. normal for in-situ or site work) so designs will likely have to accommodate much greater variations if incorporating hybrid structures or interfacing with concrete slabs or other construction.

Connection and joint design

Concealed connections and panel joints are cheaper and simpler to make (as are non-visual grade panels), exposed panels joints less (as the cost of visual grade panels also increases). Greater complexity of connections and interfaces to exposed areas or hybrid elements may result in additional cost and design commitment and may impact manufacturing design time in complex cases.

CHAPTER 8 **DESIGN AND PROCUREMENT**

Accessories

CLT is generally deemed airtight but tapes, sealing compounds or isolation strips may be required between panels for airtightness, acoustic or fire performance purposes and will require particular consideration when exposed. Strategies should be agreed with consultants before detailed design is begun.

CASE STUDY EXAMPLES

FIG 8.9

To avoid the risk of movement cracking the external brick tile cladding at Cambridge Mosque, (by Marks Barfield, 2019), double height external wall panels were utilised, reflecting the inherent stability of continuous panels. Intermediate floors are supported by a housing joint to the inner face in lieu of typical platform style construction for two storey elements.

The specialist timber contractor undertook extensive analysis of external wind loads to determine the maximum deflection potential of these panels, assisting the cladding consultant verify proposals minimising horizontal movement joints without risking cracking across the tiled masonry clad facade.

Supply capacity and manufacturers data

Global demand for CLT has never been greater and since CLT is custom manufactured on demand, no stocks or buffers are held. One recent large project in London has procured and taken delivery of CLT floor elements months in advance of them being required, to an off-site location before preparatory site works are complete in order to secure sufficient production capacity.

A number of references are included throughout this book to illustrate that further guidance and detailed technical data are widely accessible to project teams, as **Figure 8.10**. Such sources can be invaluable when considering general approaches and likely performance of elements, but teams should bear in mind that any performance data or assumptions (especially regarding fire or acoustics) will likely be derived from limited tests with very specific material combinations. All figures and data should be investigated thoroughly and many projects will require bespoke calculations and possibly testing.

CHAPTER 8 **DESIGN AND PROCUREMENT**

FIG 8.10

Example extract from manufacturer's technical literature, indicating typical wall build-up with key building physics/environmental performance criteria.

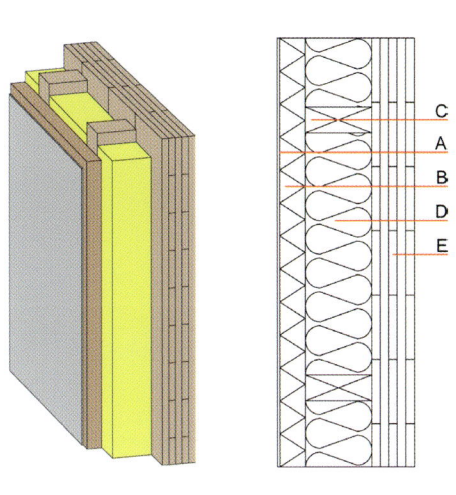

Building physical and ecological rating

	Fire protection	REI i → o	60
	max. unsupported length l = 3 m; max. load ($q_{fi, d}$) = 60 [kN/m]		
	Heat insulation	U [W/m²K]	0.165
	Sound insulation	R_W [dB]	45
	Ecology	ΔOI3	48

Building material specifications for construction, layer structure | from the inside to the outside

	Thickness [mm]	Building material	Heat conductivity λ [W/(m · K)]	Gross density ρ [kg/m³]	Flammability class EN 13501-1
A	7	Plaster facade, e.g. weberpas topdry	0.45	1,600	A2
B	60	Wood fibre insulation panel	0.042	140	E
C	160	Construction hardwood (b ≥ 60; e = 625)	0.13	475	D
D	160	Mineral wool, e.g. Isover Kontur FSP 1-035	0.034	24	A1
E	100	CLT BBS, 5-layered	0.12	450	D
Total	32.70 cm			75.74 kg/m²	

Ecological rating in detail

PENRT [MJ/m²]	GWP100 total [kg CO_2/m²]	AP [kg SO_2/m²]
779	-55.2	0.231

Classification by IBS – Institut für Brandschutztechnik und Sicherheitsforschung [Institute for Fire Protection Technology and Safety Research], A-4020 Linz
Calculation by IBO – Österreichisches Institut für Bauen und Ökologie [Austrian Institute for Construction and Ecology], A-1090 Vienna
Rated by ift Rosenheim – Schallschutzzentrum [Sound Insulation Centre], D-83026 Rosenheim and respectively Holzforschung Austria, A-1030 Vienna
Calculation by IBO – Österreichisches Institut für Bauen und Ökologie [Austrian Institute for Construction and Ecology], A-1090 Vienna

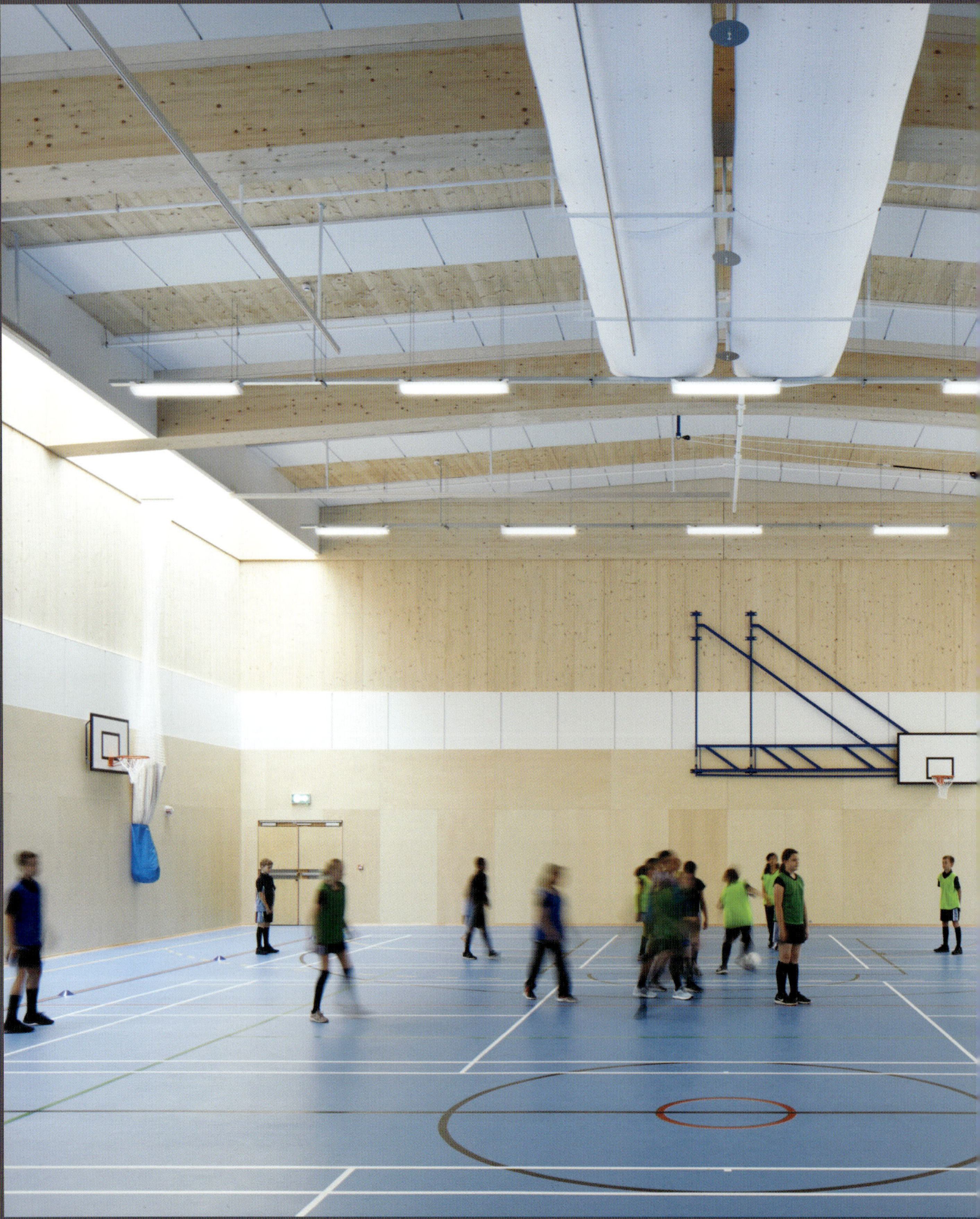

CHAPTER 9
ENGINEERING ASPECTS

In understanding the properties of CLT it is first important to understand the makeup of the raw material itself. Timber is an orthotropic material, meaning its material properties change when measured from different directions. The opposite of which (isotropic) for example would be steel where the values are the same in all directions. So, in a three-dimensional space, timber will have two axes that will have similar properties, which are perpendicular to the grain and one unique direction parallel to the grain.

CROSS LAMINATED TIMBER

> This chapter was contributed by *Alan Dowdall*, structural engineer and timber design lead with Ramboll (UK). Alan has very significant experience with many pioneering CLT buildings across different sectors.

FIG 9.0 (chapter opener)

The 715m² sports hall at Harris Academy, Sutton (by Architype, 2019), was erected in just six weeks. The large format CLT panels, seen with glulam roof beams, contributed to very high envelope performance in terms of insulation and airtightness. At over 10,000m² in area, this was the largest passivhaus project and the first passivhaus secondary school completed in the UK.

The simplest way to visualise the formation of wooden material is via a typical drinking straw, or a group of straws. Quite soft in two planes, but strong in the direction of the straws. When viewed at a microscopic level timber does indeed resemble a collection of straws. It is this cellular structure that gives the material both its strength and its weakness. The challenge in the design of any structure is to fully appreciate both the positives and constraints around a material and create a design that accommodates all aspects of the behaviour.

Timber is therefore strong in one axis. With CLT the process of cross laying the lamella is effectively reinforcing the section with more of the same material, i.e. wood reinforced with more wood. The impact is a versatile timber panel that can be used to form all parts of a structure that is lightweight, fast to construct and sustainable.

CLT BUILDING DESIGN

Understanding the material properties allows designers to apply any material where it will be working to its strengths and minimise the constraints.

Structural watchpoints

1. Avoid transfer structures. If not avoidable, loads to be light and spans short.
2. Meeting floor vibration criterion generally governs floor slab sizes (unless fire criteria is onerous).
3. Charring due to fire scenario will result in sharp reductions in capacities as char depth increases, particularly when passing a glue line.
4. Consider how exposed sections can be connected and what can/can't be seen.
5. Timber connections can be unforgiving. Front load the design intent during early stages.
6. Low density CLT is not particularly effective for resisting acoustic transmissions (additional means of mass or isolation may be required).

Building layout

CLT is a great timber product for supporting uniform loadings e.g. roofs, office floors or residential floors. The material will however struggle with large concentrated loads such as transfer loads. They may be possible but can significantly increase sizes of the elements, have large creep deflections and generally require stiffening elements (e.g. steel).

CHAPTER 9 ENGINEERING ASPECTS

Efficient layouts can be created by maintaining a simple load path to the foundations/podium structures e.g. building setbacks to be aligned with the structural grid or wall panels. It's not uncommon for the ground floor to require a more open plan structure to the layout. A podium to this area is quite regular and generally formed from concrete.

Floor spans

The main driving factor for a CLT floor structure will typically be the vibration criteria to be achieved. This should be looked at early in the scheming process and can define the setting out of the structure/architecture/material volume.

From a timber volume regard, shorter spans will significantly reduce the volume of material required and hence the cost. The sizes in **Table 9.1** give an approximate indication of expected size ranges.[1]

Building type	Typical Floor Spans	Typical Panel Depth
Residential	<5.0m	160-180mm
Education	7.5m	220-240mm
Commercial	6.0-7.5m	220-260mm

Maximise the off-site advantage

Maximising the off-site production process will lead to a smoother construction process. Consider grids/layouts to suit the ideal transport section and reduce wastage, front load services coordination where possible and the potential to pre-install roof membranes before placing panels, reducing work and risk on site and better for durability. With accurate CNC cutting, windows might be pre-ordered for quicker weather tight envelopes.

CLT FRAMING

Structural openings, such as large doors and windows will tend to require a lintel of some sort as **Figure 9.1**.

FIG 9.1

Methods of forming openings, from left to right: 1. Two-way spanning slab over openings (no lintel), 2. Wall panels with punched openings, 3. Lintel support.

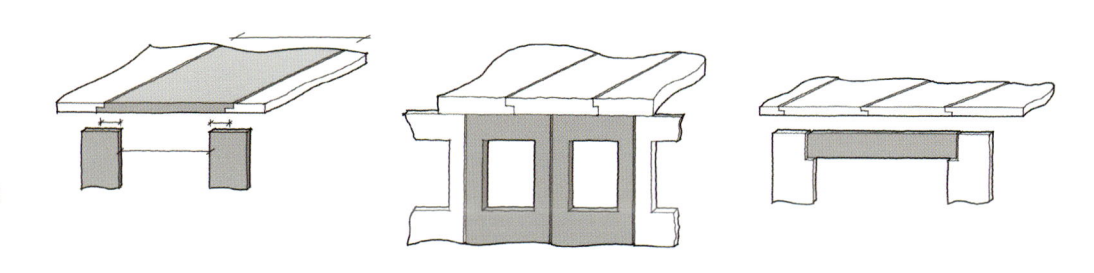

Method 1: Two-way spanning slab

The two-way spanning nature of the CLT panels can be utilised over openings where the width of the opening does not exceed the width of the panel and the bearing requirements. Supporting the slab in such a manner uses the two-way spanning nature of the CLT where the inner layers perpendicular to the main span are now acting in a larger structural capacity. The floor slab panel arrangement will need to be cut to suit the locations of the openings. This type of method is best suited as a window opening where no downstand is permitted, possibly due to daylight requirements.

Method 2: Punched holes

A punched panel arrangement can be used mainly for smaller window or door openings and is subject to the width of a panel. Openings are cut to a high tolerance so fixtures can be fitted almost straight away. However, in terms of the material's efficiency the timber cut away to create the opening needs to be included within the costs. In this case the inner layers provide the structural capacity. For high loadings the shear capacity will tend to be critical due to the reduced structural width.

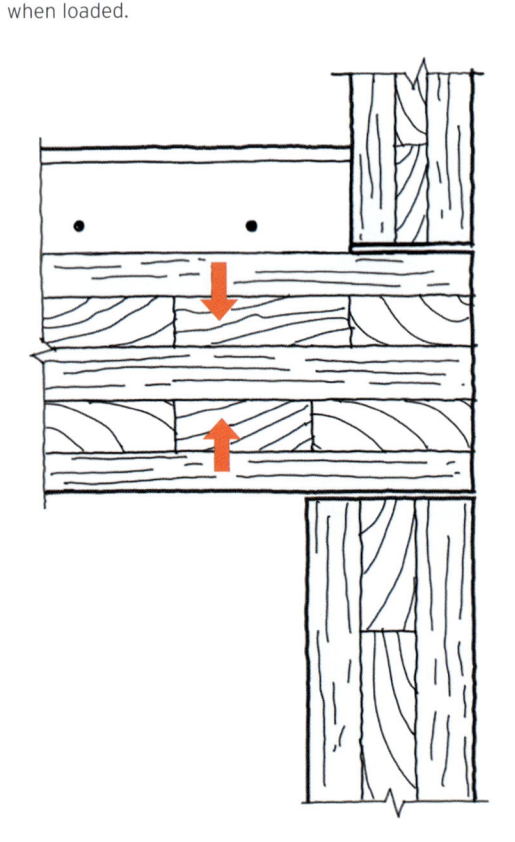

Method 3: Lintel

The majority of large openings will require a lintel support. A panel is rotated 90 degrees to form a downstand beam. The external layers are now the structural elements and offer greater capacity for the same depth compared to the punched panel arrangement. With a lintel design it is typically best practice to design the opening so the lintel and wall panel are the same thickness. This can avoid complicated finishes details and bearing issues.

UNDERSTANDING MOVEMENT BEHAVIOUR

While CLT reinforces the stability of the product it does so in one direction only. The typical construction method for CLT is to support the floor panel by directly bearing onto the CLT wall (platform construction, as **Figure 9.2**). The next wall then bears onto that floor panel. This means that the building load is applied across the grain of the floor panel which is more susceptible to the displacement and to moisture drying shrinkage effects.

Understanding the movement of the structure is necessary in ensuring that the details' design can be developed to either resist or allow for this change in dimension. Areas where this is particularly relevant include:

- Lift shafts: The predicted movement/settlement and tolerance to the lift should be communicated to the lift installation company to ensure

FIG 9.2

Section through floor slab (platform style construction) indicating direction of movement when loaded.

enough allowance is made in the connection details and to enable a consideration of potential lift realignment once the building settlement has occurred.
- Stacked facades: Where a facade is stacked from the ground floor, consideration should be given to the differential deflection at windows and parapets, e.g. a brick facade will expand in certain conditions while the timber structure will settle over time.
- Fixed facades: A rendered solution would likely need a movement joint at the floor level to avoid potential cracking uses due to shrinkage. It is also typical to fix heavier facade solutions (brick/stone) at each floor level. This limits differential movement issues but will add to the load in the timber, which could result in to reinforcement to avoid crushing of the floor.

Detailing for vertical movement tends to fall under one of two approaches:

1. Allow the timber floor to move and detail the design around this.
2. Restrict the level of movement that can be experienced in the structure.

In limiting the vertical movement the aim is to reduce the amount of loaded perpendicular grain to the floors, so the load path becomes an end grain to end grain solution. This can be accomplished by using castellated timber walls or grout pockets.

CLT ELEMENT DESIGN

The structural analysis of a CLT element is not as straightforward as reinforced concrete slab or steel section. The structural elements of the section are the layers with the grain direction parallel to the span direction. The layers in between contribute very little to the stiffness other than increasing the lever arm between the parallel layers.

FIG 9.3

Floor panel section indicating potential for fibre rolling effect of intermediate layers (cross lamella) when loaded.

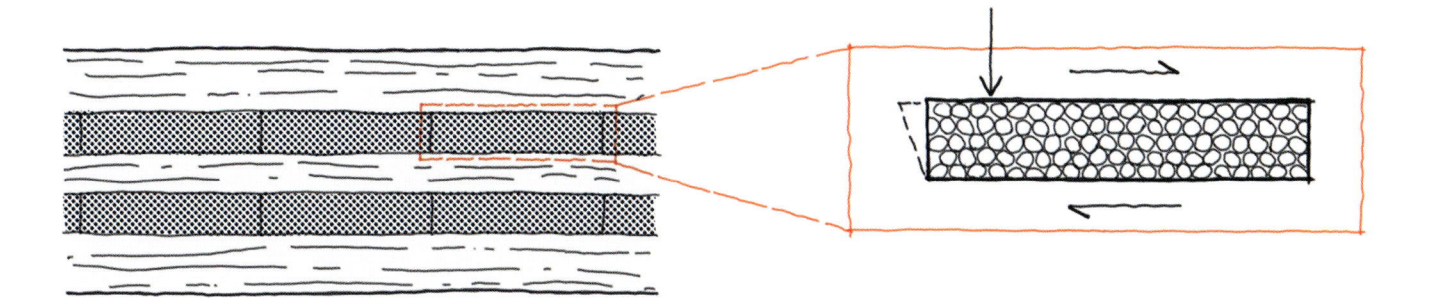

In analysing the stiffness of the CLT panel a critical factor is the rolling shear in the perpendicular grain. This will need to be considered when calculating the moment of inertia (I value), as the timber fibres can 'roll' and create a slippage in the element as **Figure 9.3**. Parallel layers cannot therefore be assumed to act in a fully composite manner. This leads to a counterintuitive situation where the longer the floor spans the more composite the section becomes. This is due to the area of the perpendicular layers increasing longitudinally and hence there is more resistant to rolling shear forces.

There are several methods of calculating such properties, however the most common is the 'Gamma method' where an approximation of the shear deflection is calculated. Annex B in BS EN 1995-1-1 gives guidance on the calculation of a mechanically jointed beam.[2] This gives a method of calculating the slip in between the joint members called the Gamma value. This value is based on the slip modulus of the fastener which it assumes is either a screw, bolt, dowel, staple etc.

On this basis, the sectional properties of the CLT panels can then be calculated by taking into account the fact that the fasteners between the structural panels are perpendicular timbers where shear failure is critical. Once this value has been obtained it can be applied to the structural layers using parallel axis theorem to calculate the stiffness of the panels. From this, the stresses and deflections in the panel can be calculated to ensure an appropriate design.

With the analysis of a beam section the layers in line with the span are taken into account during the design for moment, shear and deflection. The buckling of a beam is not usually an issue as the beam is typically restrained by the support slab. However, in certain situations this may not be the case, therefore a buckling check is required.

The total width of a CLT beam may be used for the critical bending stress calculation if the outer layers are aligned with the span. If they are not, they should not be included in the buckling calculation.

The analysis of walls and columns follows the same principles to that of a beam i.e. selecting the correct structural layers for strength and buckling checks.

Stability to a CLT structure is typically provided by the floor panels acting as a diaphragm and directing the loads to the vertical stability wall elements. Where CLT walls provide the stability to the building, the floor-to-floor heights can impact on the capacity of the walls to resist horizontal wind loads or limit building deflection.

FIG 9.4

Stability wall arrangements and potential for deflection under load.

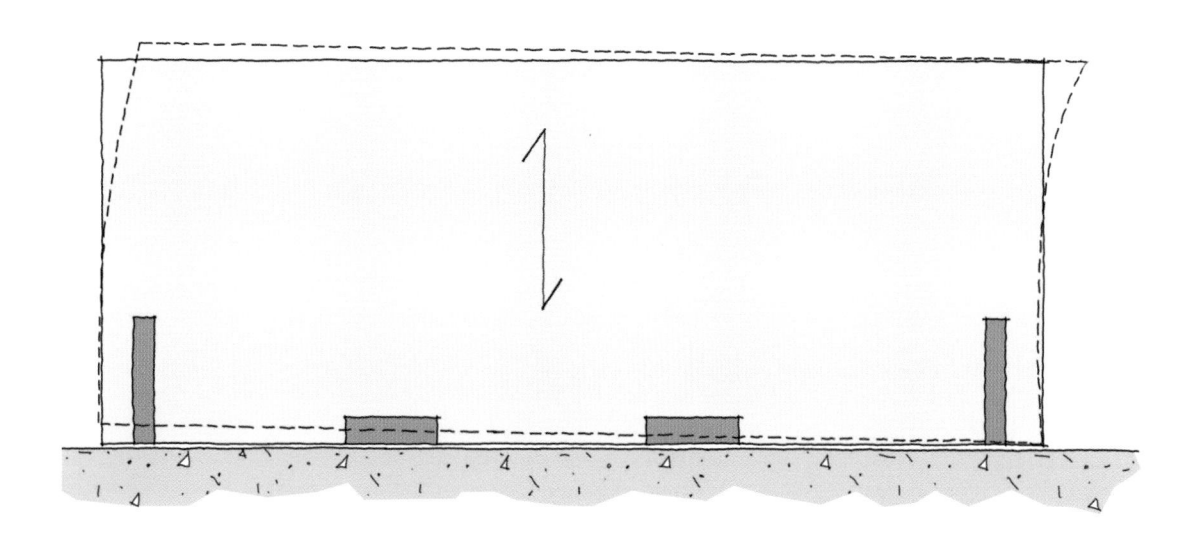

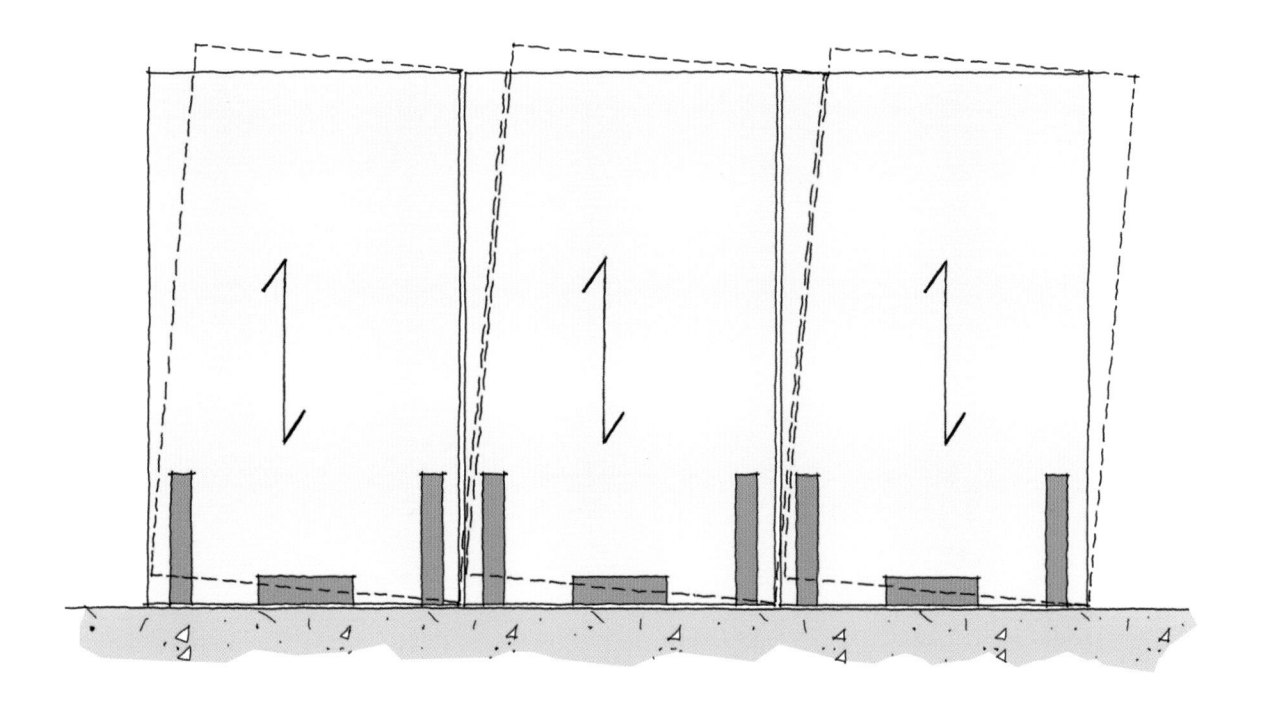

ACOUSTIC CONSIDERATIONS

Sound transmittance and soundproofing remains a key issue between uses, dwellings or areas within the same building, such as adjacent office floors or school classrooms. Timber is significantly less dense than concrete, typically around 20% of the density. Therefore, an approximately 500mm thick CLT floor slab would be required to achieve the same level of sound insulation as a 100mm thick concrete floor slab. Simply increasing the thickness of a timber slab is not often a viable solution.

A better way to increase the level of sound insulation is by acoustically decoupling the elements within a separating construction. This can be achieved by the inclusion of cavities separating two mass elements and/or resilient fixings. The inclusion of an absorbent material within cavities can further help to improve the level of sound insulation by reducing resonances. Adding mass is another commonly adopted mitigation measure, this might be in the form of a screed topping over CLT slabs or dry laid high density boards, typically lap jointed, above a slab.

Manufacturers usually offer detailed guidance regarding sound insulation, focusing on airborne sound (such as music or voices) and structure borne sound, including impact sound (e.g. footsteps or moving furniture). Accessory manufacturers offer separation strips that can be used to improve the acoustic performance of panel joints or fixings and test data is widely published for various elemental build-ups using different materials; this is typically reflected in manufacturers technical approval documents such as European Technical Assessments (ETA) or software tools.

CHAPTER 9 **ENGINEERING ASPECTS**

PANEL CONNECTIONS

FIG 9.5 & 9.6

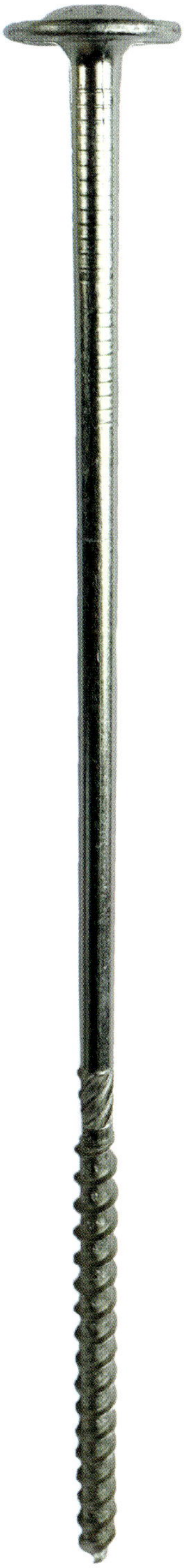

Different screws are used to connect panels in various ways and a broad range of brackets and accessories are available to suit specific fixings and functions.[3] A washer head screw, as shown, may be from 50-480mm long. Indicative axonometric and section sketches show options for forming wall/floor connections (from left: platform style with verticals built off horizontal panels, right: floors fixed from continuous wall vertical panel) and below, joining floor panels (from left: with cover strip, lap joints and butt joints).

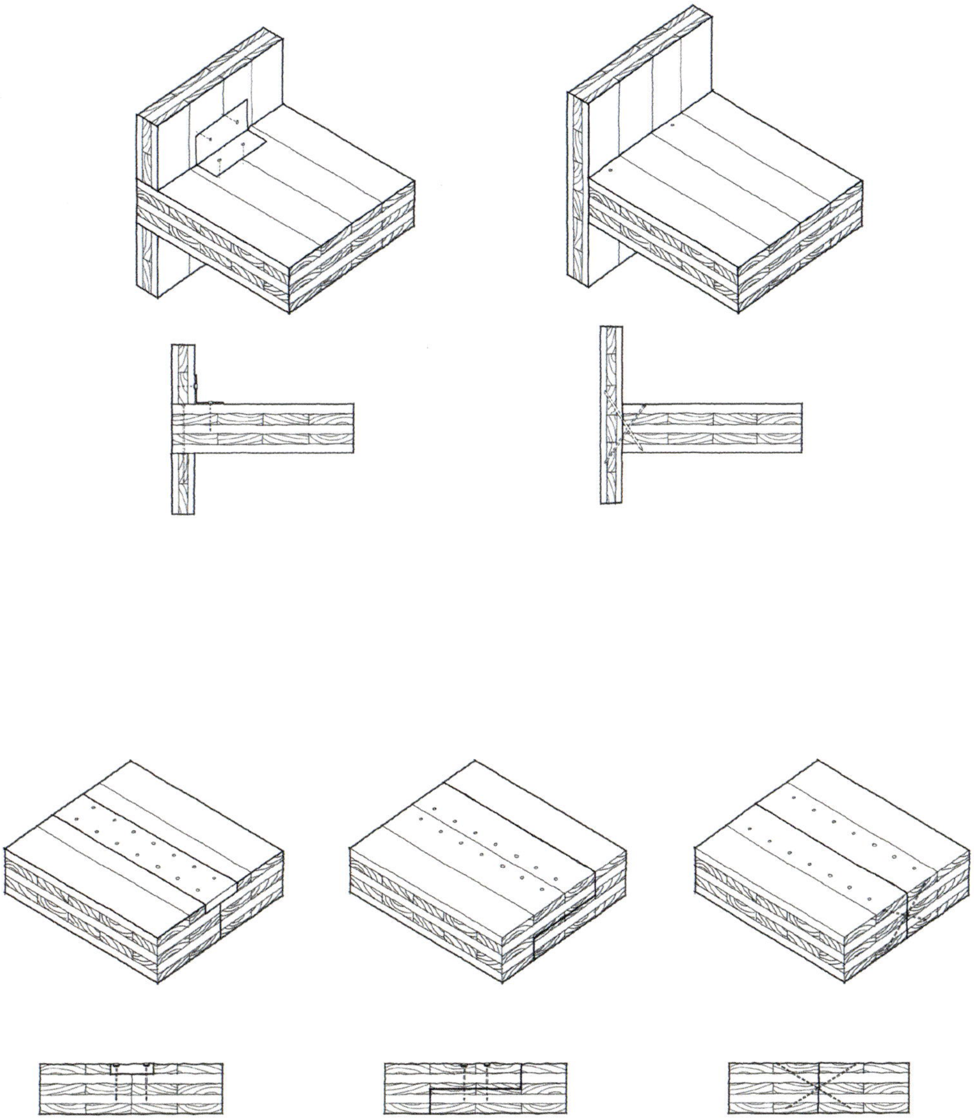

91

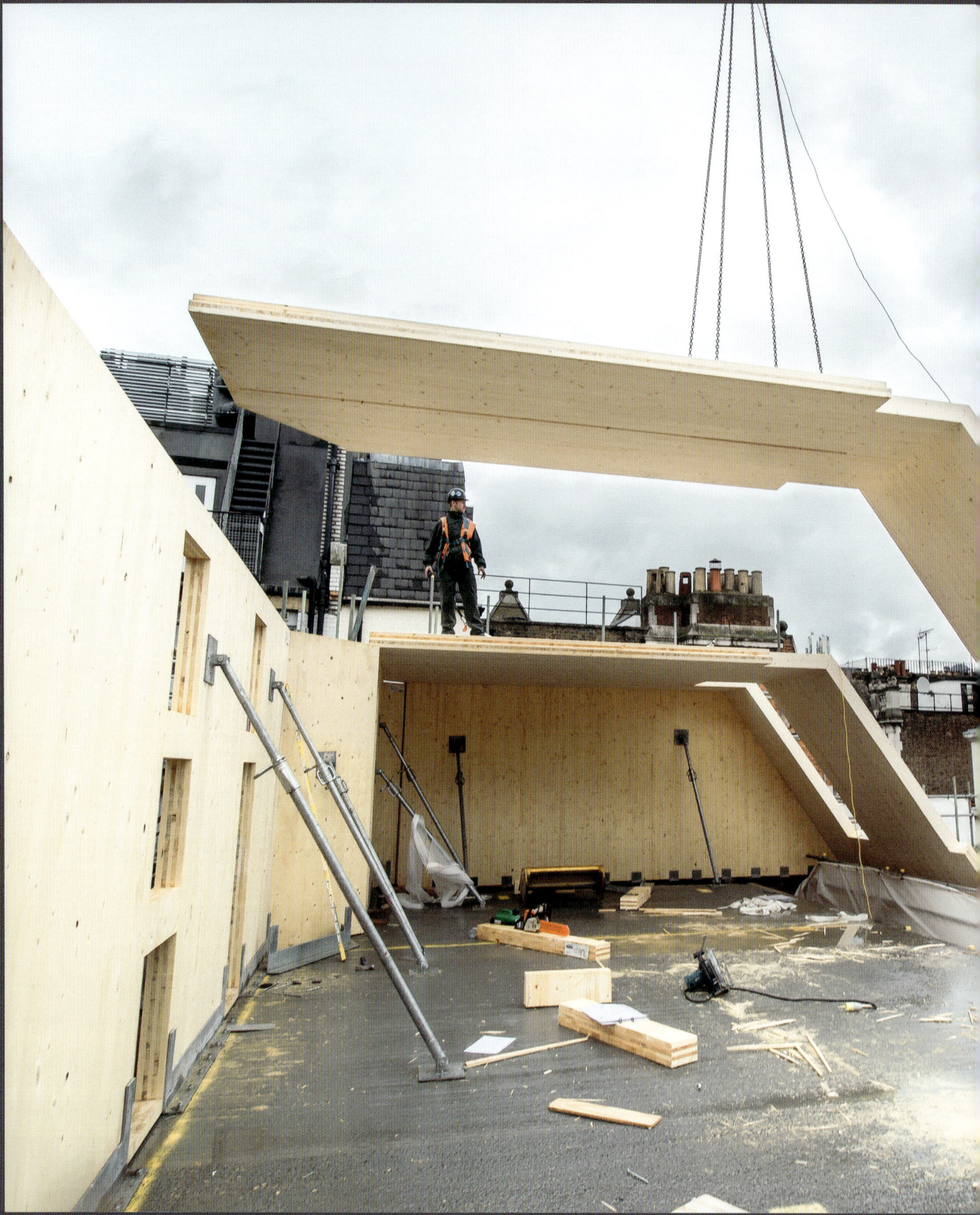

CHAPTER 10
REFURBISHED STRUCTURES

Existing buildings often have inherent excess structural capacity. Through investigation of original drawings and exposing and testing the structure on site, it is often possible to adapt and extend a building for the needs of a new market, rather than demolishing and starting again. The use of lightweight CLT not only represents an efficient form of construction but also can enable the creation of additional floor area upon existing structures, realising greater value from retained elements.

CROSS LAMINATED TIMBER

> This chapter was contributed by *Kelly Harrison*, structural engineer and timber specialist at Whitby Wood Engineers (UK). Project experience includes extensive adaptation and innovative retrofit work undertaken with CLT and mass timber at Heyne Tillett Steel (UK).

FIG 10.0 (chapter opener)

Mansard roof panels being lifted into position on a constricted site using a mobile crane to create valuable new top floor mezzanine volumes atop an existing listed structure (Lower James Street, London by Hale Brown Architects with Heyne Tillett Steel Engineers, 2016).

REFURBISHMENT SPECIFIC OPPORTUNITIES

The most significant refurbishment challenges include the reuse of foundations and adaptation of existing superstructures to allow alternative uses or create additional accommodation. In addition, the buildability of proposed extensions in and around existing buildings can create logistical and viability issues especially where some areas remain occupied.

Engineered timber and CLT provides an excellent solution to these challenges, mainly due to its high strength-to-weight ratio. Consequently, strengthening of existing structures and works in the ground may also be drastically reduced. If there is a limitation on new foundations or existing below ground infrastructure restricting load-bearing capacity (such as rail tunnels, services or drainage), additional storeys can often be justified compared to alternative materials.

The lightweight nature of CLT also makes deliveries, lifting and erection much easier and significantly safer than with other materials. Panels can easily be adapted or sized to suit cranage limitations on restricted or congested sites and if a mobile crane is required erection is so quick that any associated road closures can be limited

A limitation on new build commercial timber structures is often the grid that is achievable, typically less than that expected by commercial tenants. Forming open plan floors with long spans using CLT typically requires deep beams (whatever their form) pushing the building height upwards. For refurbishments however, older buildings often have a smaller grid which must be retained, often within the span capabilities of CLT panels, meaning an extremely efficient timber structure can be used to complement existing spaces.

DESIGNING A TIMBER EXTENSION

The most common types of existing structures can be adapted and extended using full CLT, or with timber and other hybrid frame elements:

- **Reinforced concrete (RC) frames** – RC buildings frequently have inherent excess capacity built in and are relatively simple to extend; timber connections can be anchored into the existing structure. A survey will be required and scanning to ensure the position of the existing reinforcement is highly recommended to avoid delays on site.
- **Steel frames** – As the connection pieces for timber frames are predominantly steel, this is no different to extending using a more traditional steel construction. If the building dates from the first part of the 20th century it may have rivets on the existing beams and columns, which should be surveyed in detail prior to detailing and production of the connections.

CHAPTER 10 **REFURBISHED STRUCTURES**

- **Load-bearing masonry** – CLT load-bearing walls can be used to extend masonry structures in the same form but in a more lightweight fashion. The connection between the two walls, whether on top or to the side should be carefully considered. A typical method to extend upwards is with a steel shoe junction, which may require fire protection and lateral extensions can be fixed with standard timber brackets, but again will need to be considered aesthetically.

CASE STUDY EXAMPLE

FIG 10.1

Lower James Street, Piccadilly, London by Hale Brown Architects (2016) posed challenges as a rooftop office extension located on a narrow public road within a busy one-way system. The architects worked with Heyne Tillett Steel Engineers to create a lightweight load-bearing CLT (with a bespoke design resin-dowelled cranked connection detail) which could be delivered during off-peak hours, in two-hour slots over a series of days. These panes were stored in the existing building then erected using a mobile crane within two weeks, creating a striking, high value space atop a 1930s Grade II listed building.

One of the key risks with existing buildings is being unable to survey some areas of a building at tender stage, but if considered early the design team can develop solutions in case the worst is found.

Survey everything, at various stages – early, post strip out and post-demolition. Existing structures will not only have different tolerances to the precise nature of engineered timber (with typically only 2mm tolerance), but may also have moved over time and may not have been built to regular grids. A survey of all retained elements, including marking rebar positions, and the exact level and position of the timber connection will be required to ensure there are no interface issues. Timber products are square and precise, details should be developed from early stages to take out any differences between the two structural elements and ensure that any extension is buildable and visually pleasing. Regular element sizes should also be considered within the parameters of the existing structure, along with how to minimise wastage of the panel cuts and how the position of joints can work with the aesthetics of the existing space.

CASE STUDY EXAMPLES

FIG 10.2 & 10.3

Republic Masterplan, Import and Export Building, Tower Hamlets, London by Studio RHE with Heyne Tillett Steel Engineers (2019). Existing RC framed office buildings were extended using a new glulam frame with CLT floor plates, including partial infill of a 10-storey atrium, achieved with minimal strengthening works. Careful coordination and floor by floor scanning of rebar position (or options for alternate anchor/fixing positions) enabled pre-manufacturing for on-site assembly. Components, including factory fitted connections, were sized to suit the limited access and moved to position on trolleys and hoists and steel connectors for mass timber elements to existing elements included alternative fixing positions should they be required.

CHAPTER 10 **REFURBISHED STRUCTURES**

Connection and interface design

Designers must be aware of the connections they are proposing to the existing structure from the start of the design process. Timber subcontractors, and therefore often the connection designers, work predominantly on new build projects and aren't always prepared for the alterations required to deal with existing structures in terms of cost and programme. Connections should be designed early by the consultants, or with early input from the fabricators, to ensure the client and team understand the aesthetic nature of the connections and so the

---

CASE STUDY EXAMPLES

FIG 10.4

Republic Masterplan, Tower Hamlets, London (completed 2019) by Studio RHE with Heyne Tillett Steel Engineers.

Part of this office building redevelopment was built over an existing retained basement and foundation arrangement and the lightweight of CLT slabs and glulam elements resulted in significant area (and value) uplift. The use of an engineered timber solution has allowed a six (potentially seven) storey extension to be proven achievable, as opposed to a maximum of five storeys with steel frame and concrete/metal deck over the existing elements. The sketch sections in Figure 10.4 show the uplift potential of differing structural solutions, from left: Existing building (basement extends further than building); Justifiable new floors of steel frame and metal deck slabs (five new floors); Justifiable new floors of glulam frame and CLT slabs (six to seven floors, additional storey if no roof terrace incorporated); As delivered: two floors of glulam and CLT with connections installed for subsequent expansion.

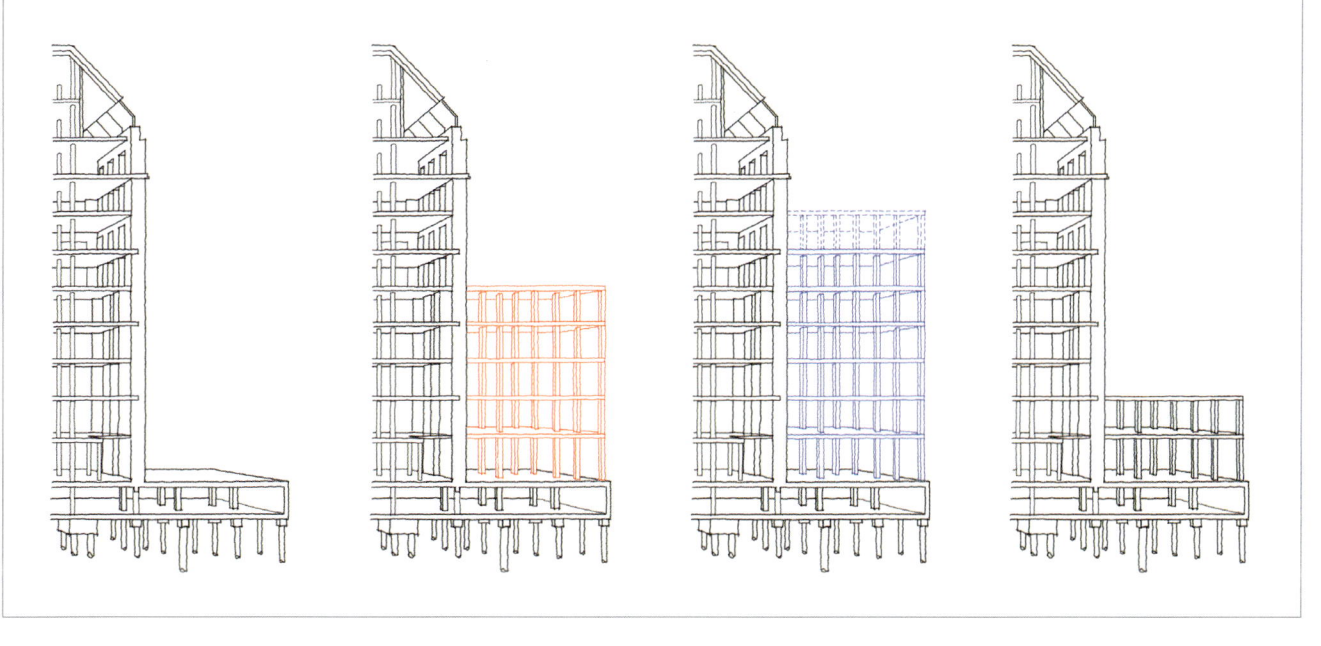

97

subcontractor can investigate their buildability at pricing stage. Mock-ups may be useful in gauging how interfaces could be resolved.

The fire protection of connections impacts the sizing of initial elements. Timber can provide protection to steel connections through its calculated ability to char (based on test data). Long-span beams have high connection forces and the spacing allowances for bolts and screws are very particular to ensure the timber doesn't split. Early design of these connections to ensure the member is large enough to take the number of fixings required and protect them from fire is key.

The thermal conductivity of steel connections however risks charring to the timber from the inside. Steel elements can conduct heat prior to intumescent paint activating. Timber chars at a lower temperature and so all connections must be encapsulated or protected to ensure that members do not char from the inside, as well as the outside (unless specifically designed to do so).

KEY ISSUES TO CONSIDER

Impact on fire performance

When extending a tall building laterally or vertically the fire rating and performance of the structure must be considered. A fire engineered solution may be appropriate to ensure that the extension does not create a higher risk than in the original building. Specialist inputs and analysis should be considered at an early stage as outlined elsewhere. If extending vertically for a residential development increasing the height, any restrictions on combustible materials in the exterior wall build-up must be observed.

Moisture control

Waterproofing details, temporary and permanent, should be well thought through. If the existing building may be occupied at lower floor levels or in part, a temporary roof may be appropriate. If not, the temporary situation should be assessed to ascertain whether any potential areas are susceptible for ponding during construction. This could well be at junctions with the existing structure and a temporary drainage solution might be proposed during construction, to ensure water is routed away from these areas so there is no damage to the timber.

New CLT slab positions

Existing buildings may have tight floor-to-floor zones so careful consideration of the grid and building services solution are required when extending laterally. The timber may not be placed at the same level as the existing adjacent slab for the best structural solution, but how will that appear visually and is there a good detail to address the junction of the two?

CHAPTER 10 **REFURBISHED STRUCTURES**

FIG 10.5
New office floors under construction showing CLT panels running above a new glulam frame – floor levels were coordinated with existing floors elsewhere as part of the Republic Masterplan, London (2019) by Studio RHE with Heyne Tillet Steel Engineers.

Weight and depth of acoustic build-ups

In phase one of the Republic Masterplan, a deep acoustic build-up was adopted, weighing almost as much as the CLT slab itself. During the time between the first and third phases, the acoustic protection providers had conducted further developments and testing and a much reduced build-up was used giving a significant weight saving for the design of the supporting elements. Such issues can have a dramatic impact on matching existing levels if extending laterally. Further work is still being conducted around the world to ensure different build-ups for CLT slabs are fully understood by acoustic consultants.

Disproportionate collapse

When extending an existing building it is necessary to assess the classification of the development in terms of disproportionate collapse. An extension may increase the classification of the original building and compliance due to age could be an issue.

Design of vertical or horizontal ties can be informed by structural Eurocodes, strong floor approaches might be considered or CLT walls can act as deep beams (minimising other transfer elements).

In many large engineered timber developments, it may be appropriate to categorise the building as consequence class 3 and complete a risk assessment so that some parts, such as transfer structures, might be designed as key elements rather than for the tie forces mentioned above.

Of all the emerging uses of CLT in recent years in the UK and beyond, the use of the material for maximising the potential for cost-effective and value-creating refurbishment may have been overlooked initially. However, it has since generated significant interest as teams better recognise the benefits and potential value of working with existing structures.

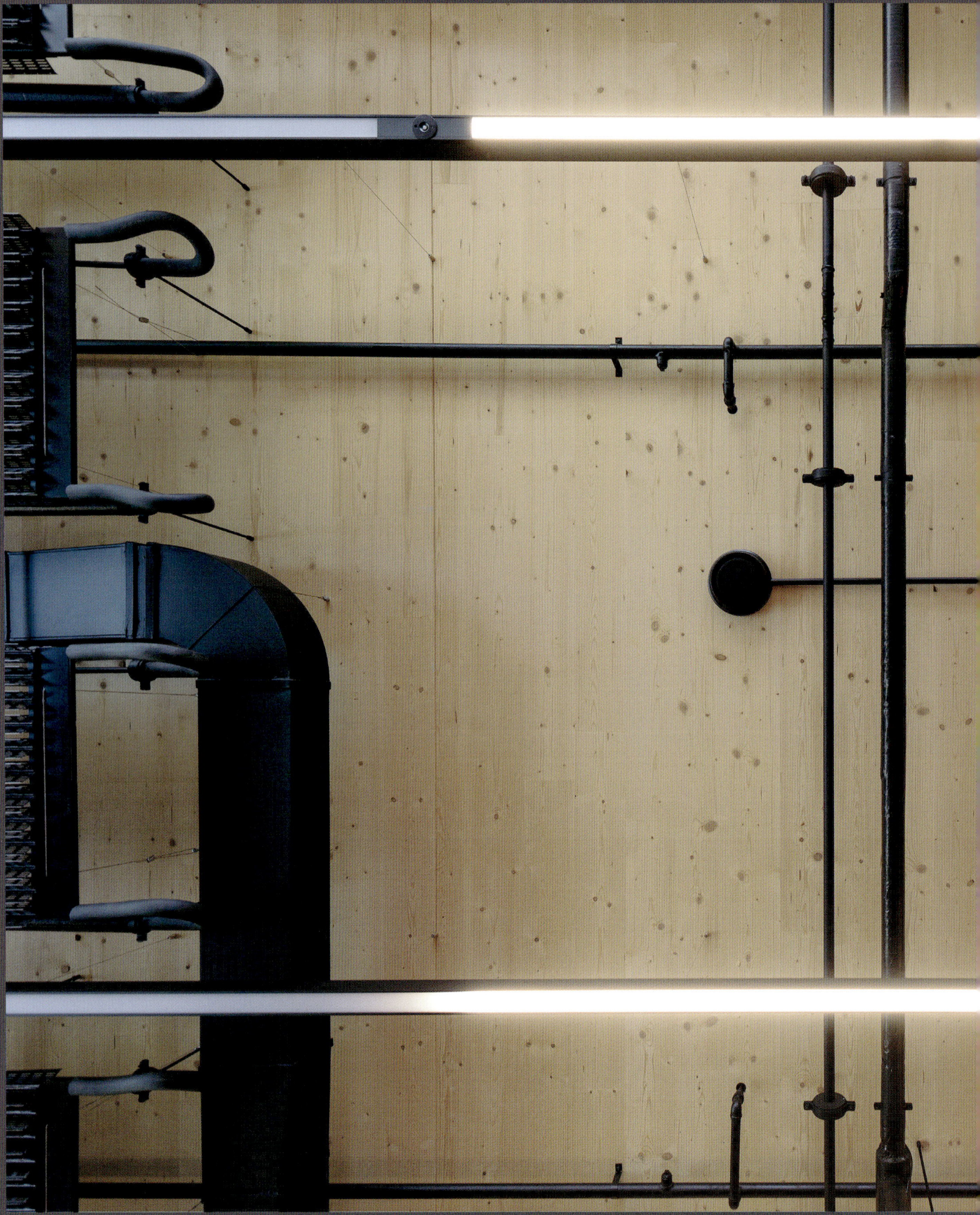

CHAPTER 11
SAFETY

Construction site safety and wellbeing remains a key concern and the use of smarter materials can displace old fashioned, and more hazardous, ways of working. It is also very obvious that building with a combustible material will pose specific challenges and this chapter introduces a number of fire safety issues specific to CLT use that must be considered and addressed by competent teams during design, construction and use.

CROSS LAMINATED TIMBER

FIG 11.0 (chapter opener)

Services, including sprinklers and smoke detectors, can be coordinated and easily fixed, or modified, on a CLT soffit as illustrated at International House Sydney (by Tzannes Associates, 2017).

CONSTRUCTION SAFETY AND WELLBEING

Across UK construction, the fatal injury rate on-site remains stubbornly steady at around 40 deaths per annum (roughly four times the all-industry rate).[1] Around 82,000 workers a year suffer from work-related ill health and after asbestosis, silica dust (typically from working with concrete, sand, bricks, blocks and mortar) is the second greatest risk to health resulting in the additional deaths of over 500 construction workers in 2005 alone.[2] Aside from the tragedy and human costs of such, annual costs to the industry for ill health and injury are estimated at £1.06 billion with 2.4 million lost days of work per annum.[3,4]

> 'Construction work is undertaken in an industry that is structured and cultured in ways unfavourable to the health and safety and well-being of its people… The world over, a harm that is evident in diseases, injuries and fatalities is endemic in the construction industry despite increasing evidence that the situation could be different.'[5]

The situation can be quite different when building with CLT elements.

Fabrication work is displaced from sites to a controlled factory environment and construction is much quicker with significantly reduced site programmes. Site logistics, sequencing and panel assembly can be planned, refined and communicated using 4D tools and existing BIM data with no need for on-site 'fitting' so risks can typically be considered in advance and designed out or better managed. Vehicle movements are hugely reduced with a fraction of the number of deliveries (benefitting site operatives and the general population).

Panels are typically installed by small specialist teams trained in working at height requiring far fewer workers on site. Manual handling of heavy materials is virtually eliminated and lifting directly from a trailer minimises the need for double handling panels (a panel lift of up to 50m^2 might be completed in 20 minutes). Teams typically work in isolation from other trades with few interface issues, hot works are eliminated and little cutting is required – limited to the smallest openings or possible bracing left in situ for transportation. Fixing processes are relatively simple with less equipment and fewer tools required. As such, projects can be managed and overseen more effectively which is particularly beneficial for dense urban sites or multi-phased and complex projects.

The use of CLT limits, or offsets, many other significantly more hazardous operations, whether they involve materials of higher mass or those harmful to health (such as cement and concrete or gypsum board) and reducing working at height (itself responsible for around half of all annual site fatalities). There are well understood risks from wood dust,[6] but these, like other risks, are best controlled in a factory environment where all processing and finishing is undertaken by machine, avoiding on site working and modification of panels.

CHAPTER 11 **SAFETY**

The risk of workforce harm across the project life cycle is also reduced. Follow-on trades can usually begin work straight after installation of panels within a significantly improved working environment. A weather-tight envelope can be achieved rapidly and CLT provides a degree of insulation before a shell is complete. Working with a CLT substrate involves screwing fixings directly into timber rather than drilling into steel or concrete and as a consequence sites are quieter with reduced dusting. End-of-use risks are also reduced: CLT can be readily designed for disassembly and if elements cannot be unscrewed, there will be no need to demolish or cut reinforced concrete or steel.

Edge protection for upper floors may be fitted before panels are lifted above ground and scaffolding is not required for CLT installation. Panels forming outer walls can provide workforce protection and temporary protection can be easily fixed to panels and readily modified to suit changes on site.

The challenge for teams remains communicating such benefits to decision makers when making comparisons with other forms of construction.

CASE STUDY EXAMPLES

FIG 11.1 & 11.2

Highpoint Terrace, Southwark is an eight storey residential building of 115 apartments by Rogers Stirk Harbour and Partners & Axis Architects (2017). The contractors reported that 25% less labour was required to assemble the building with only eight site operatives during superstructure works as opposed to around 35 if it had been a concrete structure. The CLT contractor, Eurban, used and shared 4D BIM to plan sequencing and logistics and communicate issues to the wider construction team before work started on site (as illustrated with a BIM view and subsequent site photograph in Figure 11.1 and 11.2). They also calculated that 64 deliveries to site were required rather than an estimated 250 if traditional methods had been used.[7]

NB: This building was fully code compliant when built but is now taller than that permissible for new construction under revised UK residential regulations due to the presence of CLT in the external wall zone.

FIRE SAFETY DESIGN

The behaviour of any material in fire conditions needs to be carefully considered and addressed and timber is a combustible material that presents a potential fire hazard. There are however, well-established means of ensuring safety in fire situations for smaller, non-complex buildings whilst larger or taller buildings that must involve a more considered, holistic performance-based design by specialist fire consultants, being beyond the scope of guidance such as Approved Document B or Eurocode 5 (at the time of writing). Such buildings may represent greater risks due to height, scale, complexity, use or the amount of timber exposed. It remains the responsibility of team members to ensure that designs are safe irrespective of published guidance and teams who are limited in relevant experience or uncertain of the risks must not be shy of saying so and insisting upon appropriate input and support. Aspects considered within this section include: regulations and testing, CLT behaviour in a fire situation, design and construction stage and handover/use issues.

Regulations and testing

The global upturn in CLT adoption has exposed inconsistencies in existing standards and test procedures between territories, few of which were developed with an awareness of mass or engineered timber. Around the world, new standards are being established that offer greater certainty to designers around the use of CLT.[8] Extensive best practice guidance and test data is however already available that enables designers and teams to design safely.[9]

The current situation might be compared to the end of the 19th century and early 20th century when steel-framed multi-storey construction was commonly built in the US before being adopted in Europe. In time of course, standards 'catch up' and it has been interesting to follow how forthcoming standards in the US have undertaken a clear-eyed approach to consider CLT application (including much testing) unlike the UK where it has been prohibited in limited circumstances following lobbying by those representing alternative material suppliers.[10] Readers should ensure that they are aware of relevant guidance and legislation as it affects their projects from the outset, wherever they may be located.

It is likely that building control or fire authorities may call for project specific modeling or testing of particular details or interfaces unless adopting a guidance based approach for a relatively straightforward building. These aspects should be factored into project planning in terms of preparation, cost and time, including that of any necessary response to results.

A note of caution re: standards and regulations
Teams must be aware that standards and regulations typically define what is deemed to be the lowest acceptable threshold for safety, and that

buildings are not always delivered as intended. The so-called 'performance gap' is applicable to many aspects of construction and it is not appropriate to expect that all work will be executed or maintained as intended.[11] As such, there are plenty of opportunities to incorporate additional fire safety measures and further layers of safety should always be considered.

UK regulation

Fire safety legislation and guidance is undergoing significant and long overdue broad-ranging revision in the UK. Following the Grenfell Tower fire tragedy, subsequent changes to Building Regulations (applicable to England and Wales) in 2018 introduced a prescriptive ban on the use of combustible elements within the external wall build-up of relevant (taller) residential buildings. Notwithstanding any outcomes of the new building safety regulatory framework, such a limitation does not ban CLT use in general but specifically prohibits the use of combustible materials within external walls of tall relevant (residential) buildings. Subject to other aspects, a CLT structure may still be considered appropriate for tall residential buildings (above 18m in height) as long as the wall construction, including any embedded structural elements, is entirely non-combustible and other safety criteria can be satisfied. Compliant facade solutions have been developed – typically prefabricated unitised facades more akin to those found on commercial buildings. The case studies for Fenner Hall and Brock Commons illustrate how taller CLT structures might accommodate such steel framed external wall modules.

CLT behaviour in a fire situation

If the timber surface is not exposed, boarded protection (frequently termed 'encapsulation'), typically using gypsum board may provide a limited degree of protection but this will fail in time. CLT may not ignite as readily as smaller section timber (with greater surface area) but will burn when exposed to a sustained flame or higher temperatures, contributing to a fire load and influencing possible fire break-out, internal fire spread and the self extinguishing potential of compartment fires.

Combustibility can be limited (delayed) by the specification, careful application and maintenance of appropriate surface-applied retardants and once alight, CLT chars at a rate that may in some cases be calculable (although fire circumstances will differ widely). Char layers form, protecting timber beyond from pyrolysis, slowing the rate of combustion. CLT panels are thus typically sized to accommodate loss of mass from anticipated periods of fire exposure whilst maintaining the necessary residual performance in the remaining (unaffected) section of panel.

Beyond maintaining structural integrity, some adhesives might pose a challenge when the char line approaches a glue line. Delamination can occur when some types soften, with the risk of charred lamella falling

CROSS LAMINATED TIMBER

away in parts and exposing fresh timber beyond, potentially fuelling fire regrowth and raising the risk of secondary flashover or extending a fires decay phase. Thermosetting or modified fire resistant adhesives have been proven to mitigate this issue with no such fall-off or degradation of integrity under fire conditions.

Design stage issues

As with other forms of construction, most projects beyond the simplest forms will require specialist structural fire engineering input. Such expertise and competent decision making must be involved, potentially undertaking a qualitative design review, to clearly identify, and then address the hazards introduced through the use of engineered timber for specific building types, scale and occupancy.

Understanding the objectives

Teams will need to consider and set out structural objectives, whether that be to allow adequate time and conditions for escape and external access for fire fighting operations (primarily life safety) or for other higher risk buildings, not so readily evacuated, the acceptable likelihood of surviving burnout. For commercial buildings, asset protection from a value point of view or business continuity aspect may be additional considerations.

Reaction to fire

How a material will contribute to the development of fire and its spread will affect how internal conditions impact the escape of occupants over

FIG 11.3

Protective charring, as shown on the face and in the cut section of a small sample, over remaining timber need not readily compromise overall panel integrity if sized accordingly.

time.[12] Relevant performance aspects include: ignitability, flame spread and heat release, smoke production and the propensity for producing flaming droplets and particles. A physical barrier provides the best protection, but this is often not essential and flame retardant surface treatments may satisfy local standards and the requirements of a fire strategy by reducing the rate of flame spread across a surface. A broad range of such specialist treatments are commonly available for mass timber use, including intumescents, clear or coloured finishes and are typically applied in situ following panel installation. Common to all is the absolutely critical need for appropriate quality control during application to ensure that potential performance is as intended at the design stage.

Fire resistance
This is the ability of an exposed element to maintain load-bearing capacity and resist the passage of fire, smoke and heat to adjacent areas for defined periods.[13] Again, passive measures are often most effective and CLT elements are typically sized, by calculation using known rates, to allow for charring whilst maintaining appropriate protection over required time periods.

Connections, joints and edges: Beyond considering the behaviour of a panel surface, fire resistance at edges and connections needs to be considered. Panel joints and edges may burn differently under sustained fire conditions with the risk of burn-through if continuity of material or protection is not maintained. Although timber has a relatively low thermal conductivity, providing good insulation, steel connections and fixings may conduct heat beyond any exposed or heated element resulting in charring beyond the surface which could compromise structural load-bearing capacity or integrity.

Compartment design: Appropriate fire stopping products for service penetrations, joint filling and interfaces are available. Choices may be limited in some markets and should be investigated in good time. Installation quality is again of critical importance during site works.

Manufacturers and suppliers: Typically publish test data, including the fire performance of different build-ups. Such information is particularly useful at early design stages to ensure that space allowed for elements is sufficient to provide the anticipated performance. As with all materials use, teams must review every aspect of product and test data in the finest detail to ensure that any reliance or assumptions made based upon previous modelling, testing or resultant certification are applicable to project proposals. Changing arrangements slightly or using alternative products (or slight variants) may invalidate such an approach.

New building warranty providers and insurance companies: Such bodies are typically conservative and may challenge the use of CLT for more complex or taller projects and are seen by many as the greatest obstacle to wider scale adoption of mass timber construction. Limits to potential cover can prove very significant and early engagement is again key to avoiding surprises whether through inexperience, lack of education or uncertainties around basic data about performance or risks.

Construction stage issues

The extensive use of timber is a high-risk hazard that must be addressed during the construction phase with risk assessments reflecting changing hazards as works progress. Issues for the project and contracting team to consider (from before tender) include:

- Fires on construction sites do occur (whatever the form of construction) with two out of three fires (in the UK) started deliberately.
- Most timber buildings offer limited resistance to fire until the later stages of construction when areas of exposed timber may be concealed or limited by compartmentation or enclosure. Contractors may wish to limit the amount of exposed timber on a site at times.
- Mass timber elements are however less readily ignited than traditional stick systems of thinner section timber.
- Sites may be more susceptible to extensive damage from high intensity timber fires that may in turn pose greater risks to neighbouring properties.

The Structural Timber Association's '16 Steps to Fire Safety' guidance is relevant to all sites involving CLT and defines best practice guidance covering aspects such as roles and responsibilities, inspections, detection and warnings and the planning and integration of fire protection throughout a build programme.[14]

Handover/in-use issues

In terms of handover strategy, the use of CLT and any associated protection (such as fire resisting linings or surface applied retardants) must be recorded in full, unequivocal detail. This may be part of a fire strategy and should in turn form part of any building manual, operations and maintenance file or handover information so it can be understood and used by owners, tenants, occupiers and all those managing buildings.

Uncovering a timber soffit above a boarded ceiling may be considered an attractive 'improvement' by future occupants so it makes sense to highlight the function of any in-situ protection to mitigate such risks. Where board lining is integral to a designed fire strategy that may in time be modified, some contractors have taken to physically marking the concealed panels or including notes within deeds or legal documents to make it clear beyond doubt that the integrity of the underlying protection should not be compromised.

For owner/occupiers, it's worth repeating that occupants should use and manage the building as intended and any deviation from this could compromise safety – this may include structural alterations or any changes to building services. Insurance providers may have particular views regarding the management of a building, particularly for taller or larger buildings.

Anecdotal evidence regarding integrity following a fire event suggests that of a limited number of small (contained) fires known to have taken place within CLT structures to date, few, if any have posed a risk to the structural integrity. Affected areas would always need to be assessed which may result in areas of panels being cut out and replaced locally or simply being covered over.

Safety considerations, including fire safety, are critical to the development of CLT projects (and insufficiently developed related strategies remain one of the most commonly cited reasons for not progressing CLT proposals). Like other aspects of the materials application, there are particular challenges as well as advantages to CLT use and it is imperative that teams seek appropriate advice and competent input and consider the challenges and consequences of likely performance throughout the entire project life cycle.

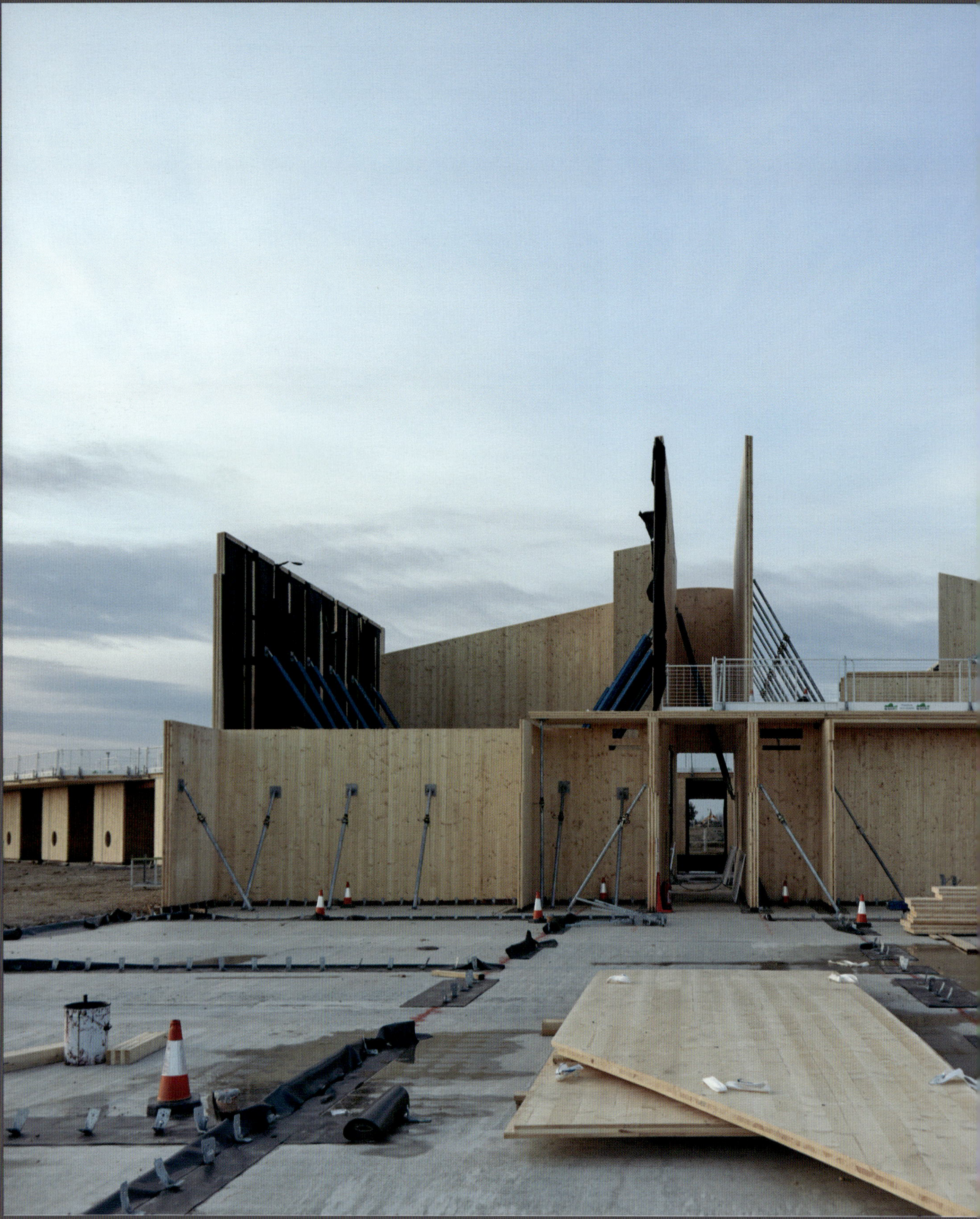

CHAPTER 12
BUILDABILITY AND ASSEMBLY

CLT use requires a different, smarter approach to construction. Digital design and manufacturing enables better and more efficient coordination, reducing risks and improving quality.

To best realise this potential, issues should be considered and communicated early by the team and with potential contractors or suppliers, not just at tender or construction stages. Beyond safety, key issues during manufacturing and construction include moisture control and durability, surface protection and the work of follow-on trades.

CROSS LAMINATED TIMBER

CASE STUDY EXAMPLES

FIG 12.1 & 12.2

For the Dyson Institute of Engineering and Technology (2019-20), WilkinsonEyre Architects were assisted by an external CLT advocate who assured the team that the proposed solution was not only achievable but also relatively straightforward and helped optimise the initial design strategy. Pods are mounted above a ventilated cavity for moisture protection and pulled away from an adjacent earth bank to avoid moisture risks. Dramatic cantilevers of 3m increments, up to 6m total, were made possible by utilising the planar strength of CLT panels. This arrangement was tested with a full scale mock-up when a checking structural engineer was engaged to review the contractors' designs and proposals.

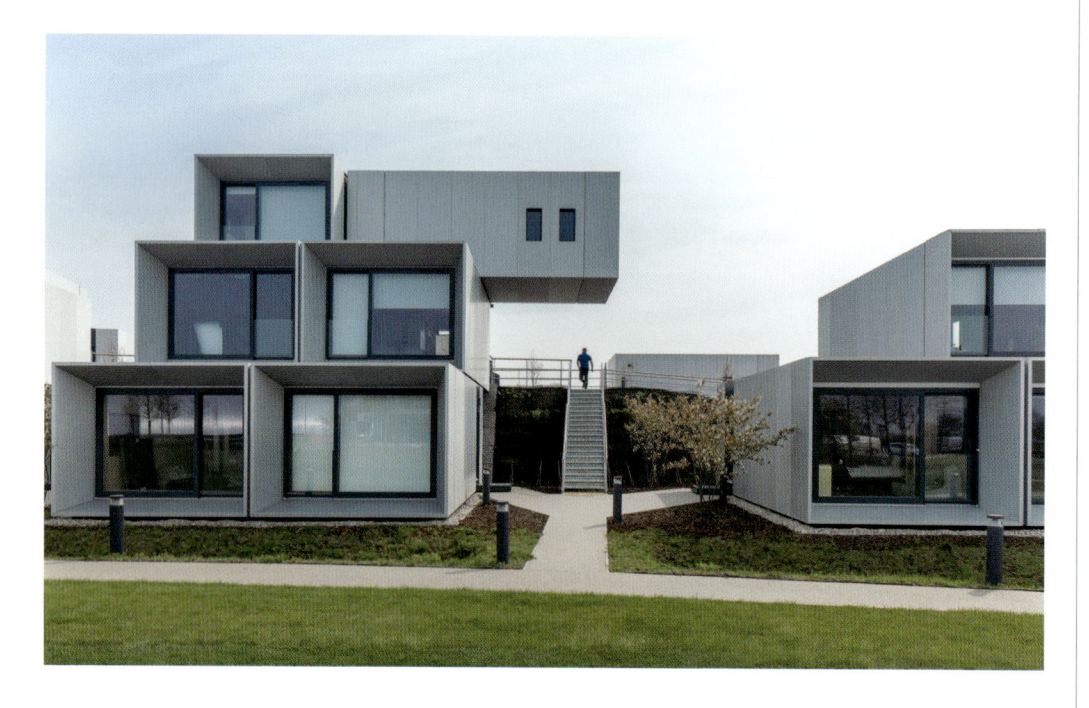

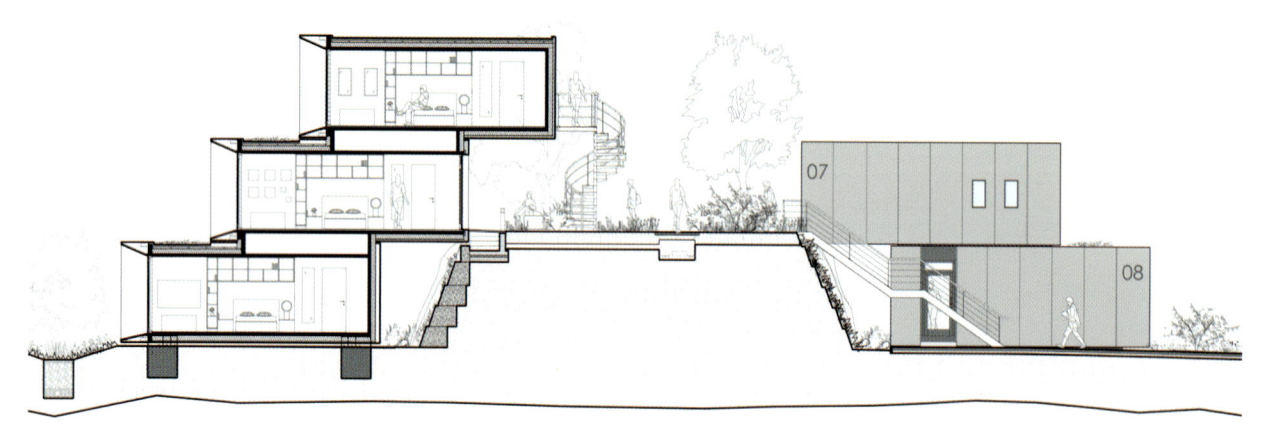

CHAPTER 12 **BUILDABILITY AND ASSEMBLY**

FIG 12.0 (chapter opener)

A typical low-rise CLT site (Ermine Street Church Academy by AHMM, as described in subsequent case study).

DURABILITY AND MOISTURE CONTENT

Whitewoods are versatile timbers but not typically durable. Moisture content is controlled in factories and panels arriving on site are reasonably consistent at around 12% moisture content (MC). They can accommodate normal site conditions and exposure but timber will begin to degrade if moisture levels exceed 20% for long periods of time. Water trapped during construction, from weather or leaks from service installations (the source of which may not be obvious or immediately recognised) and unforeseen site delays or stand-downs, which are not uncommon, all pose risks to long-term performance. Each must be addressed in a moisture control strategy or method statement with associated responsibilities clearly defined within appointments. Regular checks using a hand-held moisture meter should be made at the panel surface or within the panel depth for those exposed to excess moisture for extended periods.

Keeping moisture out

Some sites have used temporary roof decks to partially cover the footprint of a new build, like a hat that is lifted into place at the end of each day. This is clearly not an option for a very large building but most schemes are generally built with upper floors exposed to the elements as they extend upwards. Others have used tarpaulins or waterproof ply boarding to provide a degree of protection or a sacrificial temporary membrane installed in optimum conditions once uppermost panels are placed (or even before they are lifted). The most robust approach will be to manage water on site, away from completed areas and detail subsequent construction whether roofs or other forms of enclosure, to allow the substrate to 'breathe' and dry out if required (this may impact ventilation paths, membrane positions, insulation specification etc).

FIG 12.3

Moisture meter used on site to determine moisture content of slabs before being sealed under other construction.

Surface applied sealants

Panel edge sealant can be applied on site and this can be particularly useful in temporarily reducing risks for wall panels that may otherwise be exposed to rain along their top edge or be standing in water at their foot. Some installers may apply a flashing tape to exposed edges. Some manufacturers offer a factory applied water repellent coating to full panels and although it should be noted that this is not intended to provide long-term protection, it may offer some reassurance for projects considered to be at risk (including of site delays) and has the added benefit of limiting marking of the panels from regular site actions, footprints etc during assembly. Any sealants should not interfere with other anticipated coatings, fire retardants etc.

Drying out

Force drying saturated panels with heaters or dehumidifiers should be avoided to limit surface cracking and risk of delamination. With sufficient access to air (which may require stripping of finishes or other materials) natural ventilation is the best means of reducing moisture content below 20% (subject to favourable ambient temperatures and regular measurement).

The integrity and performance of CLT is typically unaffected by short-term exposure to water on site but run-off may mark either soffits or vertical elements. As outlined elsewhere, ensure that someone is responsible for moisture management during the construction period to handover to minimise risks. Beyond managing (limiting) surface water and ensuring sites are kept clean as far as possible (particularly in urban areas to avoid dirtying any water present), marking may be minimised by not forcing the rapid drying of wet areas. Beyond lightly sanding affected areas, wood cleaners and colour restorers are available that remove traces of water marks and restore the original timber (lignin) colouring to overly exposed or patchy surfaces.[1]

Covering up

CLT should only be covered up when moisture content is appropriate (falling below 20% to avoid decay). Moisture may be 'locked in' by impermeable membranes or finishes that don't allow drying-out, causing either delays in reworking/refixing areas if short-term damage is observed or longer-term structural damage if not.

FOLLOW-ON TRADES

Trades may gain immediate access since props do not need to be retained once panels are fixed (unless an in-situ topping screed is placed). Panelled enclosures subsequently provide a reasonably dry, weatherproof working environment with a degree of insulation and first/second fixes can be

FIG 12.4

On-site water marking to underside of soffit and glulam beam – subsequently removed with a specialist wood cleaning product.

CHAPTER 12 **BUILDABILITY AND ASSEMBLY**

CASE STUDY EXAMPLES

FIG 12.5

The planar strengths of CLT panels were exploited for Blackwood, a private house in Wiltshire, by Seymour-Smith Architects (2018) forming a cantilevered roof, minimising structural obstructions to clerestory glazing below with soffits exposed externally but protected from wind-driven moisture and tracking rain. Inclined CLT walls with an exposed internal finish reflected the client's vision for a legible, honest building (and their dislike of plasterboard). Exposed service coordination and careful protection during construction were important issues during design and assembly and very high thermal efficiency was helped by good airtightness and tight tolerances to interfaces.

undertaken promptly. The working environment is typically quieter without drilling/fixings into concrete nor the risks associated with silica dust, and subcontractors frequently remark about the quality of the working environment, commenting on it being warmer or quieter than other sites.

CASE STUDY EXAMPLES

FIG 12.6

First Tech Federal Credit Union, Hillsboro, Oregon, United States by Hacker Architects (2018) provides workspace for 900 people over 14,500m² (156,000ft²). BIM was used to coordinate buildings services requiring early resolution of MEP information but resulting in manufactured CLT products arriving on site just five months from the award of the timber contract.

During construction stage, concealed incorporated fixings enabled speedy assembly although extreme weather posed some challenges in terms of weatherproofing between phases of the project where there was risk of exposure to moisture for extended periods of time.

Projects have reported unnecessary delays due to follow-on trades not being ready for the completion (or partial completion of CLT works) with subcontractors expecting superstructure works to take longer. This could be communicated to trade contractors before tender, along with noting the potential advantages of working within a CLT structure. Anecdotal evidence suggests that some lift installers offer better pricing for fixing within CLT cores due to the high degree of accuracy expected from CNC-cut shafts.

CHAPTER 12 **BUILDABILITY AND ASSEMBLY**

SURFACE PROTECTION

Most readers will have come across signage, graffiti and damage, accidental or otherwise, on project sites and beyond the CLT contractor, subsequent site trades are typically used to conceal structural elements and substrates beneath other materials or finishes, ceilings, plasterboard etc. As with any exposed installed surface, it is important to cover and protect exposed panels and particularly edges and corners, until after completion to avoid having to refinish panels. To avoid surface discolouration before completion, ensure that any protection blocks UV light (particularly in territories with strong sunlight/UV radiation – the effect is accelerated) and is breathable or sufficiently ventilated to avoid any moisture building up beyond – any trapped moisture should be able to be ventilated away.

Other important Stage 5 issues include:

Cranes required may be smaller or lighter rated and are often mobile (**Figure 12.7**). Some projects have reported delays to CLT crews when having to share cranes with other trades since the speed of CLT assembly can often be underestimated. Building with CLT is typically not dependant on weather conditions, apart from strong wind. It can be installed in cold and wet weather, snow and frost. Cranage strategies should reflect any expected windy conditions or smaller panels could be designed to reduce the likelihood of delays.[2]

FIG 12.7

Mobile cranes may be sufficient to install CLT panels, even with a long reach requirement.

117

Panels are typically airtight with limited joints in most cases but edges and joints can be sealed on inner or outer junctions to suit. Interfaces around apertures are typically low risk due the tight tolerances achievable between fittings and openings.

Care must be taken to ensure other elements can be accommodated if tolerances with panels are down to +/- 1 or 2mm. Little else on site will have this degree of control or accuracy so flexibility regarding accommodating all other elements should be taken into account.

Should problems arise on site, prompt resolution may be required to avoid disrupting extremely compressed programmes and just-in-time panel delivery programmes. Teams should consider processes for how issues will be raised and actioned promptly, in advance, to minimise any delays.

Whether planning current or future projects, good data is critical and teams may wish to keep track of key metrics. Understanding any unforeseen occurrences or areas where efficiencies have been made (or could be made next time) is fundamental to assessing the success of decisions made. Detailed feedback with metrics and comparisons with other forms of construction or general best practice will also be of interest to commercial managers, programme managers, trade subcontractors etc and can help reduce risks, better inform programme planning and realise greater value from CLT use.

ANATOMY OF A TYPICAL SITE

1. Panels delivered and unloaded to suit installation sequence, minimising handling
2. Pre-fitted lifting straps improve lifting efficiency
3. Site open to elements during assembly process
4. Concrete ground slab pre-prepared with angle base brackets and moisture barrier
5. All significant cuts made off site including lap joints and service penetrations
6. Panels to single-storey elements in landscape format (longer horizontally)
7. Taller/double height spaces formed by panels in portrait format (taller vertically)
8. Props and bracing to incomplete elements removed when panels are secured
9. Panels precut to accommodate upper level structural elements
10. Full height openings between panels ensures efficient materials use (no cills/spandrels)
11. Irregular (circular) apertures precut for small windows, no lintels required
12. Edge protection readily fixed to slabs (and re-positionable) for safe working for follow-on trades

CHAPTER 12 **BUILDABILITY AND ASSEMBLY**

FIG 12.8
A typical site (CLT contractor KLH UK at Ermine Street Church Academy by AHMM).

119

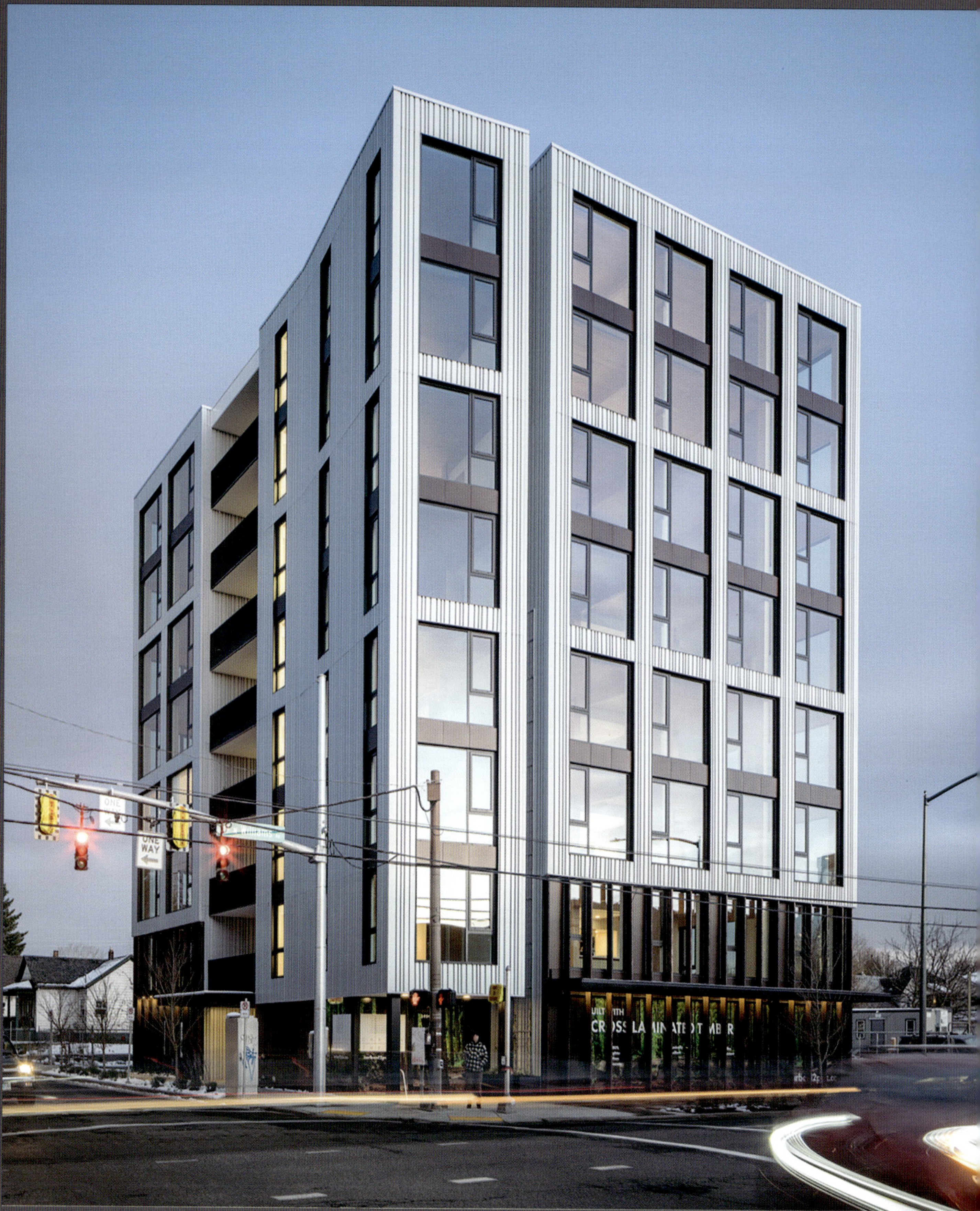
ONE WAY

CHAPTER 13
THE INTERNATIONAL OUTLOOK

Global interest in CLT is booming. The surge in interest and application in English-speaking markets, beyond the materials predominantly central European region of origin, has been dramatic and continues apace.

This chapter outlines the emerging situation in Australia (driven by use and demand) and the slightly better established scene in North America (with a broader manufacturing/supply base) in terms of diverse application, market issues and other local challenges and opportunities. Despite differences in forest resources, timber quality and domestic manufacturing, designers in both regions are pushing the boundaries of what can be built from CLT and mass timber as much as anywhere else.

This chapter was contributed by *Nicholas Sills* and *Ninotchka Titchkosky*, with the case study example on page 125 by Nic Crawley.

Nicholas manages customer and technical services at Structurlam Mass Timber Corporation (North American CLT manufacturer and timber specialists), with extensive experience of timber construction, processing and engineering.

Ninotchka is an architect and co-CEO of BVN (Australia) and continues to push the boundaries of what is achievable with digital fabrication and the use of CLT and mass timber at scale for residential, educational and commercial buildings.

FIG 13.0 (chapter opener)

Carbon12, Portland, by Kaiser Group and Path Architecture was the tallest multistorey post and beam timber structure in the US (when completed in 2018) at 8 storeys tall. CLT soffits and a glulam timber perimeter frame are exposed through residential areas.

FIG 13.1

Wood Innovation and Design Centre, Prince George, British Columbia by Michael Green Architects (2014). Layered CLT floor slabs create service zones unobstructed by downstand glulam beams to this mid-rise timber hybrid.

THE NORTH AMERICAN EXPERIENCE

By Nicholas Sills, Structurlam Mass Timber Corporation

With over 90% of single-family residences composed of light-wood framing materials, a large bias towards wood construction exists in the North American market. While traditional light-wood framing construction is only applicable to single-family homes and small-scale commercial buildings, the Wood Innovation and Design Centre (WIDC) (**Figure 13.1**) has demonstrated the feasibility of mass timber (MT) to build higher and provide a unique value proposition over conventional construction typologies.

In North America, very little value is placed on the environmental benefits of using mass timber, and the top three decision-making criteria for the design of a project are typically costs, general performance criteria, and availability. Solid wood panels simply cannot compete with the value or air between studs in light-wood framing. This has shifted focus for mass timber in North America towards large-scale multi-family residential and office projects, driving expertise in larger on average projects than typically seen in other markets.

A single unified product standard PRG-320, published by the American National Standards Institute and APA (The Engineered Wood Association), exists for CLT to ensure all manufacturers adhere to the same panel production quality control requirements for inclusion in the building code. This standard is relatively rigorous in terms of glue bonding capability and is such that CLT panels produced in a vacuum press cannot pass the quality standard. As a result, small to mid-size CLT players as well as offshore groups have significant barriers to implementing their non-conforming products to projects in North America.

The early development and inclusion of these standards for stringent quality control has allowed code officials to revise building codes in both Canada and US to allow up to 12 and 18 storeys respectively for mass timber buildings in each country. This unified standard and code development has signalled a clear path for an all-out revolution in the construction industry for mass timber structures to be become a standardised staple of modern construction. There is much speculation throughout North America that the cost-driven environment paired with simplified and unified building code systems will allow mass timber construction to flourish and possibly pass volumes currently undertaken in Europe over the next five to ten years.

KEY ISSUES AND LESSONS LEARNT

Moisture control

A major hub for mass timber construction in North America is in the Pacific Northwest, including the very rainy coastal areas of British Columbia, Washington and Oregon, where it is common for rainfall days on site to

CHAPTER 13 **THE INTERNATIONAL OUTLOOK**

FIG 13.2

MEC flagship retail Store, Vancouver, 2020 by Proscenium Architecture & Interiors, Fast + Epp Structural Engineers and Structurlam.

FIG 13.3

Brock Commons, British Columbia, 2016 by Acton Ostry.

FIG 13.4

Virtuoso apartments, British Columbia, 2018 by Rositch Hemphill Architects – the first North American condo scheme to use CLT.

exceed 20 consecutive days. This has caused many concerns around moisture and risks associated with mass timber construction, as well as hard lessons learnt with other less dimensionally stable products such as Dowel Laminated Timber (DLT) and Nail Laminated Timber (NLT). These products require a moisture protection strategy and covering during construction to ensure they stay dry, monitoring the moisture content, and only sealing off any CLT when it is below 18% MC. If a project is left wet for two months or longer significant risks are involved, however prior to this the risk can be easily managed by closing in the building on time.

Coordination of installation and tolerances

Hybrid construction systems for mass timber are very popular. The tolerances around concrete to mass timber interfaces and steel to mass timber interfaces vary greatly by trade and further standardisation in understanding these tolerances and design deliverables for these interface points need to be developed.

Fire performance

Fire performance and safety has been a key concern for allowing greater heights and floor areas for mass timber buildings. Full-scale fire testing was performed on a variety of projects to demonstrate both structural capacity and the ability of the building to self-extinguish in the event that sprinklers failed, and fire services also failed to respond. A new PUR glue has been developed that exhibits the same char-rate of solid wood to ensure no char fall of or reignition capacity existing in large buildings. These enhanced fire performance glues are key to life and structure safety for large CLT projects.

Project insurance

Construction insurance and operational insurance can be sticking points for new mass timber buildings. While reference data points are not extremely plentiful, insurance providers tend to see these types of structures as a riskier project set. However, risks and hazards can be greatly mitigated from traditional construction methods with a few easy solutions. Operational insurance is based on current risk analysis, however the new code requirements and associated testing have very much proved the background of mass timber construction beyond testing that has been done on other building typologies. Due to the in-depth code requirements there is sense that these are some of the safest buildings on the market and thus may see some insurance benefits in the future. Currently that is not the case.

123

CROSS LAMINATED TIMBER

FIG 13.5

Forte, Melbourne, Australia (2012) by Lendlease was the tallest CLT residential building in the world when built when local codes did not ordinarily permit timber buildings above three storeys.

THE AUSTRALIAN EXPERIENCE

Australia, whilst not always in the geographic heart of the action, is often an early adopter and recent projects have pushed the application of CLT and mass timber hybrid forms to new levels for commercial offices, education and residential forms as well as adaptive reuse and projects augmenting existing structures.

Environmental and Wellness Market Value

Leading Australian companies and institutions have adopted triple bottom line measures for their reporting. This has driven a considerable uplift in demand for environmentally rated projects which now have a 'value', defined through tools such as Green Star, WELL and One Planet. Such tools don't yet fully recognise the benefit or reduction in embodied carbon and this can be a limiting factor in the decision-making process.

SUPPLY, PROCUREMENT AND LOCAL EXPERTISE

Like most countries, Australia's construction industry productivity is poor and CLT use with associated higher levels of prefabrication and coordination is increasingly recognised as a means to significantly reduce on-site labour and construction time while improving safety and productivity.

A key challenge has been competitive supply with a single manufacturer using domestic timber (at time of writing) and others processing a broader range of European products locally. As demand increases, local expertise will evolve (including medium-sized contractors) and international suppliers are now striving to increase their presence. This will help reduce supply and pricing barriers and enable competitively tendering for supply with better early engagement with specialists and suppliers.

Informed and experienced developers, designers, consultants, cost planners and trades are required to capture the full value that timber can offer. There is still a lack of knowledge in the market regarding the additional and diverse benefits of CLT, leading to risk adversity and inadequate costings with savings in construction time and finishing not yet widely quantified and therefore remaining undervalued.

Commercial office projects have traditionally aspired to large column grids, not readily achievable using mass timber due to the increase in cost in beam and floor slab depth. Mass timber offices (as opposite) have been leased by major tenants, proving the market can overcome its prejudice for large grids when other benefits such as ecological footprint and staff wellness are considered in the decision-making process for tenants.

CASE STUDY EXAMPLES

FIG 13.6 & 13.7

International House, Sydney, Australia, by Tzannes (2017) utilises a 6m x 9m grid. The developer Lendlease has iterated upon the hybrid form of CLT slabs and shafts with expressed glulam vertical structures and chunky bracing with continued success: with nine office floors (above a ground floor plinth) at 25 King Street in Brisbane (2018, by Bates Smart Architects, also a 6m x 9m grid) and most recently on an adjacent site in Sydney, with Daramu House (again by Tzannes, 2019 with a larger 9m x 9m grid).

CASE STUDY EXAMPLES

FIG 13.8 & 13.9

At Our Lady of Assumption Catholic School, North Strathfield, Australia by BVN (2018), countering a typical 'knock down and rebuild' mentality from contractors, programme savings and avoiding modifications to existing footings led to adaptive reuse of elements with CLT walls and prefabricated ribbed/box section floor slabs.

The procurement process was challenging due to the restricted number of industry contractors with expertise at the mid-scale and locally defined performance criteria informed specialist input from European timber specialists and suppliers.

FUTURE OUTLOOK

The Australian market continues to be enamoured by CLT and mass timber construction prompted by the success of projects to date, and an increased focus on embodied carbon. There are many very significant projects currently underway, including university buildings, large-scale offices (including high-rise) as well as adaptive reuse for commercial and residential buildings.

However, with recent closures of some timber processing and engineering companies, it remains to be seen if this impacts market confidence or in fact opens supply chains into Australia. Additional barriers to uptake, such as open source or universal fire testing, more robust cost planning and wider expertise in design and engineering, would improve uptake and limit risk.

CASE STUDY EXAMPLES

FIG 13.10 & 13.11

At the Marie Reay Teaching Centre, Australian National University, Canberra, Australia by BVN (2019), a fire engineered approach with limited compartmentation enabled the connectivity of a dramatic series of open stairs and voids. All lift cores, stairs and services cores are CLT with a ribbed CLT floor slab. Services are exposed, requiring significant beam penetration coordination before fabrication.

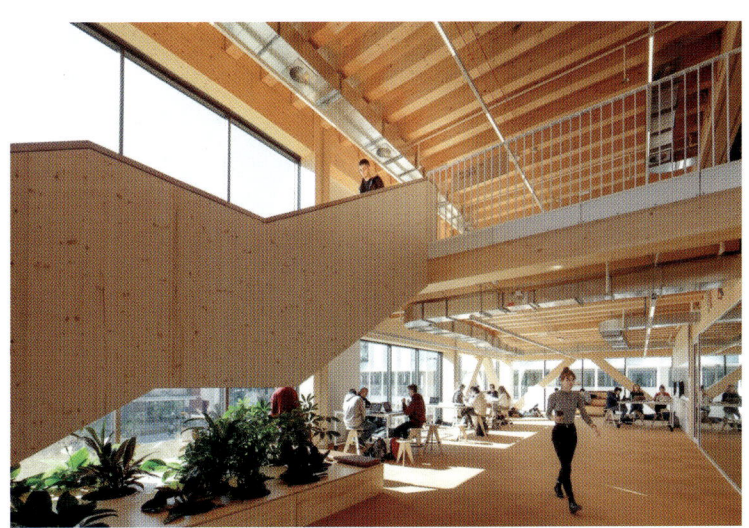

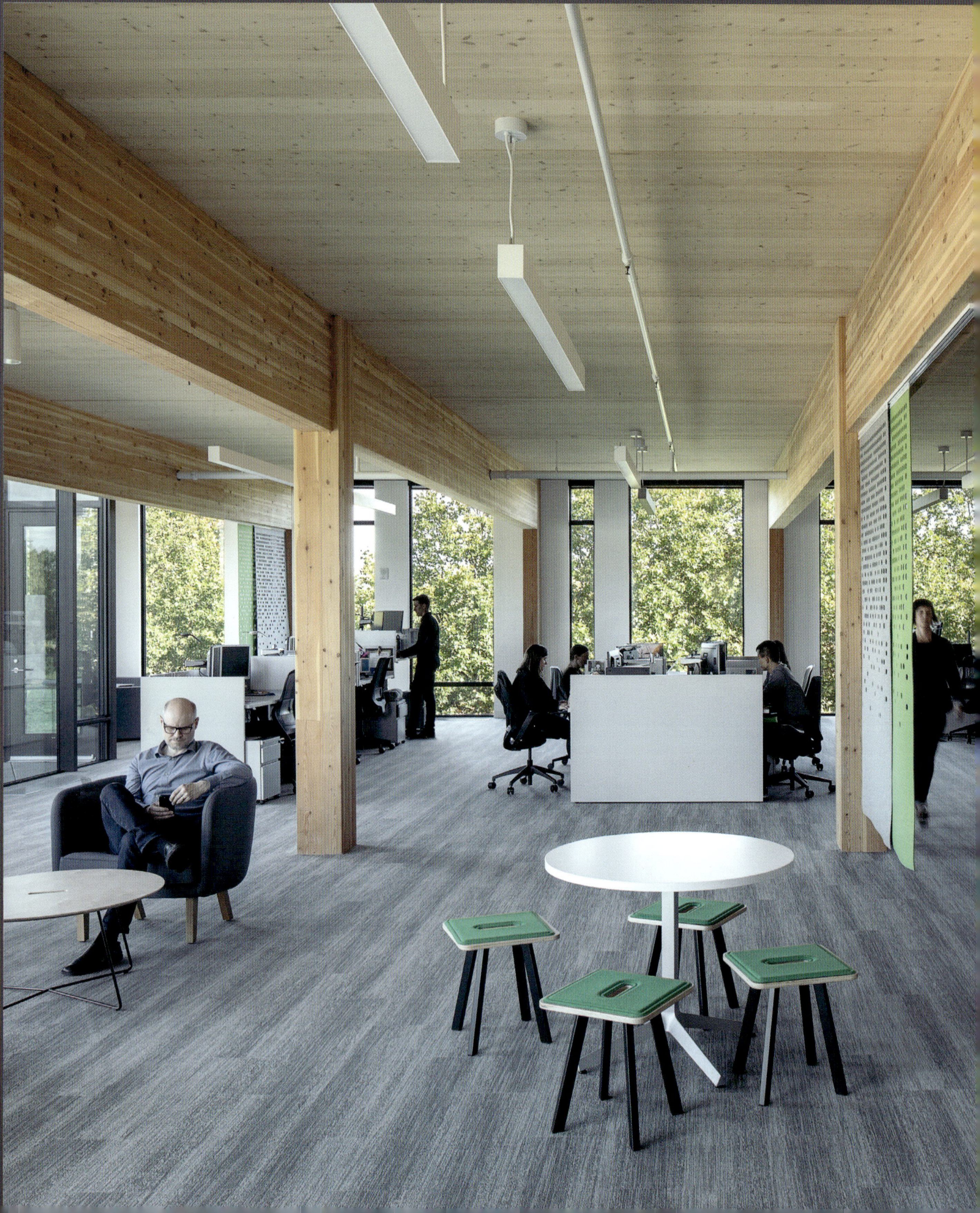

CHAPTER 14
FLEXIBILITY, USE AND LIFE CYCLE ISSUES

This chapter considers issues around building use, flexibility and life cycle impacts, including carbon accounting aspects and end of life considerations. The stage structure and impact categories used to frame this chapter are based upon definitions within EN 15978 as illustrated by **Figure 14.1**.[1]

Life cycle issues can be complex, especially investigated in detail. Teams will need to adopt a practical approach to suit their level of experience and may wish to engage specialist support to assist compiling (or reviewing) data.[2]

CROSS LAMINATED TIMBER

FIG 14.0 (chapter opener)

Floor slabs make up the majority of a commercial building's superstructure, by mass, volume and associated lifecycle impact. CLT floor slabs and a glulam frame create flexible interiors and are conspicuous when viewed on approach through extensive glazing at the First Tech Credit Union, Hillsboro, OR, United States by Hacker Architects (2018).

RELEVANT ELEMENTS

As reflected within Life Cycle Assessment (LCA) common tools, CLT use may influence the following materials and sub-groups:[3]

- Substructure materials: foundations/lower floor elements.
- Superstructure materials: external walls, structural frames, internal walls and partitions, upper floors slabs, roof elements, stairs and ramps.

Floor slabs typically represent the bulk of a superstructure's material use and impacts and therefore might be used for initial comparative studies and calculations.[4]

CARBON FOOTPRINTS

FIG 14.1

Assessment stage and impact categories relevant to CLT structures.

The global warming potential (GWP) of a product's use is typically a key focus, increasingly so regarding net zero carbon aspirations, considered in terms of carbon footprint: the total of the direct and indirect greenhouse gas emissions caused by that product. This is typically expressed in terms of CO_2 equivalent ($kgCO_2e$) per cubic metre.

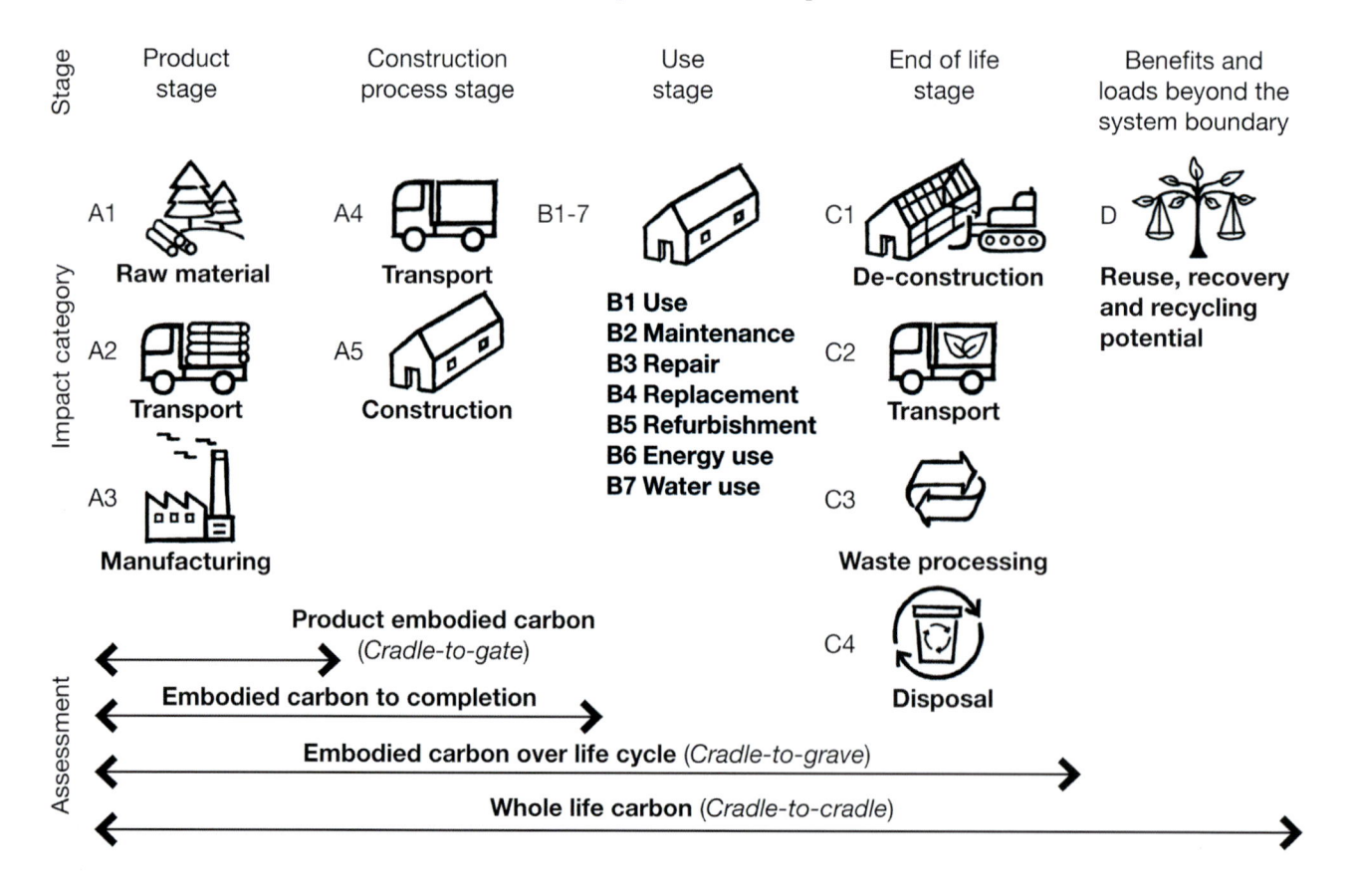

Stage	Product stage	Construction process stage	Use stage	End of life stage	Benefits and loads beyond the system boundary
Impact category	A1 Raw material A2 Transport A3 Manufacturing	A4 Transport A5 Construction	B1-7 B1 Use B2 Maintenance B3 Repair B4 Replacement B5 Refurbishment B6 Energy use B7 Water use	C1 De-construction C2 Transport C3 Waste processing C4 Disposal	D Reuse, recovery and recycling potential

Assessment:
- Product embodied carbon (Cradle-to-gate)
- Embodied carbon to completion
- Embodied carbon over life cycle (Cradle-to-grave)
- Whole life carbon (Cradle-to-cradle)

Data sources and variance

Carbon calculation and measurement can be a challenge. Assumptions and simplifications need to be made regarding likely impacts but the underlying issues are complex and frequently misunderstood.

Figures for CLT will vary by geographic location, available suppliers, species used as well as by data source. The means of calculation is key when comparing to inform decision making.[5]

For this reason, along with the potential for changes over time and regional specificity, specific metrics are not included here. Teams may want to build up their own catalogue of trusted metrics relating to local availability from suppliers, preferably prepared and certified by third parties.

Comparison methods

When comparing likely carbon impacts, it is common practice to assume a benchmark based on the default solution for the element being considered.[6] Alternative forms of construction, materials, structural arrangements etc can then be indexed to this when assessing relative value, including embodied carbon impacts.[7]

Carbon storage and end of life assumptions

Impact metrics may be quoted with and without biogenic carbon storage. Long-term storage may be taken into account if timber is sustainably sourced subject to certain conditions at end of life (and this aspect remains a bone of contention as attitudes towards LCA methods evolve).

Impacts of manufacturing will be varied in magnitude for any material (reflecting impacts from gathering raw materials, transport and manufacturing). Overall, these are typically much lower for CLT than other materials. Impact considerations that include carbon storage assumptions will reflect the sequestration properties of CLT (how much carbon is sunk or locked away in the timber), and will be therefore negative in magnitude. For CLT, such impacts can be significant. Net figures for CLT tend to be negative in magnitude (highly unusual for building materials) – the impacts of manufacturing representing a fraction of potential carbon storage (in some cases less than 10%).

Environmental Product Declarations

Environmental Product Declarations (EPDs) may be produced on behalf of manufacturers by independent third party organisations to communicate comparable product information, including life cycle impacts. The scope of each may vary but they are a good source of key data. Cradle-to-gate figures for various impacts (modules A1–A3) are calculated and information relating to subsequent stages may be included.

Product stage (cradle-to-gate impacts)

Raw material (A1)
Timber is a renewable resource and prehaps the ultimate key material for a circular economy (if used carefully). Powered by sunlight, trees convert CO_2 into polymers (such as lignin and cellulose) – particularly during their growing phase – while releasing oxygen. The resultant fibre is a versatile material with a very low environmental impact.

Forest stewardship and responsible environmental assessments schemes vary but specifying certified timber (such as PEFC or FSC) ensures that resources are generally well managed with trees replaced upon harvesting. There are however other concerns over the impacts of monoculture plantations on ecosystems and habitats that are not always considered by such schemes.[8]

Transport (A2)
CLT manufacturing tends to occur close to forest resources and factories are often co-located with, or close to, sawmills. Timber may be sourced from further afield but transport impacts during manufacturing are typically modest.

Manufacture (A3)
Little material is wasted even though only about half of the tree, by mass, becomes dimensioned timber. By-products are used for lower grade products or as a fuel source, powering heating or kilns. The drying process (required to achieve dimensional stability before manufacture) remains the most energy intensive aspect of manufacture.[9]

Panels are manufactured under highly automated and controlled environments, fabricated to order so the potential for waste is limited and adhesives used are generally environmentally friendly, formaldehyde and solvent free. They make up a small proportion of CLT by volume.[10]

Construction process stage

Opportunities for material efficiency arise throughout the entire project life cycle but design stages offer the maximum potential to reduce impacts.[11]

Transport (A4)
EPDs may describe manufacturing locations that can be used to calculate transport impacts. These may be flagged as a significant consideration but based on sample figures,[12] suggest that transport to the UK from Austria, for example, represents just 3.7% of the biogenic carbon stored. Figures vary elsewhere and relative proximity to a manufacturer remains a key feasibility driver in many cases.

CASE STUDY EXAMPLES

FIG 14.2

CLT soffits are exposed within 14 dwellings comprising Carbon12, Portland by KAISER+PATH, where (unusually for residential application) internal planning flexibility and long-term adaptation potential is enabled through the use of glulam beams rather than a honeycomb CLT form. An early understanding of design and CNC capabilities of the timber manufacturer Structurlam enabled the team to make cost-effective decisions around material use, cost and programme efficiencies and early vibration analysis aided the design of one-way spanning CLT floors. These incorporated insulation and screed over to mitigate airborne and impact sound and building services (including sprinklers) were concealed wherever possible – aided by early, and extensive, team collaboration sharing 3D models.[13]

Construction (A5)
This is difficult to measure and compare but is relatively modest. CLT-related activities include lifting by crane, fixing with screws and brackets or steel connectors with any sealant strips and accessories required. There are no hot works requiring energy (or posing risks) nor typically any associated wet works requiring drying out. Site impacts are reduced by having far fewer workers on site for superstructure works (undertaking less hazardous work) over a relatively short programme: both may be reduced by up to 70% (possibly more) representing huge improvements over traditional construction.

Use stage (Stage B impacts)

Use (B1)
A key issue around use is maximising the potential lifetime of the building – if the life of a building extends to 120 years rather than 60 years, embodied impacts of structural materials may be halved. Beyond spatial generosity and the potential to accommodate alternative uses, CLT specific considerations might include the inherent flexibility to adapt panels, for additional openings, soft spots for stairs and other modifications over time.

Long-term durability of CLT is mostly dependent upon managing moisture risks whether from external or internal sources. Buildings of any form are not typically replaced due to failures of structure but maintaining internal systems (including ventilation and sanitary installations), regular envelope inspections and preventative as well as reactive maintenance are crucially important. Moisture ingress and retention may cause decay if undetected and beyond design and construction stages, in-use risk reduction, should be a key area of attention for those managing such buildings.

Occupant health and wellbeing aspects can be improved by using CLT, changing internal environmental conditions with physiological and psychological benefits.[14]

Biophilic design patterns addressed by exposed CLT might include *visual connection with nature* (natural material and patterns), *non-visual connection* (haptic and olfactory connections), *non-rhythmic sensory stimuli* (evoking physiological responses), *biomorphic forms and patterns* (natural grain/texture and variation), *material connection with nature* as well as *complexity and order* (spatial hierarchies similar to those in nature).[15]

The role of exposed CLT in creating healthier, more human-centred buildings may also include reducing the need for other installations such as ceilings or linings (which will also save costs and materials use and may reduce fire safety risks); the haptic properties of timber – how it feels to the touch; perceived and actual surface temperature variations – timber is deemed to be a warm material and the materials ability to absorb and release moisture – CLT is hygroscopic so can help regulate internal environments. The presence of wood has been shown to reduce stress and promote a better emotional state (even reducing the perception of pain).[16]

Maintenance (B2)
Visually, most exposed CLT is not decorated so requires little if any maintenance. Timber is one of few materials that is generally felt to improve with age, developing a patina of use and wear. Fire retardants will need to be inspected and repaired if damaged and manufacturers should be consulted regarding applied products.

Repair (B3)
Minor damage can be sanded out and if significant, could be filled, however the variance in surface patterning typically conceals most surface damage. Severely damaged CLT should always be assessed by a structural specialist. Damaged sections may be left in situ and/or concealed or cut-out and replaced locally depending upon circumstances.

Replacement (B4)
Damaged areas will require analysis but may not need to be replaced. Compromised panels may be cut out and replaced as necessary, typically after fire incidents or discovery of rot.

CASE STUDY EXAMPLES

FIG 14.3

Radiata pine CLT panels are exposed and celebrated alongside other timber elements throughout the Seed House, Castlecrag, New South Wales, Australia, by fitzpatrick + partners (2019) who describe this as 'an adaptable healthy home that is of its [semi-bushland] site, that will age gracefully, developing a patina of use' (James Fitzpatrick, architect and owner). Panels are untreated where possible with edges highlighting lamella expressed including to CLT door leaves with complementary wooden fittings exposing the character of the material with the expectation of worn edges, dents and scratches over time adding texture and character, reflecting life in a family home.

Refurbishment (B5)

Working with CLT elements does not generally involve noisy or disruptive works. The installation or removal of fit-out elements can be undertaken with hand tools, and dust production and risks are minimal compared to working with concrete slabs, reducing the potential impact on other occupants. Surface-mounted installations can be reconfigured easily and screw fixings leave little damage and this may be attractive to commercial tenants regarding dilapidation considerations.

Inserting new elements within a CLT shell is typically straightforward and quicker and easier than other construction. There is much flexibility in where fixings can be made but the integrity of any passive fire protection or boarding to panels or penetrations must be maintained.[17]

Where the appearance of any exposed timber is deemed undesirable, it can of course be readily refinished, painted or concealed with standard linings or finishes.

CROSS LAMINATED TIMBER

Energy use in operation (B6)

Impacts should be considered, particularly if displacing high mass construction that might otherwise offer thermal mass advantages (CLT offers a fraction of the thermal storage potential of concrete) which may influence servicing strategies.

Panel size and low conductivity typically results in more readily achieved good levels of airtightness and the limiting of cold bridging issues reducing energy losses. Light reflectance from timber surfaces that may change tone over time, is however much lower than from white surfaces (to soffits for example) and this might be considered when designing lighting installations.

CASE STUDY EXAMPLES

FIG 14.4

The Greenwich Peninsula Design District, London, includes two CLT buildings by Mole Architects (completed 2020). The central building pictured, the 'Ziggurat' uses timber SIP wall panels on a glulam frame with CLT floors (with soffits exposed to appeal to design-conscious creative tenants), cores, stairs and feature rooflight structures. To the left, the 'Rhomboid' is full CLT, including external walls, where apertures are smaller punched openings. Internal walls to both buildings will be lined with phase change material, calculated to provide thermal mass-type benefits to these lightweight structures, improving occupant comfort and limiting operational as well as embodied impacts.

End of life stage (Stage C impacts)

Deconstruction and transport (C1, C2)
Design for disassembly techniques and accessible/obvious connection details may ease future works whatever a material's ultimate destination. CLT buildings have generally not reached the end of their intended design lives so there are no precedents to study. The material is however easy to work and lightweight and likely to be in large sections that can be handled efficiently as well as being readily separated from other elements.

Waste processing (C3)
Timber recycling is an emerging industry and becoming increasingly accessible as landfill becomes less acceptable. Of 5 million tons of UK waste wood available for recycling and recovery per annum, around a third is recycled and reused into other products and a third used as biomass feedstock, termed 'recovery' (2017 figures).[18]

Disposal (C4)
A common criticism levelled at early life cycle studies around CLT use is that at the end of life, the material is expected to be burnt, releasing about half of the solar energy used to form the timber and all of the stored (biogenic) carbon, or alternatively, buried in landfill (in which there is a risk of methane, a highly potent greenhouse gas, escaping as a consequence of anaerobic decomposition). Future generations will likely do neither. Emission standards regarding energy recovery will likely to be stricter, limiting burning waste and this option is most attractive when providing energy from waste displaces fossil fuel use which will be phased out over time.

Existing recovery and recycling figures (as above) suggest that only a limited amount of timber waste goes to landfill, space for which is already limited with related taxes escalating over time. Alternative options will likely be better developed and offer better value at the end of the life of today's new construction.

FIG 14.5

End of life options for CLT products based on established waste hierarchy to illustrate impact preferences for various material strategies at end of first use.

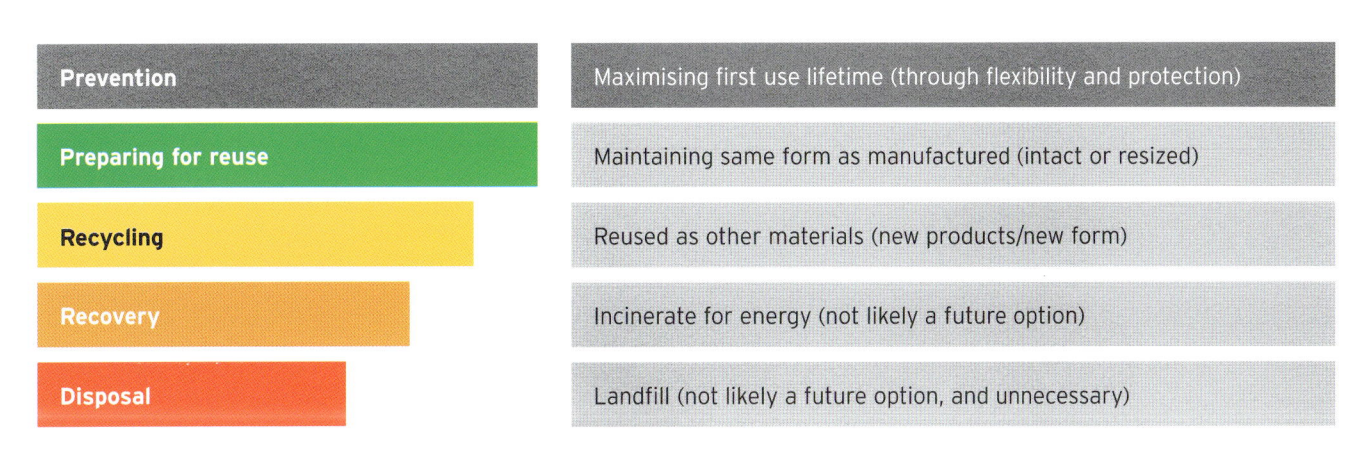

Prevention	Maximising first use lifetime (through flexibility and protection)
Preparing for reuse	Maintaining same form as manufactured (intact or resized)
Recycling	Reused as other materials (new products/new form)
Recovery	Incinerate for energy (not likely a future option)
Disposal	Landfill (not likely a future option, and unnecessary)

Benefits beyond initial life cycle (Stage D impacts)

CLT panels are relatively stable and consistent in performance compared to non-engineered, smaller format timber sections. They are therefore well suited to re-use, enabling a circular approach to materials use and the consideration of redundant buildings as assets rather than liabilities or waste. In doing so, the economic value of such structures may be realised, challenging how buildings should be valued in the future when there will be even greater pressure on resource use.

Where panels may be reused (i.e. going beyond a cradle-to-grave consideration), there is no widely accepted means of accounting for such carbon impacts or benefits. A true cradle-to-cradle consideration would recognise the embodied content of such panels reused in a form as close as possible to their original.

Subject to access to fixings (not being covered by screeds, bonded finishes etc), screws and brackets may be removed without significant damage (refer to the Triodos Bank Office Building case study where 165,312 screws were recorded, with other measures, to ensure the building is fully demountable in the future with minimal loss of value).

Designing panels to be of regular or smaller modules may make reuse of elements more attractive but recording as much detail about the panel, physical characteristics, geometry etc is critical. This may be facilitated by BIM or so-called material passports where buildings are treated as material banks or assets suitable for future resource 'mining', ensuring better use is made of scarce resources whilst ensuring value is retained wherever possible.

Given that all panels arrive on site with a detailed label (based on strict quality assurance procedures and the processing undertaken), such information could be marked by other means directly onto the panel (printed/branded/plated) to leave no doubt about the identity and value of the material to future generations.

FIGURE 14.6

The Multiply pavilion by Waugh Thistleton with Arup, was produced for the American Hardwood Export Council to showcase the use and variegated nature of tulipwood, forming some of the worlds first hardwood CLT, and first installed in the V&A Sackler courtyard for the 2018 London Design Festival. Using local expertise and the only CLT press in the UK, over 100 panels were produced at the Construction Scotland Innovation Centre with extremely precise digitally fabricated joints to create a lightweight but robust kit of parts that can be assembled quickly to withstand significant visitor loads and then be readily demounted and transported elsewhere. CLT is increasingly used for installations and demountable structures and the pavilion has been successfully reconfigured on several sites around Europe since.

CHAPTER 14 **FLEXIBILITY, USE AND LIFE CYCLE ISSUES**

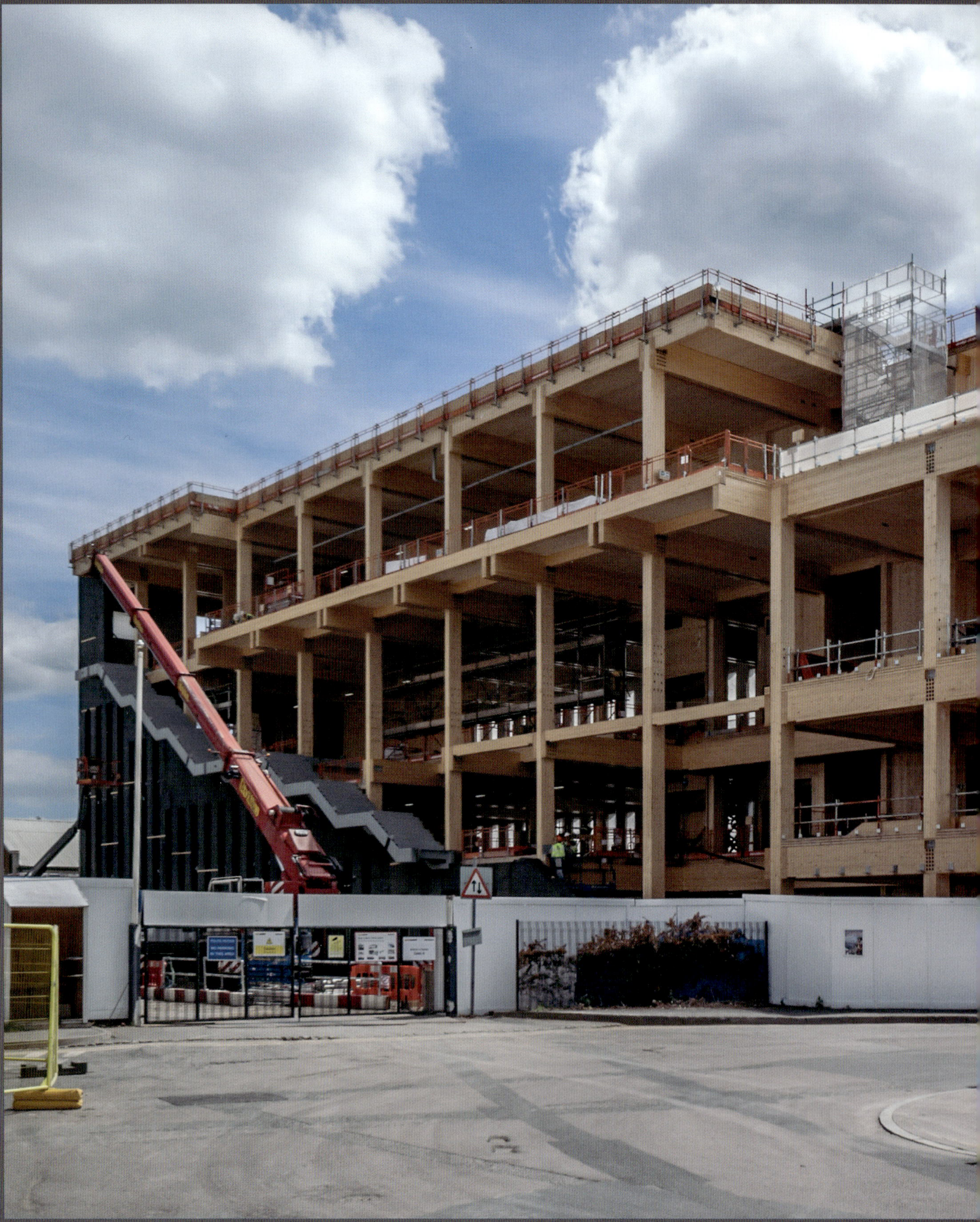

CHAPTER 15
CLIENT ISSUES

More so than aspects discussed in preceding chapters, this chapter outlines matters of particular interest to clients and their advisors (and therefore those working with them) that will be regarded differently depending upon the type of client, sector, scale of project, location, form of investment or development or particular moments in time. The only constant is change, it seems, as perception and priorities continue to evolve and shift, often with surprising speed.

CROSS LAMINATED TIMBER

FIG 15.0 (chapter opener)
CLT and mass timber are commonly adopted (and expressed to reflect corporate priorities) by high profile commercial clients. Sky's Believe in Better Building, London (by Arup Associates, 2014) was completed in record time due to early team and contractor collaboration.

Clients and developers know better than anyone involved that delivering any development can be extremely challenging and developments that innovate and endure and offer long-term value are certainly no easier.

Many are rightly cautious, particularly when it comes to resolving issues around fire safety, acoustics and durability and the priority should of course be to deliver buildings that are safe, comfortable and endure. Concerns may also extend to contractors' relative inexperience and the potential for this to limit the numbers of interested/able parties at tender stage, adding further pressure to costs.

THE DECISION-MAKING PROCESS

In some instances, CLT will be an appropriate material to consider and in others it may not be. Clients and teams may need work together, taking time to carefully consider options, communicate key issues or listen and evaluate appropriately rather than defaulting to the established way of doing things. A comparative approach is typically adopted, allowing favoured options to be identified and investigated further.

Investigating potential options

In periods of uncertainty and potential change it is even more important to maintain options and retain flexibility where possible. Whilst maximum benefits are typically achieved when CLT use is designed-in from the outset, it is in few parties' interests to preclude particular actions (whether

FIG 15.1
Simplified visual summary of a comparative exercise considering the differing impacts of various forms of slab construction and grid spacing (headline indicative figures shown with and without accounting for carbon sequestration).

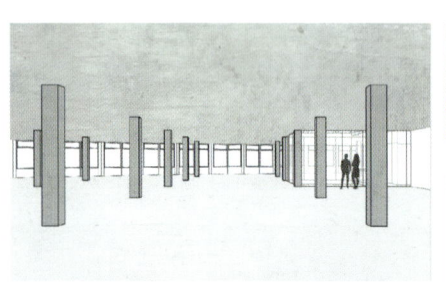

RC frame and slab (50% GGBS), 9 x 9m grid
Carbon impacts (no sequestration): 100 [baseline]

RC frame and partial CLT slab, 9 x 9m grid
Carbon impacts with sequestration: 42
(Carbon impacts without sequestration: 65)

RC frame and partial CLT slab, 10.5x10.5m grid
Carbon impacts with sequestration: 72
(Carbon impacts without sequestration: 49)

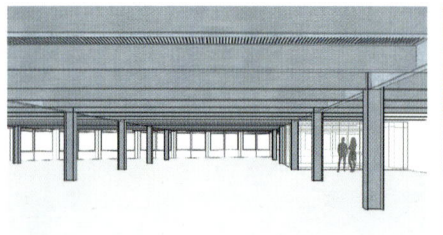

Steel frame with metal decking, 9 x 12m grid
Carbon impacts with sequestration: 68

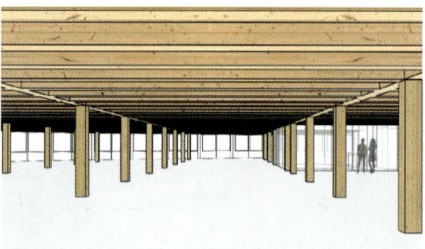

Glulam frame with Precast RC planks, 6 x 9m grid
Carbon impacts with sequestration: -19
(Carbon impacts without sequestration: 70)

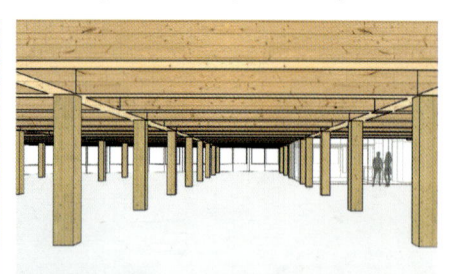

Glulam frame with CLT planks, 6 x 7.5m grid
Carbon impacts with sequestration: -66
(Carbon impacts without sequestration: 26)

that be insisting on CLT use or ruling it out) until sufficient investigations have been undertaken to make the best decisions.

Pressured decision making

A key constraint is often time. Project experience suggests that decisions around structural materials are often made early in the process, while resources are limited and perhaps before a full team is engaged. Fledgling teams exploring any approach that is not widely adopted will rightly be asked to justify design direction or materials choices, typically responding to specific technical issues, at short notice. As such, undertaking early research into CLT use may help understand whether it offers value to a project and this is a great opportunity to explore projects in other regions and countries where experience may vary.[1] Engaging specialists can also be important – seeking out parties with relevant experience, engaging the supply chain in a meaningful way and bringing them to the project in any way possible early on will also inform better decision making.

Existing precedents

Whatever material is under consideration, one of the most common questions posed when considering relatively new forms of building or construction is 'show me examples where it's been done before'.

Since many of the buildings completed with CLT to date have been developed by innovators and early adopters, such leading edge individuals and organisations are typically minded to share lessons learnt to benefit the early majority and those following afterwards. Seek out relevant precedents and contact those involved to learn more.

Resources such as this book and others referenced can signpost completed projects and sources of further information and help teams understand the scope and scale of a range of issues. Established specialists and industry trade associations are typically well positioned to assist and keen to help decision makers cross the perceived chasm from innovation to wider adoption and frequently publish precedents and guidance on a range of issues.

This is of course not always possible if proposals are novel and particularly with commercial buildings, there are many diverse ways of making use of CLT and many emerging structural solutions as further hybrid options are developed. As a last resort, mock-ups and tests can be undertaken to validate designs and achieve necessary certification or reassurance if the investment can be justified.

Residential clients

Private residential clients continue to drive interest in innovative new materials and this sector produces a large number of CLT buildings where early innovators are less burdened by institutional views or the obligations and perceived risks associated with large buildings. Feedback from owner-occupiers is typically very positive and although this should be expected (given most have made significant personal investments in a bespoke home to suit their own interests and priorities), it seems that the emotional response to exposed timber from owners and visitors alike is almost universally positive.

Many in the UK will consider the use of CLT in multi-storey/multi-family residential to be off-limits due to post-Grenfell regulatory changes to Building Regulations. It should be noted that subject to other established design approaches, combustibility restrictions are proscribed to elements within the external wall only. Large-scale residential schemes such as Brock Commons or the Australian National University, as illustrated within this book, offer proof that external wall elements can be readily incorporated with lower impact CLT superstructures in a way that would meet current UK regulatory requirements.

KEY ISSUES AROUND THE CONSIDERATION OF CLT

Risk managers, insurance and warranty providers

Any new approach will deservedly attract the keen attention of those underwriting risks and CLT take-up is no exception. Concerns will likely be raised around issues of fire safety (including during site works) and durability – particularly in terms of long-term asset value. This is not an issue that should be avoided and early engagement with warranty providers, insurance providers and others to help inform other decisions (rather than afterwards) will be time well spent. In doing so, be specific in raising any concerns, whether relating to the perception of risk or actual risks to life safety, building fabric or business continuity. Such engagement can help all parties better understand actual risks and may provide opportunities to explore or alleviate concerns over specific issues. A thorough approach at this stage will minimise abortive work if particular arrangements are deemed to be unacceptable in time.

Considering value as well as price

Development decisions reflect a huge range of considerations beyond just cost but developers and contractors are prompting teams to explore and consider value from CLT use in other ways. Programme savings are a great example where CLT panels, which likely cost more than conventional materials, are lifted and installed quickly, in panels sized up to 50m^2 at a time. The impact on site programmes, preliminaries and secondary costs can however be significant and should be calculated and considered.[2]

Telling the right story

Beyond issues discussed within the cost and values chapter, developing a story explaining the benefits of materials choices and design decisions can be key. This is frequently raised by agents who might typically want to know 'what's the story?', 'what are the three headline issues that will appeal to investors or tenants?', i.e. 'what can I sell?'. Any metrics supporting such narratives (and more importantly informing the preceding decision-making process) will always be put to good use.

Environmental and financial priorities

Until relatively recently, briefing and early stage sustainability aspirations may have focused primarily on driving down boring-but-worthy operational energy. This agenda offered little joy but plenty of restrictions and requires difficult structural change to make significant improvements beyond established (low) performance benchmarks. Over time, focus shifted to more conspicuous, more tangible issues around occupant health and wellbeing. Such aspirations are undoubtedly more readily achievable, easier to sell and create a much more positive image for occupants to buy into.

As demonstrated around the time of Brexit, there was a very significant upsurge in the awareness of, and stated concern about, environmental issues by businesses as well as individuals. This was due perhaps to a wider recognition of the climate emergency, the rise of high impact social movements such as Extinction Rebellion, global school strikes, and the adoption of (and in short order, subsequent improvements of) net zero carbon ambitions by nations, regions and leading corporations, including for the first time serious widespread discussion of zero embodied impacts from construction.

One of the most dramatic consequences of this is a marked change in attitudes regarding real estate development with agents, clients and funding bodies recognising potential risks to capital and placing a much greater emphasis on issues around environmental impacts.[3]

Net zero carbon considerations are now frequently front and centre for funders and investors, developers, owners and occupiers in a way that would have been unimaginable only a few years earlier – presenting a marked shift even during the time it has taken to compile this book. There is now an increasingly common appreciation that developments should be considering and addressing embodied carbon impacts and although these are not typically well-defined or understood, this has led to a dramatic upsurge in interest of CLT. This may be in part because using CLT conspicuously, i.e. on display, may be seen to address issues of wellbeing, natural materials, biophilia and a better internal environment and still be associated with a meaningful carbon impact (do also bear in mind that CLT need not be on display to provide myriad advantages to a project – this is often overlooked with a common fixation on visual aspects).

Carbon accounting and reporting

Carbon accounting of impacts across both development portfolios and tenant estates is now commonplace and after years of building awareness, client bodies are seriously addressing embodied carbon impacts with the understanding that doing so will likely increase capital expenditure. Legislative and/or fiscal incentives may well follow to ensure industry moves towards national net zero carbon targets but when increased reporting around such issues is commonplace, financial institutions are proving keen to change direction to protect future value. Funding bodies realise that if the market moves to lower impact buildings as it appears to be doing then most present day developments may be very unfavourably compared to newer, smarter alternatives. This may take place within a relatively short period of time - potentially the next property cycle. While lower impact buildings may or may not attract a premium, either way, it is possible that higher impact and therefore prematurely outdated and unwanted buildings may be devalued, risking becoming stranded assets, seen as dinosaurs from a previous age.

Key questions to ask at the options evaluation stage may explore the scope of carbon impacts to be evaluated, whether considered as part of a longer term, circular approach or a more limited, shorter term linear view:

- How is embodied carbon being accounted for and measured?
- Are sequestration benefits to be considered when comparing materials?
- Will considerations include manufacturing impacts only (cradle-to-gate impacts), construction related issues (such as transport) or life cycle impacts beyond (cradle-to-grave) or a fully circular approach taking into account reuse potential (cradle-to-cradle)?
- What is the potential for reuse of the building, or elements, at the end of its intended life?
- Where can comparable alternative impact savings be made, and at what cost?

New workers' expectations

Universities understand acutely that they will be judged on the quality of their campus assets and learning environments and for this reason, many of the bespoke CLT exemplars around the world (and indeed high quality/superior performance learning spaces) have been developed by the higher education sector. Students will in turn progress to the commercial workplace and in a market competing for talent will not be impressed by companies offering less attractive environments than they may be used to. This may be most apparent in the tech sector where interest in mass timber buildings has been particularly significant and huge buildings are currently on site for Google and Microsoft and under consideration by many others.

Emotional response to timber

Whether or not they are interested in how a building is put together, many agents recognise the benefits of good quality, high visual impact spaces and are amongst the best advocates for mass timber buildings. They might understand that the use of CLT and related materials reflect broader societal concerns on many levels and are more aware of the basic emotional response to timber that is typically positive, and therefore good for business. In researching this chapter, discussions with residential clients and commercial agents alike kept coming back to the positive emotional effect of timber use on occupants and users of buildings.

Whether teams have the appetite to try and address some of the challenges we face or whether they are more concerned by the preferences of others, it is hoped that this book has helped identify key issues and highlighted further opportunities when considering this exciting new material.

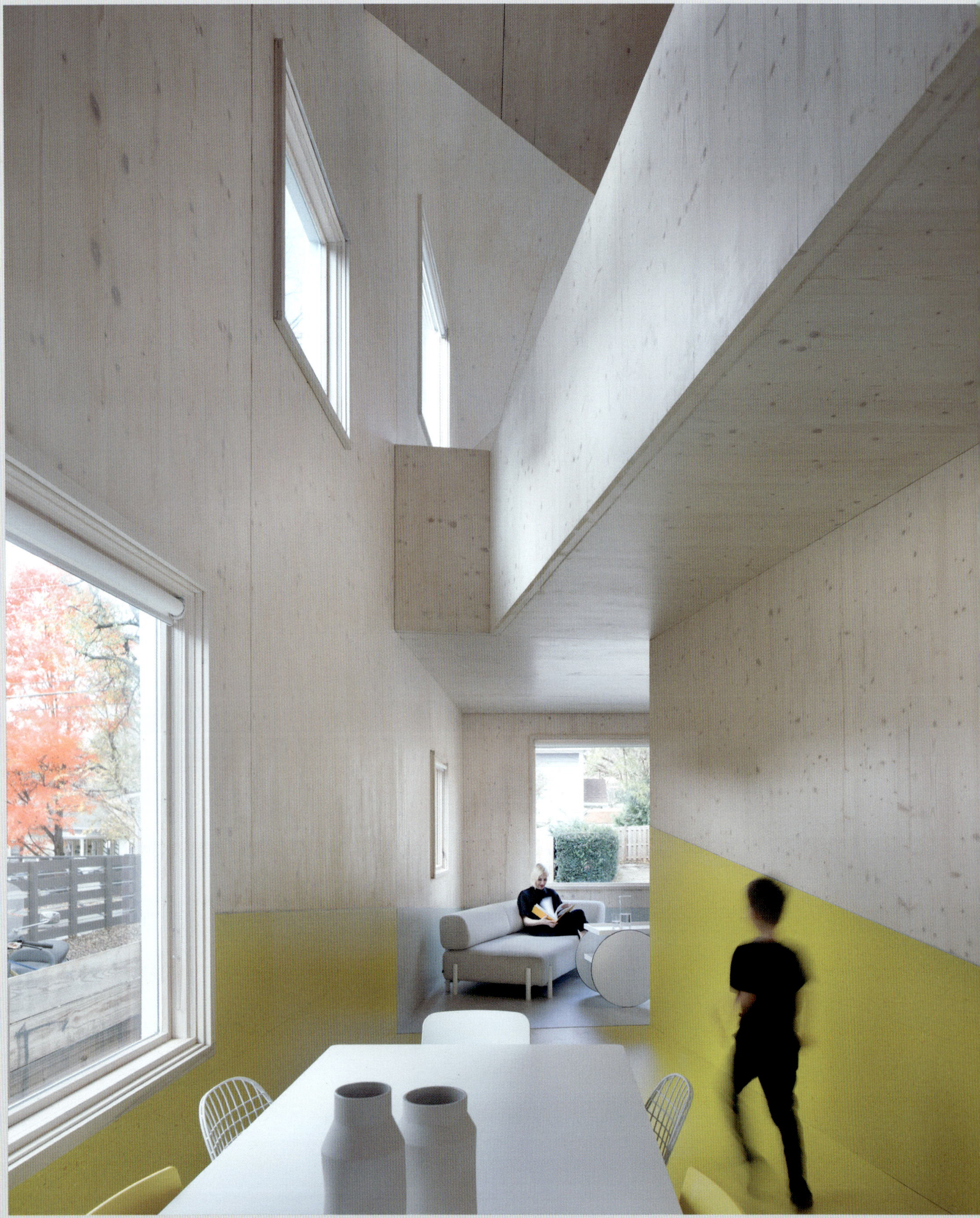

CASE STUDY
HAUS GABLES, ATLANTA, USA

CROSS LAMINATED TIMBER

FIG 16.0 (chapter opener)
Interior and exterior forms and volumes are defined throughout by CLT planes exploiting the structural and visual properties of large format panels.

Project name:	Haus Gables
Location (including local authority):	Atlanta, Georgia, USA
Sector/type:	Residential (single family house)
Year completed:	2019
Area of building (GIA):	204m²
Volume of CLT (m³):	Undisclosed
Overall construction cost (million):	Undisclosed
Total height of building:	10.1m
Client(s):	Volkan Alkanoglu & Jennifer Bonner
Architect:	Jennifer Bonner, MALL
Main contractor:	Principle Builders Group
QS:	Undisclosed
Structural engineers:	AKT II; Bensonwood; PEC Structural; Fire Tower
Timber engineer:	As structural
CLT contractor:	Terry Ducatt (installation specialist)
CLT manufacturer:	KLH Massivholz, via KLH USA

Areas of interest: Milestone US project; Roof form achieved by use of CLT panels; Combination of exposed panels with applied internal finishes.

PROJECT SUMMARY

A dramatic external form encloses and defines soaring internal volumes to this new-build single-family dwelling house on a constrained urban plot in Atlanta, Georgia, USA. CLT panels form faceted, folded and long-spanning planes, exploiting the structural qualities of the two-way spanning panels with the joyful celebration of structure amplified by a contemporary and playful approach to applied surfaces and colour (See **Figure 16.1**).

The structure is comprised of 87 unique individual panels up to 10.4m long utilising 3-ply panels for walls, 5-ply for the roof and 7-ply, up to 240mm thick, for the floor structure, all over a concrete basement plinth.

FORM

Roof form and therefore the internal soffits were informed by extensive research into roof typologies of the American South. The architect also intended to challenge the notion of a traditional dwelling, typically formed from a wood frame of small section lumber and overclad with drywall

CASE STUDY **HAUS GABLES, ATLANTA, USA**

throughout – the last thin layer of sheet material defining spaces and volumes. Instead the CLT panels form the character of different spaces as well as bearing load and enclosing volume.

FIG 16.1

Haus Gables exterior.

151

CROSS LAMINATED TIMBER

FIG 16.2

Long sections illustrating roof form, voids, level changes and faux finishes.

Section

01 Patio
02 Living Room
03 Entry
04 Bathroom
05 Bedroom
06 Laundry Room
07 Mudroom
08 Garage

152

CASE STUDY **HAUS GABLES, ATLANTA, USA**

'The process was actually incredibly liberating. This is what the architect should be doing: building, but also conceptualizing architecture, with one foot in academia, in experimentation.'
Associate Professor Jennifer Bonner, designer, developer and owner

STRUCTURE

CLT panels lend themselves well to roof structures. Without ties, the origami-like roof serves as a form of shell, a folded panel reminiscent of a card model built 1:1.

As is typical for many mass timber projects, there were a number of different structural engineers involved over the project. Beyond initial investigations and concept development, another firm picked up the design development and then outsourced detailed timber calculations to another. A fourth company designed the slab connections specifically (a key element for most CLT structures as they interface with concrete plinths or slabs) and resolved specific local code approvals based on inputs from predecessors.

FIG 16.3

Aerial view of roof form after completion of panel assembly.

CROSS LAMINATED TIMBER

FIG 16.4

Roof form reflected by underside of exposed panels.

FIG 16.5

CLT panels act as a folded plate and bedroom beyond landing is hung from larger roof above.

FIG 16.6

CLT wall and roof surfaces are exposed on the bedroom interior.

INTERIORS

Interiors are defined by structural panels, the geometry creating soaring volumes expressing external form and by a range of faux finishes applied to lower surfaces. Finer materials are contrasted with the robust finish and texture of exposed panels. The wainscoting of applied finishes also conceals service chases to lower levels and creates opportunities for further expression of occupied spaces through the contrasting use of colour blocking. Timber is exposed to a greater extent in more intimate areas such as bedrooms or covered as required in wet areas and panels are also used to form stairs, balustrades and suspended elements.

PROCUREMENT AND SEQUENCING

A number of suppliers were put off by the apparently complex form, but the architect digitally designed and nested each panel within larger 'blanks' (full panels representing the optimum size available since panels were

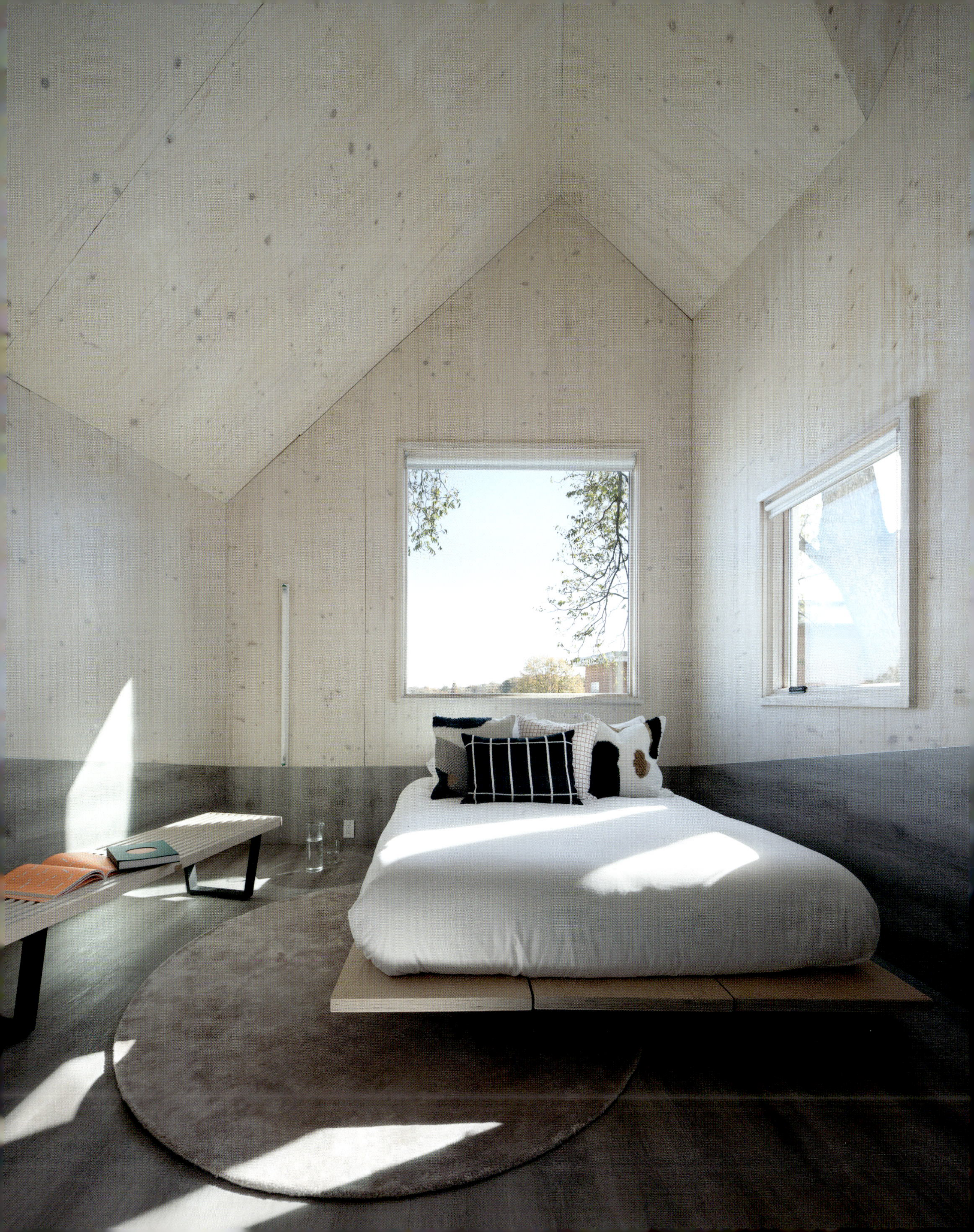

to be shipped in containers from Europe). This demonstrated the most efficient cutting arrangements for pieces forming the irregular geometry. Working closely with an Austrian panel supplier enabled the design team to draw upon the manufacturer's very extensive experience of milling and processing complex details, which proved invaluable in detailing, before checking (and rechecking) every connection detail.

The construction process required careful planning and key to this was communication between various team members, including pre-empting difficulties by scenario planning. Following investigation of the only comparable precedent, a house in Seattle, Washington,[1] the same specialist installer was recruited to help inform and guide the detailed design, preparation and assembly process. A key challenge was site logistics and providing a crane and staging area on a constricted narrow site, but panels were arranged so they could be craned from each of the 11 trailers delivered in order of assembly. A team of 4 workers installed all the panels over just 14 days before the build was handed over to the general contractor for completion.

This was one of the earlier full CLT houses in the US and the use of such panels enabled a highly efficient resolution and stunning expression of the complex geometry. Lessons learnt can of course be applied to more straightforward forms.

FIG 16.7

Volumes are defined throughout by exposed structural CLT panels and double height voids to living areas offer expansive internal views.

FIG 16.8

Site works during assembly of pre-manufactured panels.

CASE STUDY **HAUS GABLES, ATLANTA, USA**

157

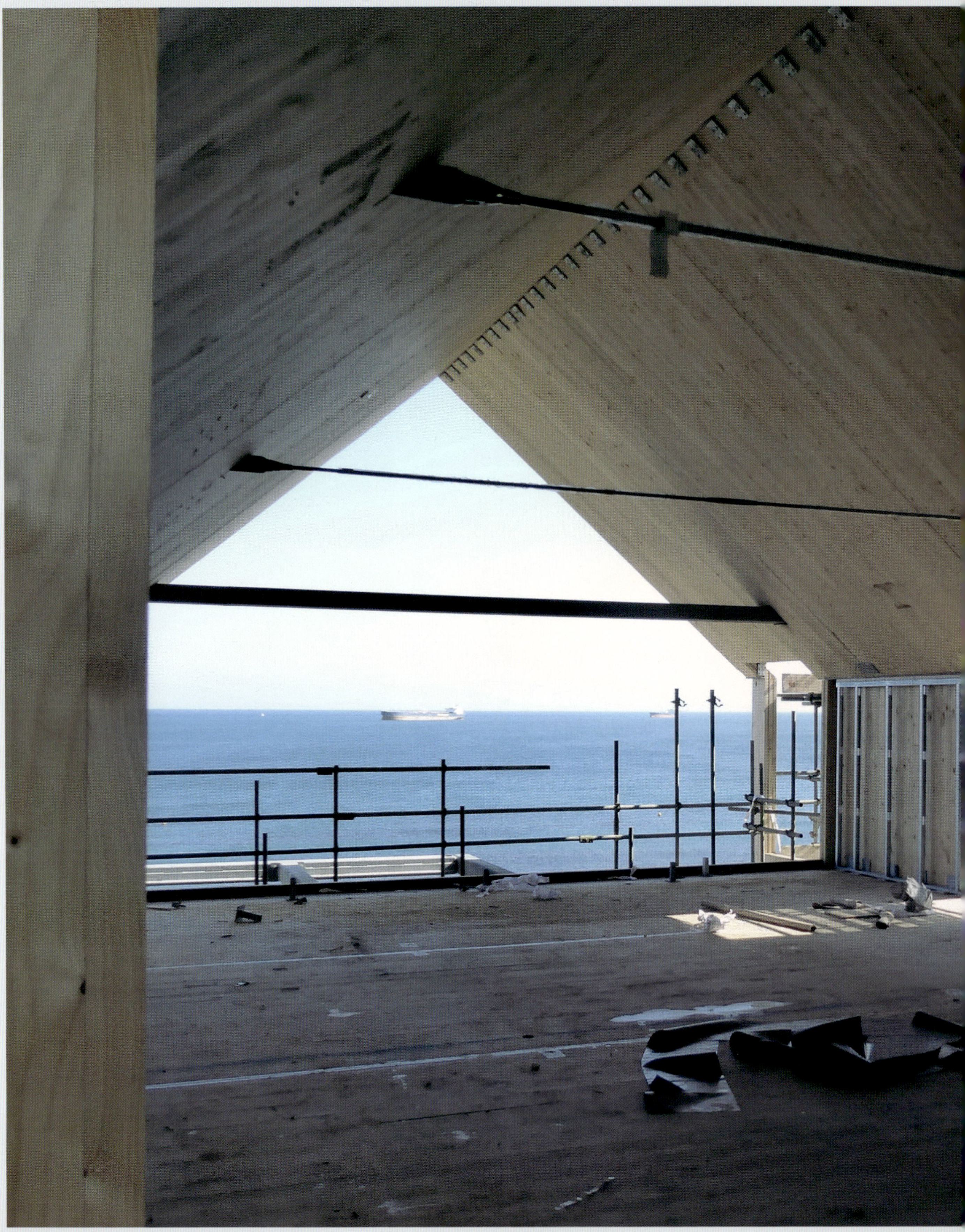

CASE STUDY
THE FITZROY, FALMOUTH, UK

CROSS LAMINATED TIMBER

FIG 17.0 (chapter opener)
Top floor special spaces are formed by combining CLT panels with limited steel ties to efficiently form double-height volumes.

Project name:	The Fitzroy, Falmouth
Location (including local authority):	Falmouth, Cornwall, UK
Sector/type:	Residential (private sale retirement housing)
Year completed:	2019
Area of building (GIA):	3,860m^2
Volume of CLT (m^3):	Undisclosed
Overall construction cost (million):	£8.0
Total height of building:	19.5m
Client(s):	PegasusLife
Architect:	Allford Hall Monaghan Morris Architects
Main contractor:	Midas Construction Ltd
QS:	PMP Consultants
Structural engineers:	Symmetrys
Timber engineer:	Engenuiti
CLT contractor:	B&K Structures
CLT manufacturer:	Binderholz

Areas of interest: Predominant use of CLT with steel supports to part; Challenging coastal site conditions; Moisture control.

PROJECT SUMMARY

This new seafront building of 34 retirement apartments represented a trial of alternative methods of construction by a specialist housing provider with an ambitious delivery programme. Single-storey apartments are accessed from a central core and decks to the rear, arranged to allow large apertures with cantilevered balconies facing seaward.

FEASIBILITY AND COMPARISONS OF STRUCTURAL FORM

To challenge initial presumptions in favour of concrete or steel, differing structural systems were scored using a comparisons matrix covering programme, cost, impacts on foundations, likely site conditions and advantages for follow-on trades. The most favourable was a full CLT superstructure that reduced site programme by an estimated six to eight

CASE STUDY **THE FITZROY, FALMOUTH, UK**

FIG 17.1

Illustrative sketches to communicate the application of CLT to the project team and local planning authority.

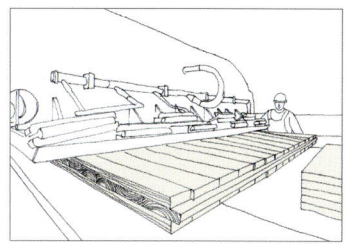

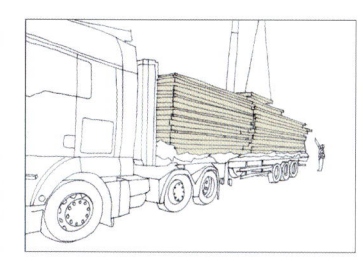

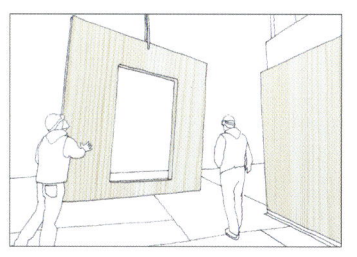

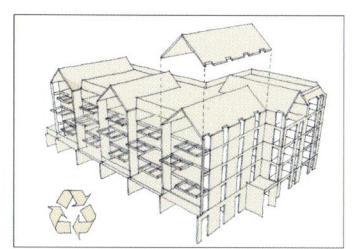

FIG 17.2

Axonometric of cantilevered balcony support with steel beams used to counter-rotational forces.

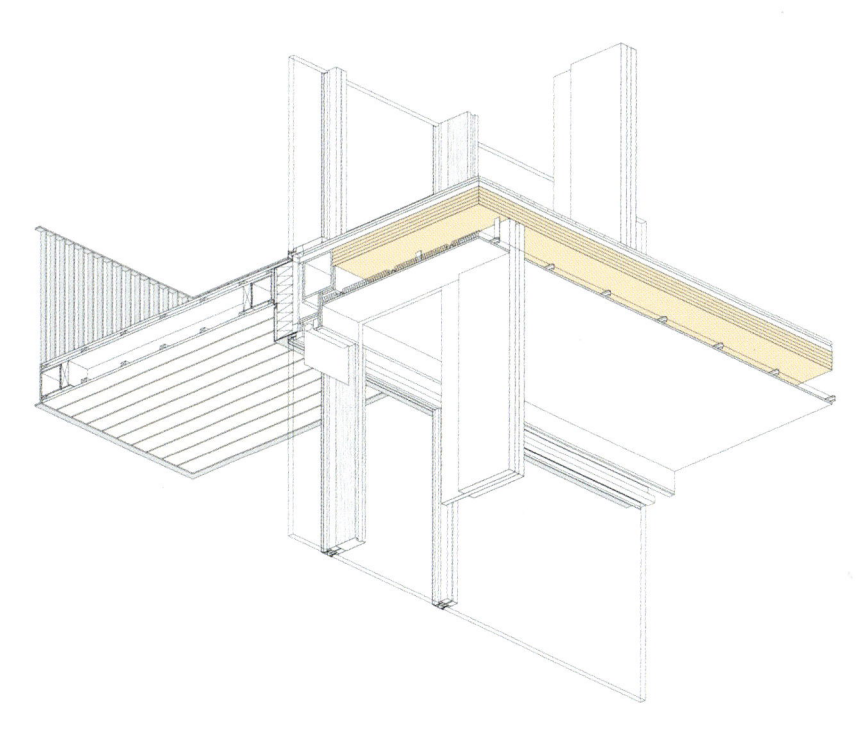

weeks, but this was subsequently modified to reduce costs by incorporating limited structural steel elements (typically horizontal elements, ties etc). This partial hybrid structure provided additional bracing and countered rotational forces from large cantilevered balconies (while retaining CLT lift cores and stairs) but resulted in much more complex detailing of interfaces and junctions. This particularly impacted the architectural team who would, without doubt endeavour to simplify the design of future projects.

CROSS LAMINATED TIMBER

FIG 17.3
Steel beams and framing supporting balconies with CLT crosswalls and slabs allowing larger openings framing sea views.

In this instance, the vertical alignment of similar apartments was well resolved and proved advantageous in avoiding significant transfers or requirements for downstands. The choice of CLT did allow slimmer floor build-ups than would have otherwise be achievable (with a considerable saving of 90mm per floor over a conventional concrete slab alternative) resulting in a reduced overall building height and reduced sizing of foundations with some, yet to be quantified, cost, programme, excavation and material (concrete and steel) savings on site.

FIRE SAFETY DESIGN

At five storeys, with double height top floors, this building is close to the maximum allowable height for CLT use in external walls of residential buildings in England and Wales following Building Regulation revisions in 2018/19. The team assessed fire risks regardless and worked hard to source fire-stopping solutions with party walls and service penetrations proving most challenging with limited supplier options at the time of specification. If the main contractor had employed a fire-stopping specialist from the early stages, this would have helped the process, giving clarity to specialist roles and responsibilities. Surface spread of flame issues were mitigated by the concealed construction with panels typically covered by gypsum boarding.

WEATHER EFFECTS DURING CONSTRUCTION

Building quickly with large prefabricated elements was an advantage in this exposed location on low cliffs to the sea but high winds caused some limitations to craning activities, having more of an impact on lifting schedules to higher levels. Construction and craning sequencing was revised when this became apparent and the contractor would reconsider their lifting strategy when planning the next project.

CASE STUDY **THE FITZROY, FALMOUTH, UK**

FIG 17.4

Top floor double height living areas are formed by inclined CLT panels using the planar action of the material to create special internal spaces with minimal steel ties above head height. These dramatic volumes are expressed on the main facade, crowning the elevation.

FIG 17.5

Initial projections underestimated the restrictions on lifting due to high winds for this coastal location affecting construction sequencing.

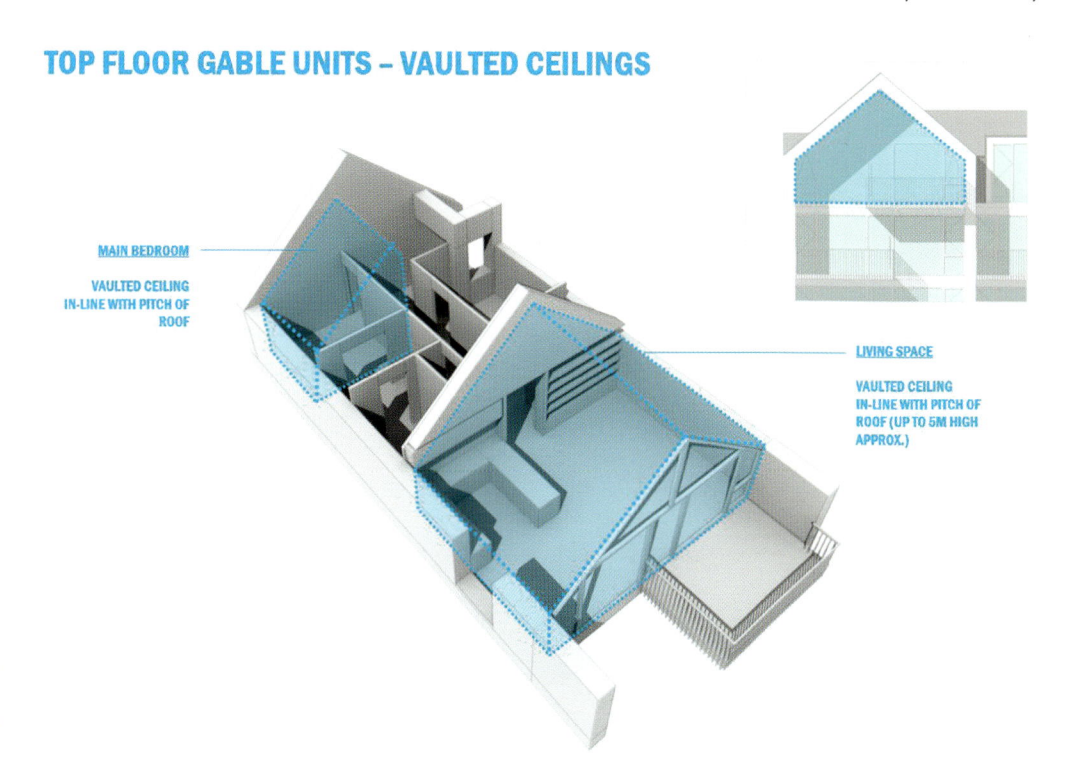

TOP FLOOR GABLE UNITS – VAULTED CEILINGS

MAIN BEDROOM
VAULTED CEILING IN-LINE WITH PITCH OF ROOF

LIVING SPACE
VAULTED CEILING IN-LINE WITH PITCH OF ROOF (UP TO 5M HIGH APPROX.)

CROSS LAMINATED TIMBER

FIG 17.6
Sea views and large openings seawards resulted in a steel supporting structure across the main facade to accommodate significant moment forces from cantilevered balconies.

As a consequence of standing water observed on some slabs before the envelope was made weathertight, temporary drainage was introduced under an improved moisture management plan. These and limited other areas affected by envelope leakages were checked and monitored by the CLT contractor taking regular moisture readings from slabs. Some areas of horizontal panels were required to be left to dry out before being covered over (requiring careful management and sequencing at later stages) although vertical panels were unaffected due to end the grain sealant applied to the head and foot of vertical panels by the frame contractor. Because of the exposed coastal location, the engineering team specified fixings and connection elements that would not be adversely affected by coastal exposure; this would not typically be an issue in other locations.

SITE OBSERVATIONS

During frame construction, it was observed that the site had a relatively small workforce present and was extremely tidy which was beneficial in terms of health safety risks as well as construction fire safety. This was the main contractor's first experience of using CLT and those on site during the erection of the frame were hugely impressed by the relative speed and ease with which the superstructure was assembled as well as the timing when follow-on trades could begin working on subsequent packages.

CONCEALED CLT

Following much consideration and team discussion, the client was hesitant about the appeal of exposed timber surfaces to the older purchasing market and all panels were eventually concealed (which also added to the acoustic and fire safety performance). The form of construction did however generate a huge amount of interest locally during the build when the timber was fully on display and this site proved to be the fastest-selling development in the client's portfolio.

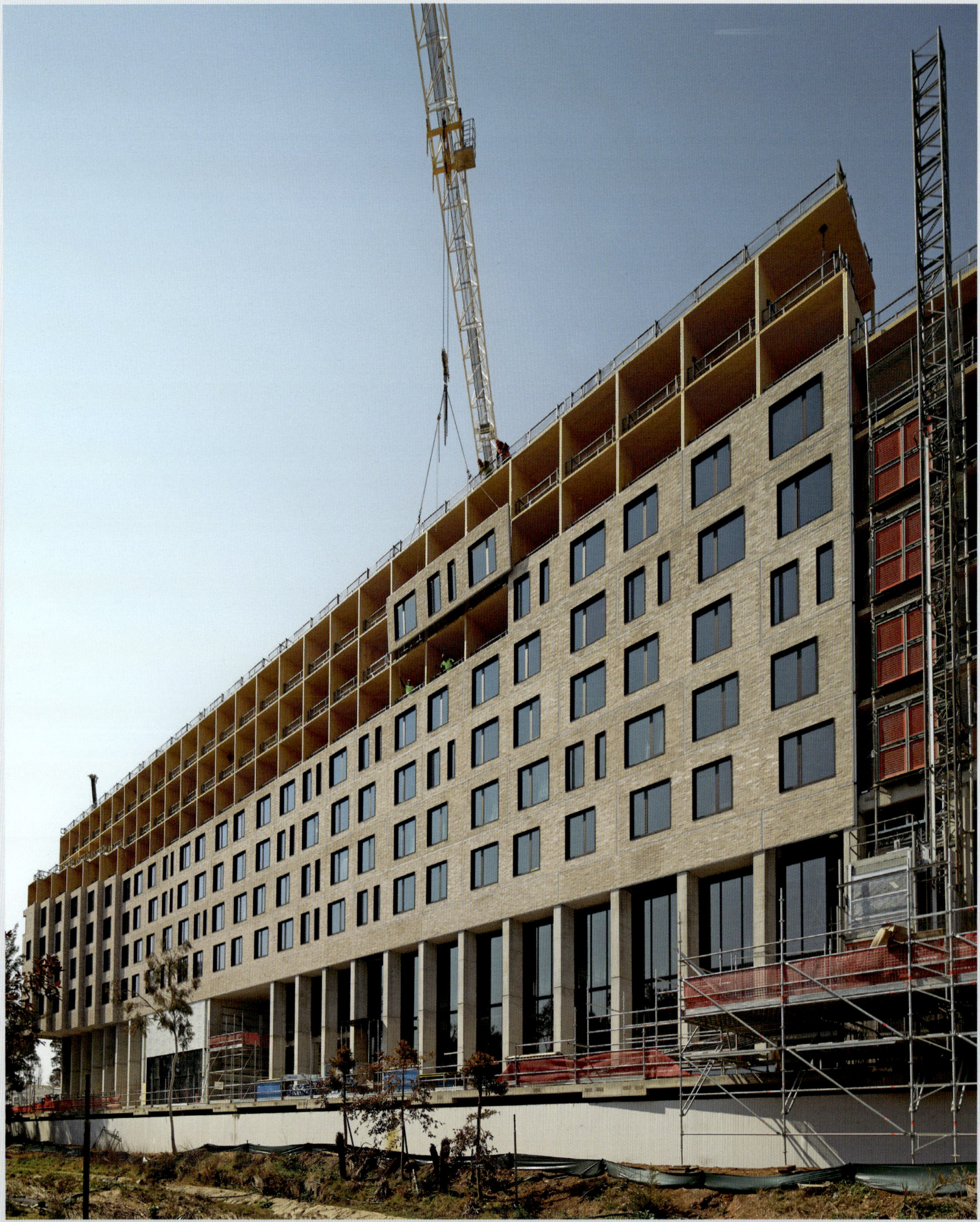

CASE STUDY
FENNER HALL, STUDENT RESIDENCES, CANBERRA, AUSTRALIA

CROSS LAMINATED TIMBER

> This case study was contributed by *Ninotschka Titchkosky*, Co-CEO, BVN

FIG 18.0 (chapter opener)

Pre-manufactured external wall modules were installed rapidly, complete with cladding and glazing, onto the cellular CLT superstructure of this large student accommodation building.

FIG 18.1

Fenner Hall, Australian National University, Canberra, Australia.

Project name:	Fenner Hall Student Residences
Location:	Kambri, Australian National University, Canberra, Australia
Year completed:	2019
Sector/type:	Student Residential
Area of building (GFA):	10,150m²
Volume of CLT used (m³):	Not disclosed
Approximate total construction cost (million):	AU$47
Total height of building:	30m (excluding basement)
Client:	Australian National University (ANU)
Architect:	BVN
Main contractor:	Lendlease
Quantity surveyor:	Lendlease
Timber engineer:	Lendlease Design Make
CLT contractor:	Lendlease Design Make
Structural engineer (non-timber elements):	Robert Bird Group
Timber manufacturer:	Stora Enso

Areas of interest: High density, medium-rise residential; Speed and buildability; Prefabricated facades.

PROJECT SUMMARY

Fenner Hall provides 450-bed student accommodation at the centre of the ANU Kambri redevelopment. Two of seven new buildings are CLT and mass timber, amongst the largest timber constructions in Australia, at the time. The entire precinct architecture was designed by BVN and delivered by Lendlease within a two-year period to limit downtime and disruption to the existing operational campus.

The ecological footprint of the new buildings were defined and measured using the 'One Planet' methodology, assessing all aspects of the project that impact its ecological footprint, including energy and embodied carbon. Under this system, the quantitative measure of human demand versus the supply of nature, the project achieved an ecological footprint of 0.7 of the world's resources which is considered 'World Sustainable Leadership' (representing a positive impact).

CASE STUDY **FENNER HALL, STUDENT RESIDENCES, CANBERRA, AUSTRALIA**

CONTRACTOR AND DELIVERY

Lendlease, a major contractor in the Australian market, has been an important catalyst in introducing mass timber construction. They were engaged as design and construct contractors in part due to their ability to handle a very large site and deliver mass timber at scale through their maturing timber business, Design Make, and existing supplier relationship with Stora Enso in Europe. This reduced risk for the university, providing time and cost certainty.

Shared spaces on lower levels were designed in concrete creating a 'table' for the CLT upper floors, primarily 10m^2 student rooms in a double loaded corridor plan arrangement with a high degree of repetition. Separating walls are load bearing, either 90mm or 140mm thick CLT and cores and risers above level 1 are also CLT.

Panels (shipped from Europe) increased the design time and coordination pre-order but accelerated the construction process on-site dramatically. Timber elements were installed in around four months resulting in a 33% reduction in the overall construction programme. In addition, time and cost savings to follow-on trades, such as service installers, were apparent but are yet to be formally calculated.

The entire timber superstructure and facade was installed by a team of ten with three crane crew. In comparison, concrete construction would require a team of 50-60 people, including multiple trades such as scaffolders, formworkers and concrete contractors. This considerably

FIG 18.2

Kambri campus, Australian National University, Canberra, Australia. Precinct under construction highlighting timber buildings.

reduced construction labour costs from 50–60% to 20–30% for the timber components. This reduced team and working hours increased site safety with fewer high-risk activities such as moving reinforcement or forms and overhead work or risk of falls with column pours.

The timber assembly team were part of the facade subcontractor's team, where their proficiency in accurate and detailed setting out, as well as carpentry, was complementary to the skill set required for the timber installation.

COMPLEMENTARY FACADE SYSTEM

The benefits of mass timber construction (MTC) are realised when other elements of the design and construction can be revisited to produce compounding gains in cost, time and quality. The prefabricated timber structure, cost of installation and programme pressures prompted the introduction of the first fully prefabricated rainscreen panel facade of a mega scale in Australia. The system could be craned in place, eliminating scaffolding and saving AU$1.2 million. The timber structure did not require a construction apron which enabled the prefabricated facade panels to be installed in sequence with the installation of timber which in turn allowed finishing trades to progress immediately.

Fire regulations require all facade materials to be non-combustible so the team worked together to adapt a new steel-framed prefabricated unitised rainscreen facade system with a steel subframe. To reduce weight and aid fixing, Italian bricks were cut into 20mm slips and threaded on steel rails connected to the subframe. Each storey height section was premanufactured with windows, slips and mortar or aluminium cladding, all waterproofing and thermal requirements as a 'mega panel' up to 13m long before being lifted up to the CLT superstructure.

FIRE ENGINEERING, ACOUSTICS AND SERVICES COORDINATION

Each room required 90-minute fire separation. Initially, the project was designed to have one exposed CLT wall in the rooms and exposed soffits in the corridors and rooms. The combined effect of acoustic and fire separation between rooms resulted in all surfaces in the rooms being clad in fire rated plasterboard. Each panel received a subframe with plasterboard and insulation attached to one side to achieve the acoustic rating.

Meeting the requirements for fire compartmentation and acoustic separation in CLT and with all services penetrations being cut in the factory required extensive 3D-modelling. Bespoke detailing was required where no industry standards existed for items such as refuse chutes, kitchen exhausts and riser access platforms.

CASE STUDY **FENNER HALL, STUDENT RESIDENCES, CANBERRA, AUSTRALIA**

ECOLOGICAL FOOTPRINT

Adopting timber structures for the student accommodation and the other timber building in the precinct, reduced embodied carbon by more than 30% over traditional concrete. Across the project, over 31,100 tonnes of CO_2 emissions were avoided by specifying low carbon materials, clever design and construction, delivering the entire student accommodation building for zero carbon footprint.

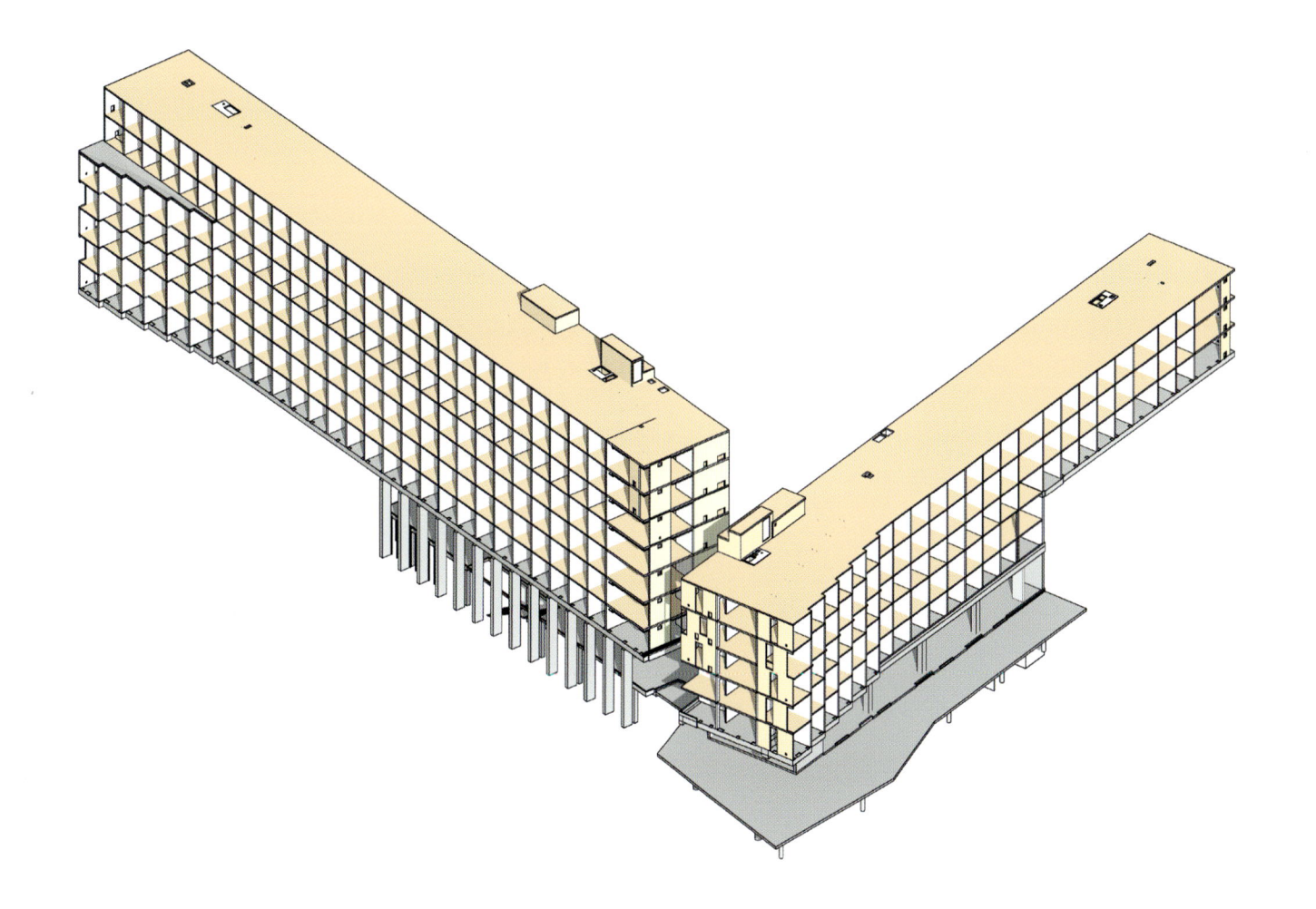

FIG 18.3

Structural system diagram illustrating cellular nature of upper floor CLT structure.

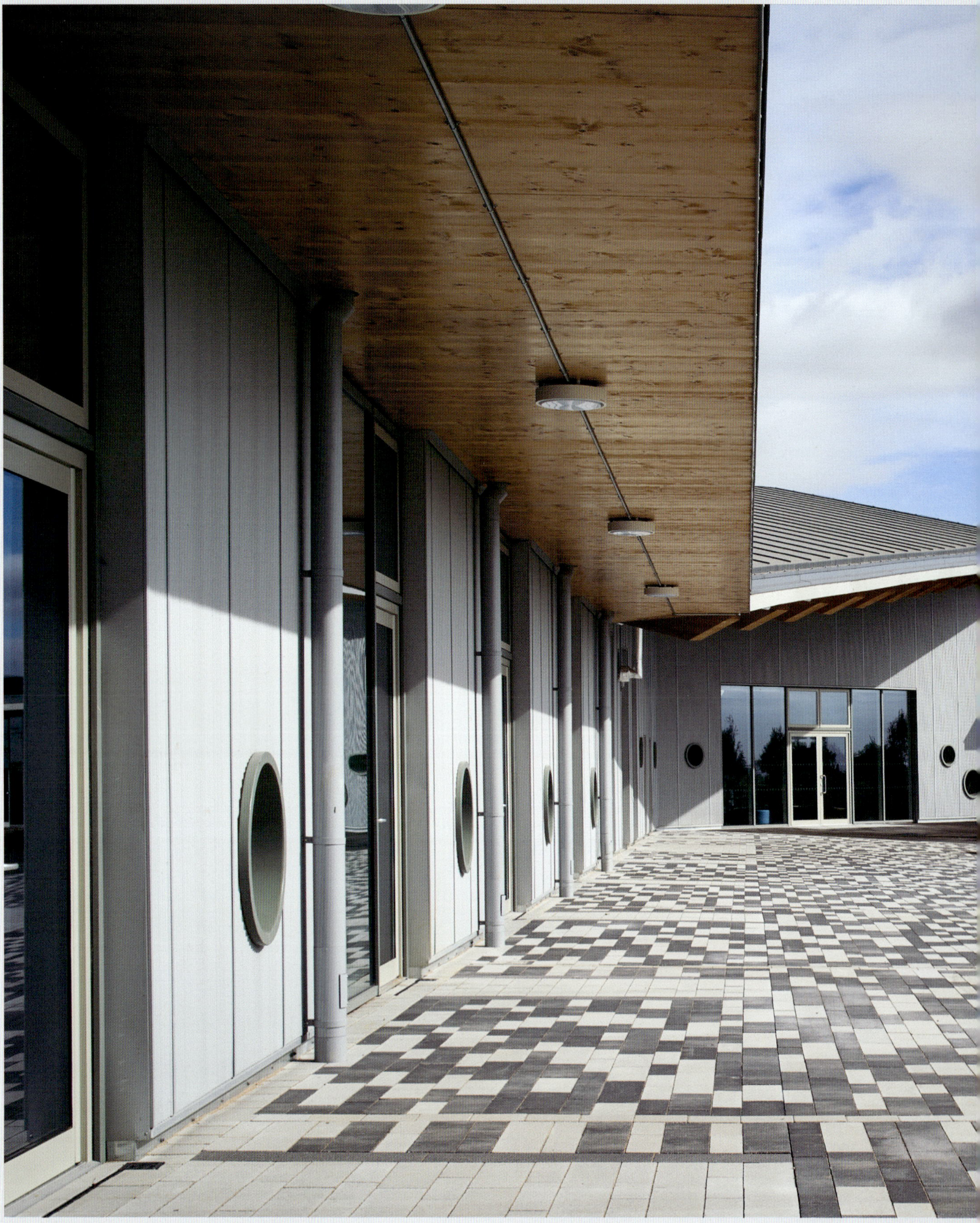

CASE STUDY
ERMINE STREET CHURCH ACADEMY, HUNTINGTON, UK

CROSS LAMINATED TIMBER

FIG 19.0 (chapter opener)
CLT panels are exposed throughout this new school and form protective soffits externally (in turn, protected from weather and moisture).

Project name:	Ermine Street Church Academy
Location (including local authority):	Huntingdon, Cambridgeshire, UK
Sector/type:	Education; new build nursery and junior school
Year completed:	2016
Area of building (GIA):	c.3,000m^2
Volume of CLT (m^3):	1,500m^3
Overall construction cost (million):	£7.8
Total height of building:	Up to 10m (single storey)
Client(s):	Morgan Sindall/Cambridgeshire County Council
Architect:	Allford Hall Monaghan Morris Architects
Main contractor:	Morgan Sindall
QS:	Morgan Sindall
Structural engineers:	Peter Dann Engineers
Timber engineer:	Ramboll
CLT contractor:	KLH UK
CLT manufacturer:	KLH Massivholz

Areas of interest: New build school; Exposed CLT throughout; Review of building in use.

PROJECT SUMMARY

This flagship new primary school was intended as a focal point for a new community masterplan. CLT panels and glulam beams are exposed wherever possible (to reduce costs, material use and maintenance burden), to external areas (creating shelter or covered play space) and throughout entrance, pupil and staff areas (including soffits and many walls). Spaces are predominantly single height with double- and triple-height common areas (as **Figure 19.1**) and extensive natural lighting and landscape views.

There are a number of issues pertinent to visual aspects of CLT use, many only uncovered during post-occupancy evaluation work several years after occupation.

DESIGN STAGE ISSUES

CLT use was initiated by the Council's framework contractor and based on past experience of similar building types was fully incorporated from

CASE STUDY **ERMINE STREET CHURCH ACADEMY, HUNTINGTON, UK**

FIG 19.1

Double and triple height hall with glulam structural beams.

FIG 19.2

Teaching rooms under construction and completed with large apertures to landscape, partial linings and suspended panels to conceal service elements (including large natural ventilation unit to roof aperture).

FIG 19.3

Cloakroom area with joinery elements contrasting with exposed CLT.

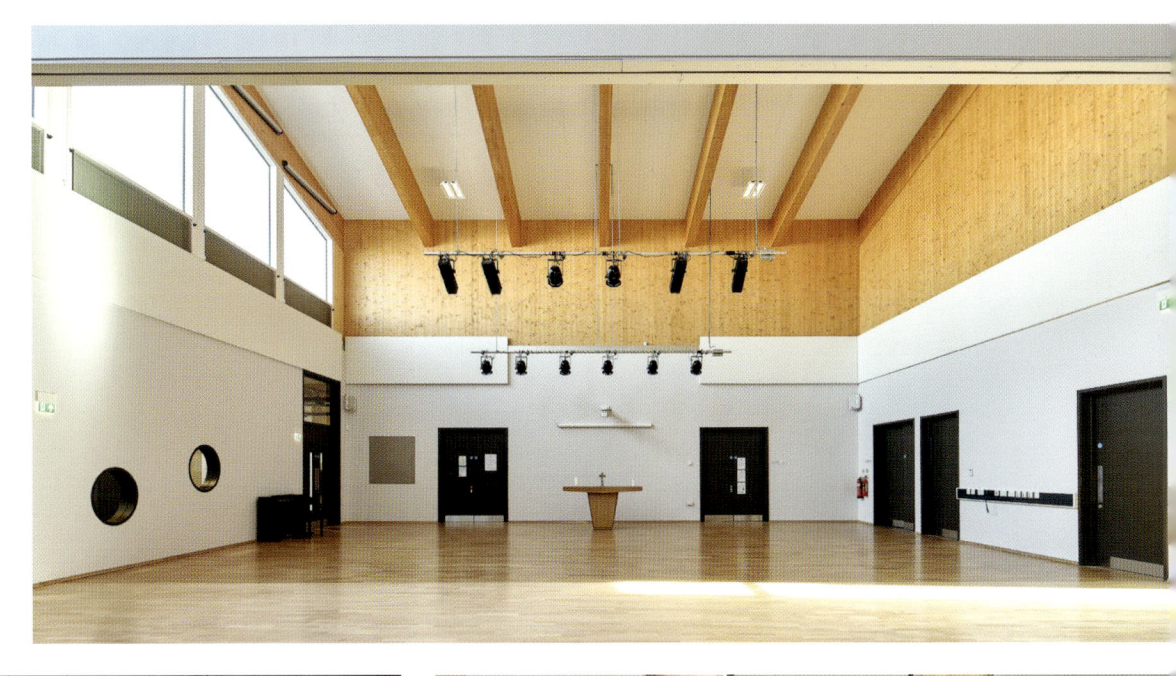

project inception. The design team were engaged after that decision was made and the application of CLT was very straightforward according to the project architect. An economical specification of surface finish grades was based on viewing distances with better-value non-domestic grade panels used in areas at higher levels above the occupied zone.

In other areas, large expanses of timber panels were contrasted with suspended panels, concealing service elements and some lined walls accommodating display zones, posters, whiteboards etc (as **Figure 19.2**). The flexibility to create openings in panels without inserting lintels allowed a number of circular apertures with the exposed inner timber face contrasted with other joinery elements such as window surrounds as **Figure 19.3**.

CROSS LAMINATED TIMBER

Acoustic separation between classrooms was an early challenge. The timber engineer and CLT contractor's extensive experience was leveraged to resolve potential issues, achieving stringent performance criteria through local increases in thickness to some panels to satisfy site test requirements. No adverse issues have been reported in use.

KEY ISSUES AT CONSTRUCTION STAGE

Construction was generally straightforward on this semi-greenfield site for a low-rise building. The CLT contractor was extremely well experienced and supportive of the project team and the main contractor had recent experience of constructing other schools from CLT. They continue to undertake this kind of project together still. There were however some issues with delays caused by wind – the site is on a former airfield and is very exposed, as **Figure 19.4**. This led to an upgrade in lifting equipment after the CLT contractor experienced some of their worst ever stoppages and they now recommend smaller sized panels if similar risks are identified at design stage.

FIG 19.4

Wind issues compromised otherwise good conditions on this exposed site.

CASE STUDY **ERMINE STREET CHURCH ACADEMY, HUNTINGTON, UK**

Some UV marking of panels occurred when they were temporarily protected with non-UV limiting sheeting before the envelope was completed – this required sanding on site to remove transferred marks.

OBSERVATIONS AND FEEDBACK

The architects undertook an occupancy evaluation exercise approximately three years post-completion. Minor areas of walls marked in use have been tidied up by local sanding by caretaking staff and small quantities of sap bled from the timber in limited areas for approximately the first 18 months of occupation but were readily wiped away (this is apparently not common for CLT).

Walls, soffits and beams have visibly yellowed (so called 'aging', a result of lignin degradation by UV light) and this is conspicuous where furniture or posters have been placed against walls (despite areas of lined walls being provided, partly for this reason) leading to 'shadows', as **Figure 19.5**. Where lots of posters and displays may be fixed to walls and may not be changed regularly, this could become a more obvious issue in time.

Fire-retardant coatings along busy corridors may require reapplication after having been worn/abraded over time by passing traffic. When viewed from shallow angles, upper levels of some walls reflect light whereas lower levels (beside trafficked areas) are flat matt and lightly abraded by passing traffic, bags etc. Limited areas of CLT were exposed at high level to the school canteen kitchen area (requiring a similar fire-retardant surface treatment to these areas) and this appeared more consistent, being beyond reach but could be at risk if not considered within any cleaning regime.

The management were unsure as to how to redecorate the building as the first maintenance cycle is due (and are rightly concerned about maintaining the integrity of any fire-retardant coatings). Such information, typically from manufacturers, would be contained within Operation and Maintenance information and in the handover of fire safety information at the completion of works and finishes should be maintained in line with these recommendations.

Limited areas of fully sheltered CLT soffits are exposed externally. There is some evidence of light water marking towards outer edges and some horizontal soffits appear to be susceptible to condensation caused by exhaust air from air handling ducts below. This has resulted in some very limited white surface marking.

Overall feedback from occupants (staff and pupils) is generally extremely positive with the head teacher crediting the 'excellent learning environment' (his term) to the large amounts of timber visible and extensive natural lighting and landscape views. Having been in post since the school opened to a new cohort of pupils, he was quite convinced that the exposed timber has had a very significant positive effect on the children's wellbeing and ability to learn.

FIG 19.5

Uneven colour change to walls where lower levels previously covered by furniture retain their original pale (spruce) colouring.

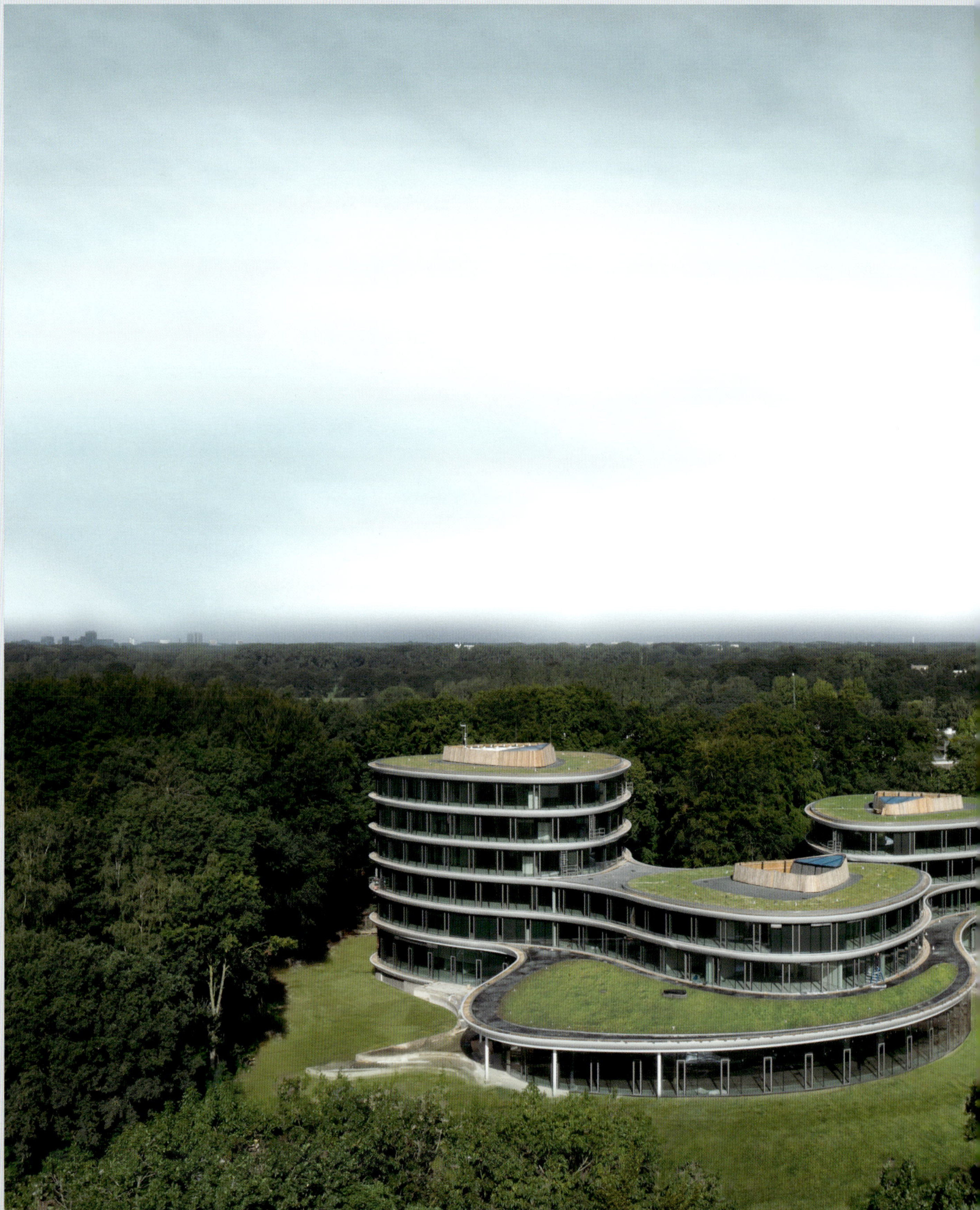

CASE STUDY
TRIODOS BANK OFFICE BUILDING, DRIESBERGEN-RIJSENBURG, THE NETHERLANDS

CROSS LAMINATED TIMBER

FIG 20.0 (chapter opener)

A predominately timber structure is an appropriate response to the bank's corporate philosophy as well as the woodland setting.

Project name:	Triodos Bank Office Building
Location (including local authority):	Driebergen-Rijsenburg, The Netherlands
Sector/type:	Office (new build)
Year completed:	2019
Area of building (GIA):	13,000m²
Volume of CLT (m³):	2,623m³
Overall construction cost (million):	Not disclosed
Total height of building:	25m
Client(s):	Triodos Bank
Architect:	RAU Architects
Main contractor:	J.P. van Eesteren
QS:	PMP Consultants
Structural engineers:	Aronsohn (Rotterdam), Luning (Arnhem)
Timber engineer:	Aronsohn (Rotterdam), Luning (Arnhem)
CLT contractor:	J.P. van Eesteren, Derix
CLT manufacturer:	Derix, Groot Vroomshoop

Areas of interest: Full timber hybrid for new office; Circular economy approach; Fully demountable design; Use of materials passport.

PROJECT SUMMARY

Commissioned by Triodos Bank, this new office building embodies the clear investment values of the occupying organisation, creating a 21st century workplace with a long-term view of resource ownership and value.

Three compact towers are connected by a shared plinth at lower levels. Above a concrete basement, cores, floor and roof elements are CLT with sculptural glulam beams and columns radiating from around the cores at the centre of the upper floor pop-ups.

FIG 20.1

BIM view illustrating central cores and plinth below upper floor workspaces. The structure above ground floor slab is predominantly CLT with glulam columns and sculptural beams.

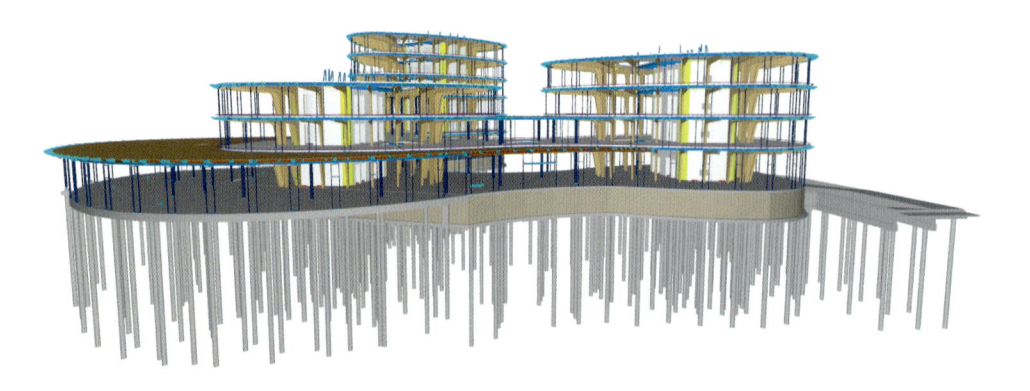

CASE STUDY **TRIODOS BANK OFFICE BUILDING, DRIESBERGEN-RIJSENBURG, THE NETHERLANDS**

FIG 20.2

CLT floors are partially masked by timber ceiling level ribs that allow access to chilled/radiant panels and services fed from risers within the CLT cores beyond.

FIG 20.3

Four storey height panels were used to create stability cores and vertical shafts.

FIG 20.4

Once lifted into position, vertical panels require propping only until neighbouring panels are secured.

FIG 20.5

CLT shafts are typically better aligned than those made of other materials due to extremely tight tolerances and allow rapid fixing of lift installations and services.

Mostly glazed externally with a flush curtain wall, a priority was creating a high-quality internal environment. A limited palette of materials is used alongside exposed timber elements with glulam columns and beams and CLT expressed to cores where vertical CLT panels form lift shafts anchoring other elements and to soffits, with screening from decorative timber elements and soffit-mounted service panels. CLT was also used for stairs and roof slabs.

Beyond the structural solutions, all CLT panels and major materials used were considered in terms of design for disassembly and maximum value reuse from the outset. This is a bank building that is also a materials bank and a very deliberate investment for the future: a great example of a low-impact building that reflects circular economy principles as well as any built to date.

PROJECT AMBITIONS

Minimising the carbon footprint of the building was a concern for the project team and as such, concrete use was limited to basement areas due to the proximity of ground water – it is never good practice to use CLT below ground level. Elsewhere, structural elements are virtually all mass timber. Glulam beams span from central cores creating generous floor heights and emphasising a free-form facade with full flexibility for glazing, shading and opening lights where required, maximising daylight penetration and visual connection to the surrounding woodland setting.

CROSS LAMINATED TIMBER

FIG 20.6

CLT stability core and shafts with glulam columns and beams before the installation of first floor CLT slabs. All timber fixings were designed to be demountable and recorded (down to the last screw) to maximise future value and potential reuse of elements and materials.

EARLY COLLABORATION

From the outset, a collaborative approach was adopted to maximise potential gains and best address technical issues. Having previously worked for the same client, the architect and many of the team were brought together at the outset with construction advisors, the contractor and its subcontractors. This has been acknowledged as a key factor in delivering what is a ground-breaking building, in terms of initial construction, timber performance and future potential for demountability and maximum-value materials re-use.

CIRCULAR ECONOMY APPROACH

The building as a materials bank

Beyond physical aspects considered, data around CLT and other key materials use was considered with every element identified and documented. Information and key characteristics are recorded within a building specific materials passport for future reference. This fundamentally changes the way the building can be valued and by adding clarity and certainty to records, better ensures that elements stand the best chance of being reused at end of first life with minimal loss of value (rather than rather than downgraded or down-cycled).

RAU Architects were instrumental in establishing the Madaster database, a commercial materials passport platform that aims to 'eliminate waste by providing materials with an identity'.[1]

Design for reuse

Using a total of 165,312 screws, structural connections including all fixing of CLT was undertaken using dry processes to maximise the potential for disassembly and subsequent highest value reuse.

During first use, such an approach facilitates maximum flexibility by enabling elements to be relatively easily moved/taken away/replaced where required and the hoped-for reuse of individual elements on other sites (second and subsequent use) is made more attractive by the relative light weight of the timber elements used. If dismantled, elements may be handled relatively easily with the CLT being around 20% of the weight of concrete alternative elements.

FIG 20.7

Extracts from the buildings materials passport, held within the Madaster database. This platform was developed independently by the architects and records key data about the materials, components and products within a building taken from BIM.

CASE STUDY **TRIODOS BANK OFFICE BUILDING, DRIESBERGEN-RIJSENBURG, THE NETHERLANDS**

TRIODOS_DER_HOUT MADASTER.IFC

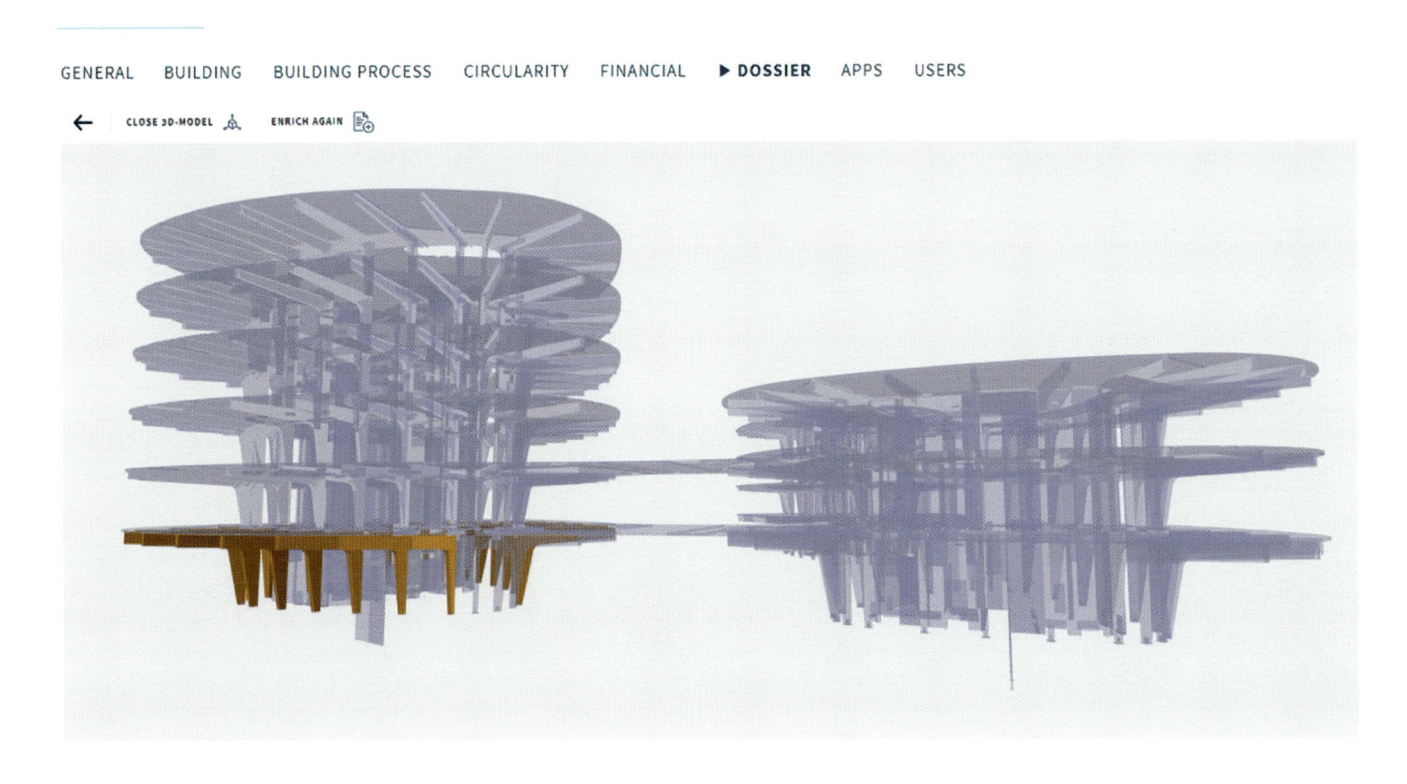

GENERAL BUILDING BUILDING PROCESS CIRCULARITY FINANCIAL ▶ DOSSIER APPS USERS

← CLOSE 3D-MODEL   ENRICH AGAIN

TRIODOS BANK

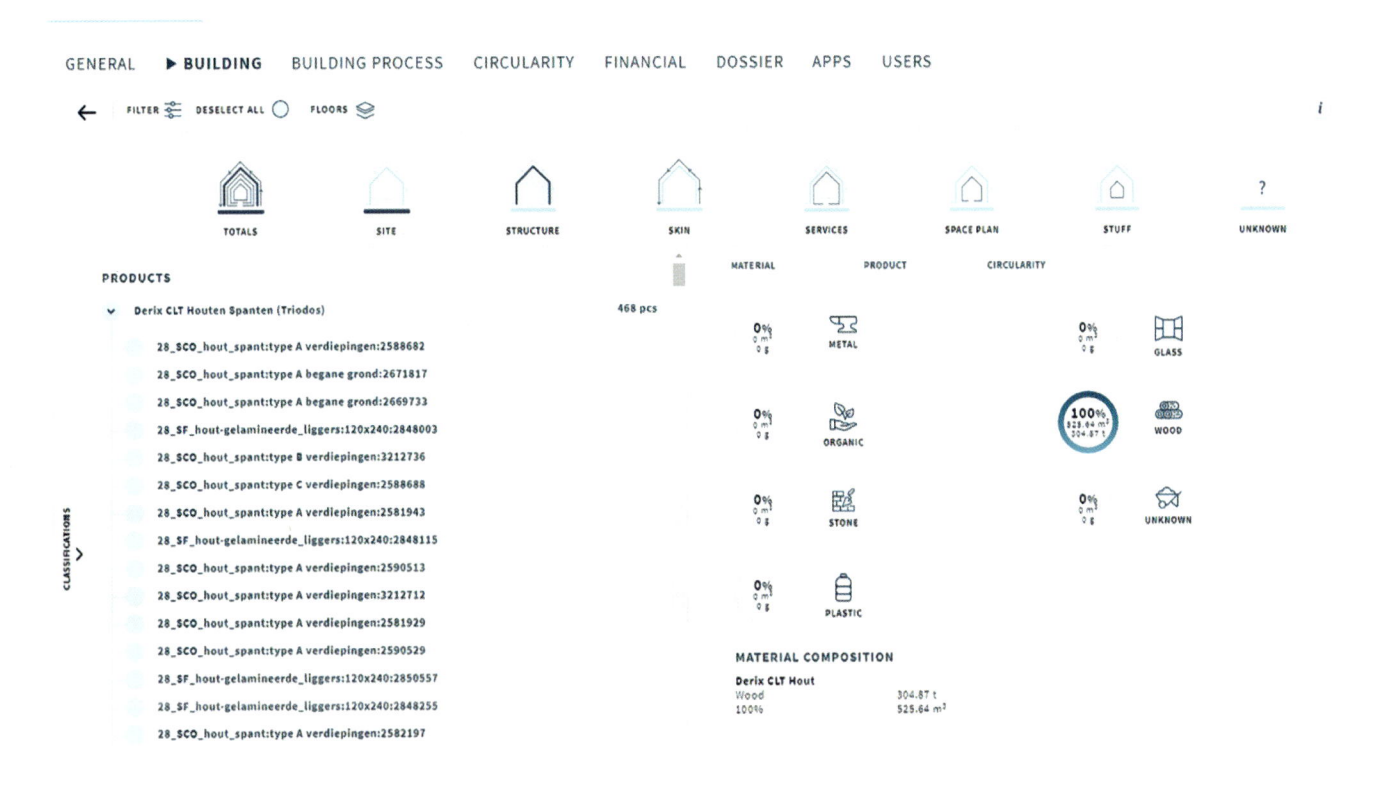

GENERAL ▶ BUILDING BUILDING PROCESS CIRCULARITY FINANCIAL DOSSIER APPS USERS

← FILTER DESELECT ALL FLOORS

TOTALS SITE STRUCTURE SKIN SERVICES SPACE PLAN STUFF UNKNOWN

PRODUCTS 468 pcs

MATERIAL   PRODUCT   CIRCULARITY

- Derix CLT Houten Spanten (Triodos)
    - 28_SCO_hout_spant:type A verdiepingen:2588682
    - 28_SCO_hout_spant:type A begane grond:2671817
    - 28_SCO_hout_spant:type A begane grond:2669733
    - 28_SF_hout-gelamineerde_liggers:120x240:2848003
    - 28_SCO_hout_spant:type B verdiepingen:3212736
    - 28_SCO_hout_spant:type C verdiepingen:2588688
    - 28_SCO_hout_spant:type A verdiepingen:2581943
    - 28_SF_hout-gelamineerde_liggers:120x240:2848115
    - 28_SCO_hout_spant:type A verdiepingen:2590513
    - 28_SCO_hout_spant:type A verdiepingen:3212712
    - 28_SCO_hout_spant:type A verdiepingen:2581929
    - 28_SCO_hout_spant:type A verdiepingen:2590529
    - 28_SF_hout-gelamineerde_liggers:120x240:2850557
    - 28_SF_hout-gelamineerde_liggers:120x240:2848255
    - 28_SCO_hout_spant:type A verdiepingen:2582197

0% METAL   0% GLASS
0% ORGANIC   100% 525.64 m³ 304.87 t WOOD
0% STONE   0% UNKNOWN
0% PLASTIC

MATERIAL COMPOSITION

Derix CLT Hout
Wood   304.87 t
100%   525.64 m³

183

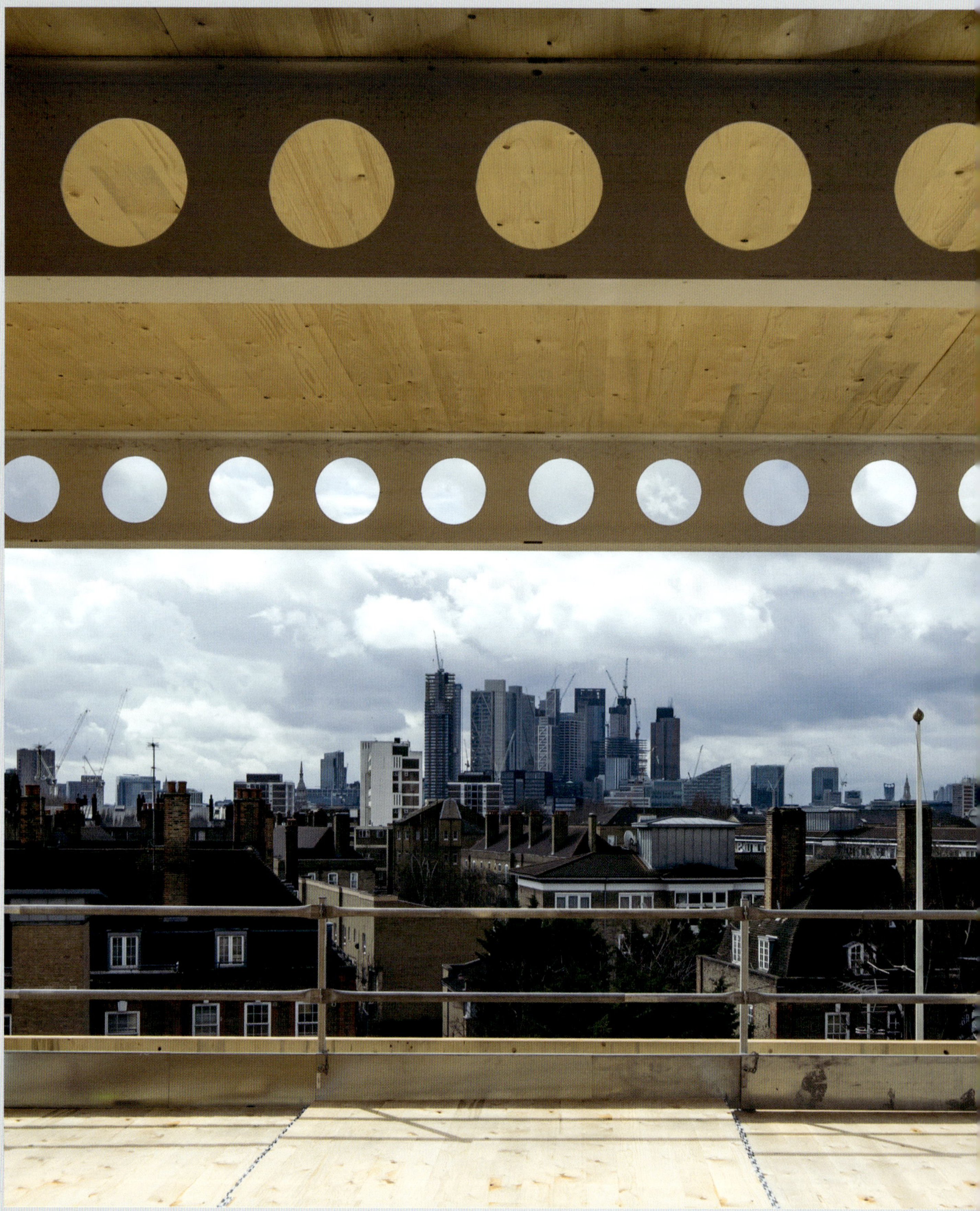

CASE STUDY
6 ORSMAN ROAD, LONDON, UK

CROSS LAMINATED TIMBER

FIG 21.0 (chapter opener)

This simple hybrid form of CLT slabs running above a steel frame optimizes the material's use to create flexible, characterful volumes.

Project name:	6 Orsman Road
Location (including county):	Hackney, London, UK
Sector/type:	Commercial/Office building
Year completed:	Base build: 2019, fit-out: 2020
Area of building (GIA):	4,678m²
Volume of CLT used (m³):	830m³
Approximate total construction cost (million):	Base build: £9.0
Total height of building:	20m
Client(s):	Base build: Boultbee Brooks Real Estate Fit-out: Storey/British Land
Architect:	Waugh Thistleton Architects
Main contractor:	Base build: RFM Construction Management Fit out: Parkeray
QS:	Base build: RFM Construction Management Fit-out: Alinea Consulting
Structural engineers:	GDC Partnership
Timber engineer:	Engenuiti
CLT contractor:	B&K Structures
CLT manufacturer:	Binderholz

Areas of interest: Significant commercial benefits to CLT use; 'First-in-class' commercial CLT/steel hybrid office development at scale; Continuation of progressive CLT use in London Borough of Hackney.

PROJECT SUMMARY

6 Orsman Road was the largest and most significant steel and CLT office building in the UK at the time of completion. This coincided with a significant upsurge in interest in CLT use in commercial projects and as such this was a highly significant development, influencing large numbers of professional visitors as well as contractors, investors and decision makers even before completion.

Waugh Thistleton Architects have done a huge amount to promote CLT and mass timber adoption, designing many of the buildings that raised global awareness of the London Borough of Hackney in this respect. This building is a continuation of themes developed on previous projects but in response to clear practical, commercial and site-specific challenges.

FIG 21.1

3D isometric of structure, indicating upstand beams to balconies on RHS (south elevation).

FIG 21.2

South facade during construction with projecting balconies and CLT upstand beams.

FIG 21.3

Overclad CLT elements provide solar shading and amenity space along the street elevation.

CASE STUDY **6 ORSMAN ROAD, LONDON, UK**

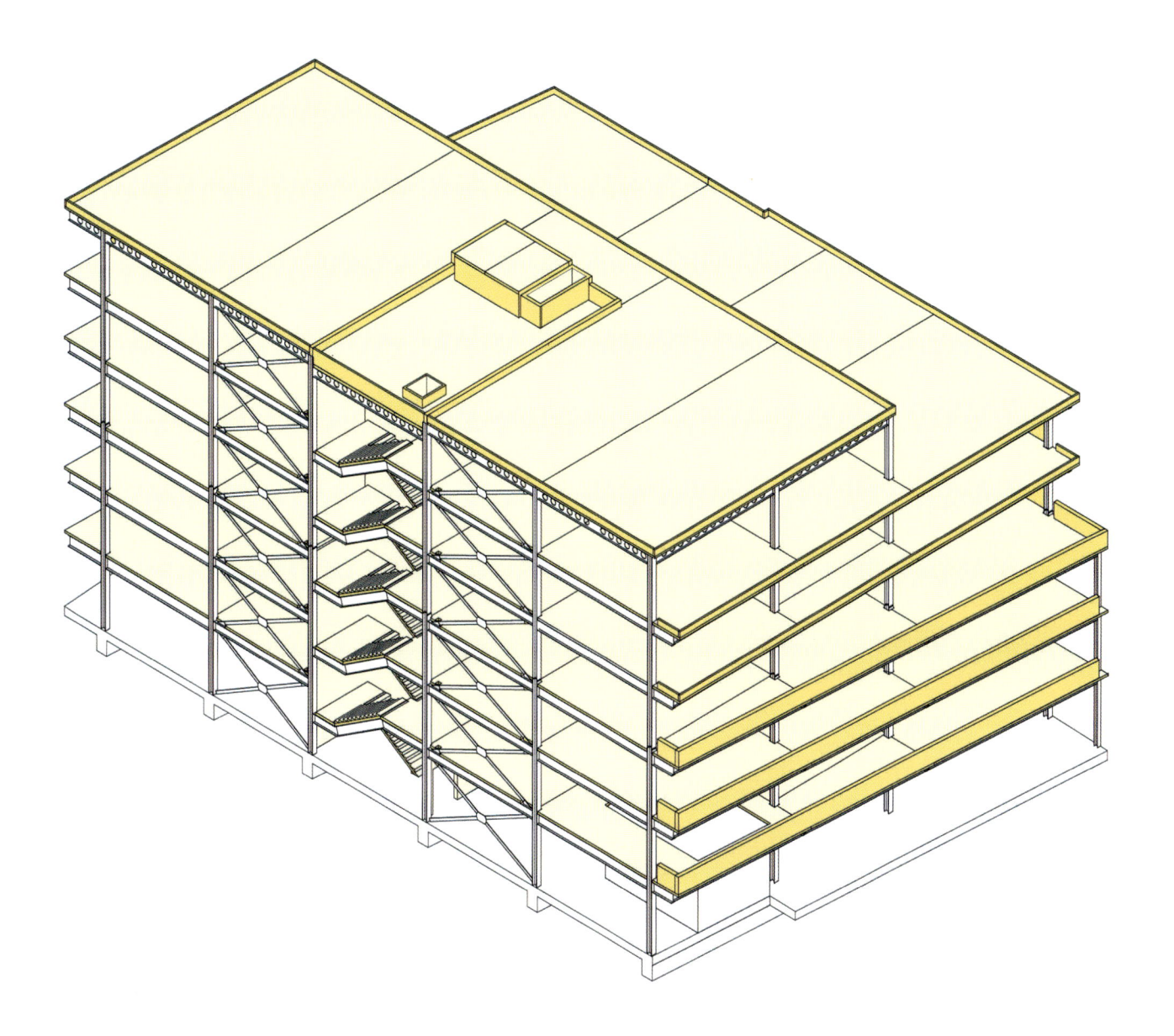

187

CROSS LAMINATED TIMBER

FIG 21.4

Clearly expressed hybrid structure: the expression of timber soffits and steel frame has been maintained with glazed facades (since constructed) overlooking the canal to the north with views towards the City of London to the south.

FIG 21.5

Section through upper office floor south facade showing fibre cement rainscreen over mineral wool insulation with 5-ply CLT panel beyond and raised floor with 3-ply CLT over cellular steel beams forming floors within.

FEASIBILITY AND DESIGN STAGE OUTCOMES

Like many other sites in London, development potential and therefore value was compromised by limited ground-bearing capacity, being within the Crossrail 2 safeguarding zone. The consequences of limited loading potential and restrictions on pile depths meant that in order to maximise the number of floors and lettable accommodation, a lightweight superstructure was essential in order to make such a project feasible.

CLT slabs with a steel structural frame and cellular beams were adopted as a hybrid means of minimising storey heights without compromising servicing potential at soffit level (as would have been the case with a glulam downstand beam alternative). The exposed aesthetic, integrating and expressing architecture and engineering, servicing and materials use is also typically highly desirable and successful in this part of London – the building is being fitted out as a vibrant, flexible workplace.

Cellular beams below a continuous CLT slab offer the advantages of economy, the ease and familiarity of steel fabrication and assembly, allowing the greatest floor to soffit heights and ensuring flexibility in service distribution while creating a flat floor for follow-on activities.[1] This project also achieved long span bays with limited numbers of internal columns. Like other case study projects, where flat roofs and terraces are formed by CLT panels, the architects advocate a shallow fall (1:60) to ensure that risks of standing water and increases in moisture content are minimised before subsequent roof coverings are installed, sealing panels with any moisture present.

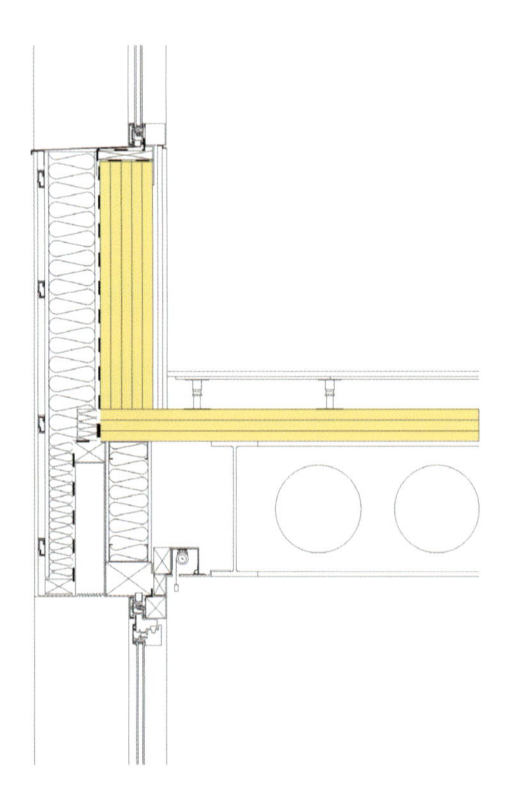

CASE STUDY **6 ORSMAN ROAD, LONDON, UK**

FIG 21.6

Fit-out proposals avoid the unnecessary use of additional materials to lower levels.

FIG 21.7

CLT and steel define the character of this future-facing workspace in fashionable Hackney.

Beyond locking away 460 tonnes of carbon dioxide equivalent in the CLT used (LCA modules A1–A3, i.e. cradle-to-gate), the architects were also keen to explore issues around resource and materials efficiency, reducing waste and the use of unnecessary materials and finishes wherever possible. The form of construction also ensures flexibility in use whilst allowing the potential for reuse of elements at end of first life, and by considering demountable fixings maximising the value in doing so by enabling elements to be reused rather than down-cycled.

CONSTRUCTION STAGE LESSONS LEARNT

The superstructure site team consisted of a four-man installation crew, a non-working site supervisor and a dedicated site manager. A single tower crane (within a CLT core formed by triple height lift shaft panels) achieved around 15 lifts a day, and the building was erected at an average of a floor every 1.5 weeks, ahead of programme at times.

Managing rainwater during subsequent construction proved to be a challenge. This helped inform the architects' policy of outlining potential rainwater and moisture management strategies in tender documentation, ensuring that this critical issue is highlighted specifically so it can be considered, priced and ultimately managed effectively throughout the build. A similar approach was suggested for a construction stage fire strategy, to be issued pre-tender for similar reasons.

Following panel installation, the building's potential occupancy was increased, resulting in the need to add a second staircase. This was relatively easily achieved by cutting out a bay of panels from each floor (the structure not requiring any further adaptation) that were manoeuvred through the building and ultimately utilised for furniture as part of the subsequent fit-out works.

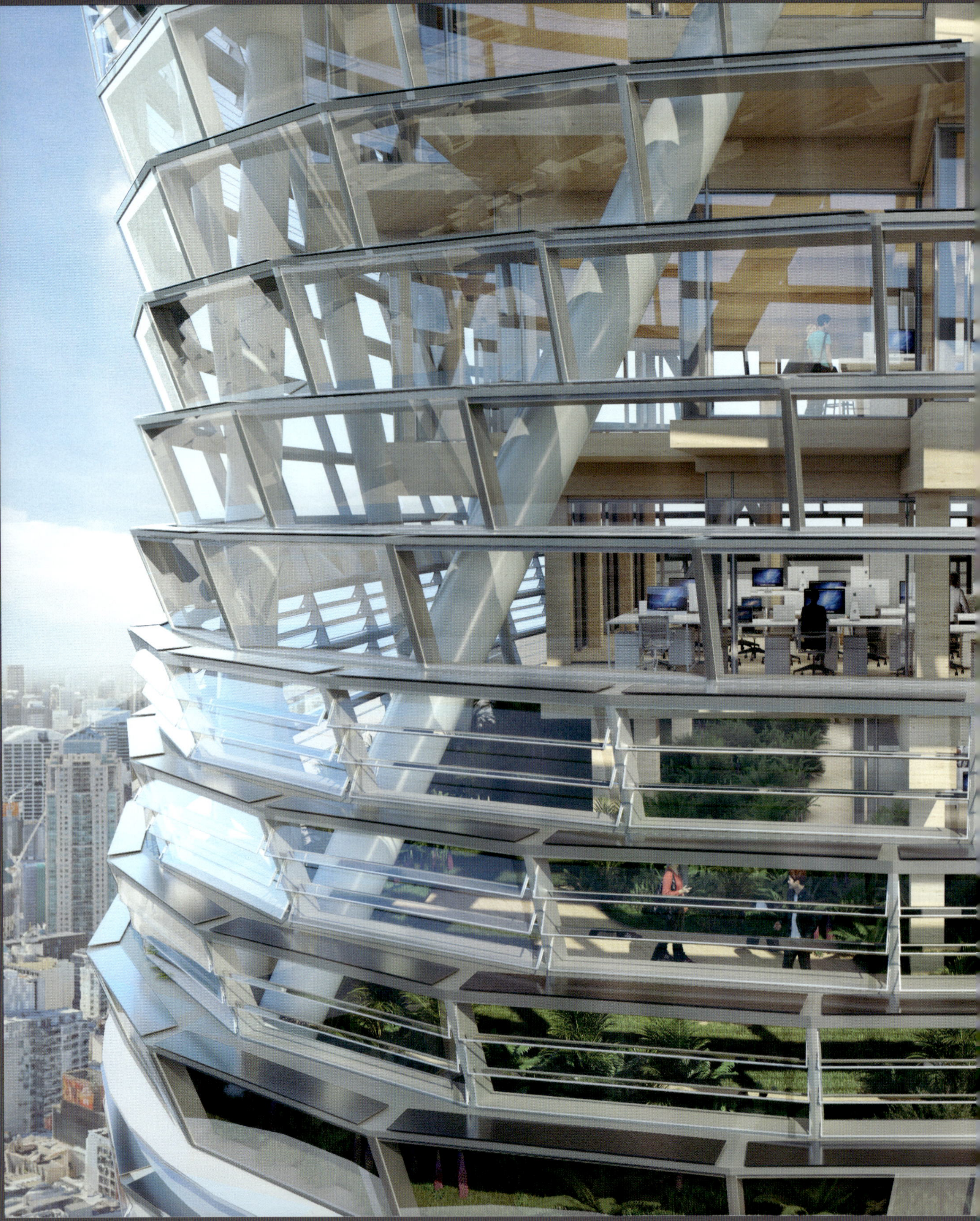

CONCLUSION: THE WAY AHEAD

CLT is an increasingly accessible gateway material that will lead teams to greater use of digital design, smarter manufacturing and more off-site fabrication. There are a number of risks that must be considered but it has many practical, commercial, social and environmental advantages and a wealth of existing information and diverse precedents are available to support project teams. Each of us should be considering better ways of building and there is a new generation of designers, constructors and developers not blinded by established ways of working or the fear of the new. Emerging patterns from recent years seem likely to continue as the market, supply and use of the material matures and this chapter considers likely future developments, in terms of the material and associated products and then by use.

CROSS LAMINATED TIMBER

FIG 22.0 (chapter opener)

Concept design for a record breaking 180m tall hybrid tower in Sydney for tech firm Atlassian, comprising CLT and mass timber elements with a steel exoskeleton to target a 50% reduction in embodied carbon impacts (proposed 2020 by SHoP Architects, USA, and BVN, Australia).

MATERIALS AND PRODUCTS

As demand for plant-based buildings increases globally, attention will be focused towards material supply issues and improved forest management to better consider impacts.

The CLT acronym has been interpreted as 'Contains a Lot of Timber'. Although the raw material does grow on trees, panels can be a little flabby. Like all other materials, elements likely contain more material than is necessary structurally for each application and further production and manufacturing advances will help address this as resources are optimised further. There will always be a trade-off between optimising elements and infinite variations in size and format and more carbon is stored the more timber is used. Technology assisted forestry operations (so-called Forestry 4.0) will introduce more data into the material supply process and in the factory, scanners might detect, gauge and track individual elements through the manufacturing process; there is potential for further refining panel composition accordingly, increasing efficiencies and minimising waste.

Future projects will likely exploit the further use of kits-of-parts such as ribbed products, with CLT slabs integrated with glulam beams or forming box panel sections. Both offer greater potential than is currently realised as well as further challenges... for example, box sections might accommodate service distribution or mass elements (potentially as 'dry' separable ballast) and whereas ribbed elements might offer even lighter slabs which may be better for foundations or constrained sites, they will provide a greater surface area for flame spread or charring and pose challenges regarding vibration and acoustics. Such issues are hardly insurmountable but offer opportunities for innovation and smart solutions from creative designers.

Beyond the wider adoption of fire-resisting adhesive in Europe to mitigate risks around potential delamination, much research is being undertaken into bonding elements, from adhesives sourced from biomass products to timber connections on a cellular level.

Dimensional standardisation may not be driven by standards in the near future but manufacturers will choose to differentiate products by other means, adding value to panels by incorporating applied finishes or additional materials such as insulation, acoustic surfaces or secondary elements to reduce site work further. Using better digital design and manufacturing interfaces, panels might be etched or printed: better labelling of elements may encourage future reuse or mark the setting out of elements to be surface mounted by follow-on trades.

Accessory and component manufacturers will respond to the growing market and diversity of forms of use with new products. A greater range of off-the-shelf components, typically connection elements either between panels, through floors or with other elements where interface issues can pose challenges on site such as concrete slab connections. More easily identifiable and therefore readily demountable methods of connection will further aid reuse and add, or help retain, future value. There is also the potential for the wider use of timber connection elements, certainly at smaller scale, typically exploiting moisture differentials and subsequent equalisation in machined homogeneous timber connectors, eliminating the need to pepper panels with steel screws that otherwise may be difficult to trace in a panel or remove once placed.

APPLICATION AND USE

As the construction transition evolves, new applications will no doubt emerge. They will be championed and refined by those with an appetite for doing things better as they further explore the material's potential, on its own or in combination. No one material is suitable for all uses but greater choice and diversity in the mix of considerations is a good thing and pragmatic hybrid forms will enable better use of all materials, utilised depending upon fitness for purpose and in doing so allowing greater economy, design flexibility and the potential to delight when expressed. Much research underway involves diverse combination forms to improve performance including composites of polymers, carbon fibre and cementitious materials.

There are very clear opportunities to better use the material as a planar form, exploiting CLT panels' unique structural and visual characteristics rather than as a substitute for other materials and in time, to better reflect local traditions and important cultural aspects around the use of timber.

CLT panels will continue to be used at greater scale, not just as superstructure elements but increasingly as components or decorative elements placed within or integrated with other elements, including existing

FIG 22.1

Timber panels sculpted and routed to create a contextual historic map of the environs beyond, Daramu House, Sydney by Tzannes (2019).

structures, particularly as links between digital design and manufacturing are explored.

Residential use, including ever taller CLT buildings (where appropriate), will remain an important market. If the UK is serious about addressing low carbon construction, we will have to use timber at heights above six storeys and demonstrate safe ways to use the material for the public, professions and importantly those managing risk in use and insuring such buildings.

The wholesale reform of UK building safety legislation currently underway offers a particular opportunity to ensure that the necessary regulatory framework is truly fit-for-the-future.

An ongoing issue will be carbon accounting, reporting and the resultant influence over how society perceives different buildings. It will be fascinating to see how buildings built with biomass perform as cultural icons, homes, workplaces and assets compared to older, alternative forms of construction, whether there are fiscal incentives introduced to encourage such an approach and beyond all this, how the value of CLT elements themselves can be maximised at end of first use.

As this book has been compiled, plans for various 'cities for the future' have been announced with Alphabet's Toronto Waterfront proposals featuring mass timber and CLT use front-and-centre and Toyota's Woven City in Shizuoka, Japan claiming to be developing the world's first 'urban incubator', to be built from timber using traditional joinery techniques and robotic production methods. Whether these schemes are realised or not, such corporations and future-facing strategists seem to agree that smarter future buildings will be made of timber with significant CLT HQ buildings underway for corporates such as Google in London, Microsoft in Mountain View and Walmart in Arkansas.

IN CONCLUSION

To address the myriad challenges we face, future material choices will involve greater scrutiny than ever before. Step-change solutions are required for our cities, homes and workplaces and we cannot be satisfied with making things a bit better. We need to reconsider our approach to big ticket items: reconsidering what we put in the ground, how we build above it, increasing density, efficiency and flexibility, significantly improving the quality and speed of construction, better addressing safety and wellbeing, slashing embodied carbon and energy impacts all while meeting the expectations of future users of buildings and in doing so, ensuring the future value of our built assets.

As a society and within our industry, we are at a point of inflection. How we build must evolve and CLT offers exciting alternative opportunities to address the challenges we face. It may well be the ultimate modern method of construction and while it is rooted in the 20th century, the 21st century is an age of enlightenment for timber architecture, engineering and construction with CLT at its heart.

APPENDIX: CLT PANEL CHARACTERISTICS

Key statistics (for European Spruce panels[1]):

Moisture content:	12% +/- 2%
Density:	480kg/m³
Example panel weight:	3,100kg (for medium thickness, 160mm thick, 3.0m x 13.5m)
Adhesive content	c. 0.6% by volume [2]
Shrinkage rates:	Dimensionally stable under normal conditions
Longitudinal:	0.010% per % change in moisture
Perpendicular:	0.025% per % change in moisture
Thermal conductivity/ resistance (λ):	0.12W/mK (to EN ISO 10456)
Specific thermal capacity (c)	1600J/kgK
Thermal mass:	Marginal
Airtightness	Airtight if three layers minimum
Fire performance (to EN 13501):	D, s2 d0 [3]
Char rate (calculable):	0.67-0.74mm/min (depending on application)
Acoustic absorption coefficient:	Low. 125 Hz: 0.2-0.15; 500 Hz: 0.05-0.1; 2000 Hz: 0.1 [4]
Service class (as Eurocode 5[5]):	Suitable for Class 1 use (dry internal area/no increased humidity) and Class 2 (not directly exposed to moisture but higher humidity)
Certification, supply chain:	Timber typically PEFC and/or FSC (or local equivalent)
Certification, production:	Europe: CE marked when certified to *'BS EN 16351: 2015 Timber structures. Cross laminated timber. Requirements'*.

APPENDIX: CLT PANEL SURFACE QUALITY

CLT panel surface quality: Surface quality appearance with respect to product characteristics[1]

Characteristics	Visible Quality (VI)	Industrial Visible Quality (IVI)	Non-Visible Quality (NVI)
Bonding	occasional open joints up to max. 1mm width permitted	occasional open joints up to max. 2mm width permitted	occasional open joints up to max. 3mm width permitted
Blue stains	not permitted	slight discolouration permitted	permitted
Discolourations (brown stains, etc)	not permitted	not permitted	permitted
Resin pockets	no clusters of pockets, max. 5 x 50mm	max. 10 x 90mm	permitted
Bark ingrowths	occasional occurrences permitted	occasional occurrences permitted	permitted
Dry cracks	occasional surface cracks permitted	permitted	permitted
Core - pith	occasional, up to 40cm long permitted	permitted	permitted
Insect damage	not permitted	not permitted	occasional small holes up to 2mm permitted
Knots - sound	permitted	permitted	permitted
Knots - black	ø max. 1.5cm	ø max. 3cm	permitted
Knots - hole	ø max. 1cm	ø max. 2cm	permitted
Rough edges	not permitted	not permitted	max. 2 x 50cm
Surface	100% sanded	100% sanded	max. 10% of surface rough
Quality of surface finish	occasional small faults permitted	occasional faults permitted	occasional faults permitted
Quality of narrow side bonding and face ends	occasional small faults permitted	occasional faults permitted	occasional faults permitted
Chamfer on L panels	yes	yes	no
Rework edge of cut with sandpaper	yes	no	no
Machining - chainsaw	not permitted	permitted	permitted
Lamella width	less than 130mm	max. 230mm	max. 230mm
Moisture content	max. 11%	max. 15%	max. 15%
Timber species mixture	not permitted	not permitted	with spruce, silver fir and pine permitted
Aesthetic surface finish with bolts, pegs, etc	permitted	permitted	permitted

NOTES

Introduction

1. Such was the impact and sentiment towards this building, much information is available online about its use, form and associated legends three decades after it was demolished.
2. During a presentation at the BAU 2017 exhibition in Munich.

Chapter 1

1. Moisture content (MC) is expressed as a percentage of dry weight. Green timber may have a moisture content of 100% or more (holding more than its dry weight of water) and for spruce, the drying process may reduce volume by 5% tangentially and 2–3% radially.
2. Drying timber can account for 90% of total manufacturing energy but is typically done artificially, rather than air drying, for expediency and consistency. See M. Ramage et al., 'The wood from the trees: The use of timber in construction', *Renewable and Sustainable Energy Reviews*, vol 68, part 1, 2017, p 345.
3. Other forms of adhesives are in use but not all perform in the same manner, particularly in terms of fire performance, curing behaviour or off-gassing. Do discuss adhesives with manufacturers before specifying, in particular with regard to fire performance. PUR adhesive may soften under fire situations, enabling delamination and modified PUR (with fire retardant properties) may not be available in all territories.
4. If an additional, non-structural, decorative layer is added (e.g. oak or beech, as offered by some manufacturers) a balancing layer on the opposite face may be required to ensure stability.
5. By way of example, a medium thickness, 160mm, panel 3.0m wide x 13.5m long may weigh around 3,100kg.
6. Any modifications on site need to be reviewed beforehand with the timber engineer and/or panel supplier – changes may be possible but care needs to be taken to maintain panel integrity.
7. British Standards Institution, *BS EN 13017-1:2001 Solid wood panels – classification by surface appearance. Softwood*, British Standards Institution, London, <https://shop.bsigroup.com/ProductDetail/?pid=000000000030025910>, 2001, (accessed 21 August 2020).

Chapter 2

1. For a solid introduction to key issues refer to Patrick Fleming, Simon Smith & Michael Ramage, 'Measuring-up in timber: A critical perspective on mid- and high-rise timber building design', *Architectural Research Quarterly*, vol 18, issue 1, 2014, pp 20–30 as well as two books by Michael Green: *The Case for Tall Wood Buildings*, Vancouver, Michael Green Architecture, 2018 and *Tall Wood Buildings – Design Construction and Performance*, Basel, Birkhäuser, 2017.
2. HoHo Wien architect Rüdiger Lainer, from 'Tall stories 188: HoHoWien, Vienna', *The Urbanist* podcast, Monocle 24 from *Monocle*, first published 6 January 2020, https://monocle.com/radio/shows/the-urbanist/tall-stories-188/ (accessed 24 August 2020).

Chapter 3

1. For a broad-ranging overview of recent history and application including many important cultural aspects relevant to CLT, refer to Oliver Lowenstein, 'Unstructured 9 extra: Where is CLT going? And where has it come from?', *Fourth Door Review*, 2019, http://www.fourthdoor.co.uk/unstructured/unstructured_09/extra/where_is_clt_going_intro.php, (accessed 24 August 2020).
2. For an excellent summary of 100 UK precedents from the first 15 years of adoption, see Waugh Thistleton Architects, *100 Projects UK CLT*, Softwood Lumber Board & Forestry Innovation Investment, London, 2018.
3. UK and Irish manufacturing has been considered repeatedly but is not currently undertaken beyond small-scale experimental presses. This is due primarily to the quality of domestic timber; CLT feedstock is typically C24 structural graded material whereas commonly available UK and Irish grown softwood is typically class C16, from Sitka spruce.
4. Mineral Product Association, 'How is the CLT Industry Responding to the Combustibles Ban?', *The Concrete Centre, News*, 2019, www.concretecentre.com/News/2019/How-is-the-CLT-Industry-Responding-to-the-Combusti.aspx, (accessed 24 August 2020).
5. Research based on 30 sectors in 20 countries from 1995 to 2014 found that while manufacturing productivity nearly doubled, construction productivity barely increased (p 22), McKinsey Global Institute, 'Reinventing construction through a productivity revolution', McKinsey & Company Insights, 27 February 2017, www.mckinsey.com/industries/capital-projects-and-infrastructure/our-insights/reinventing-construction-through-a-productivity-revolution, (accessed 24 August 2020).

NOTES

6. Mark Farmer, author of *The Farmer Review of the UK Construction Labour Model*, from Stephen Cousins, 'Is cross-laminated timber coming of age?', *Construction Manager*, 2 March 2018, www.constructionmanagermagazine.com/insight/clt-coming-age/, (accessed 24 August 2020).
7. According to an extensive survey by housing charity Shelter (2017), 51% of new homeowners in England were found to have had major problems with their properties: Shelter, 'Rigged housebuilding system means eight in ten families cannot afford new home, says Shelter', *Shelter England, press releases*, 2 March 2017, https://england.shelter.org.uk/media/press_releases/articles/rigged_housebuilding_system_means_eight_in_ten_families_cannot_afford_new_home,_says_shelter, (accessed 24 August 2020).
8. ICAEW Thought Leadership, 'Audit insights on construction: bidding for lasting value, delivering for success', 2019, *The Institute of Chartered Accountants in England and Wales*, https://www.icaew.com/technical/audit-and-assurance/audit-insights/audit-insights-industry-sectors/audit-insights-construction, (accessed 24 August 2020).
9. 32% of landfill waste comes from building and demolishing buildings and over 10% of products and material sent to site are sent to landfill unused: Daniel Brooks-Dowsett, '10 ways to make construction greener', 23 October 2018, *Construction Manager*, http://www.constructionmanagermagazine.com/news/10-ways-make-construction-projects-greener/, (accessed 24 August 2020).
10. For more, refer to Circle Economy, 'The Circularity Gap Report 2019', *Circle Economy – Publications & reports*, 2019, www.circle-economy.com/insights/the-circularity-gap-report-2019, (accessed 24 August 2020).
11. UKGBC, 'Climate Change', *UK Green Building Council*, 2019, www.ukgbc.org/climate-change/, (accessed 24 August 2020).
12. Concrete alone represents around 8% of global greenhouse gas emissions: J. Olivier, G. Janssens-Maenhout, M. Muntean and J. Peters, 'Trends in global CO_2 emissions: 2016 report', The Hague: PBL Netherlands Environmental Assessment Agency, 2016, https://edgar.jrc.ec.europa.eu/news_docs/jrc-2016-trends-in-global-co2-emissions-2016-report-103425.pdf, (accessed 13 September 2019).
13. For a broad-ranging overview of the issues around the benefits of timber use, see M. Ramage et al., 'The wood from the trees: The use of timber in construction', *Renewable and Sustainable Energy Reviews*, vol 68, part 1, 2017, pp 333–59, https://www.sciencedirect.com/science/article/pii/S1364032116306050, (accessed 24 August 2020).

Chapter 4

1. Examples in this section are all AHMM projects due to the fact that the sensitive nature of schemes at feasibility stage makes access to projects by others difficult.

Chapter 5

1. *Wabi-sabi* (侘寂) is an aesthetic view based upon on the acceptance of variation and imperfection, finding beauty in asymmetry, roughness and valuing the inherent variety of natural textures and processes.
2. For example, refer to British Standards Institute, 'BS EN 13017-1:2001 Solid wood panels. Classification by surface appearance', BSI, London, 2001, for UK/European products.
3. It is important to note that higher-grade panels are typically finished to one face only, so engage suppliers early regarding special requirements.
4. The lack of consistency in terms and acronyms is not made easier by the fact that definitions may be varied due to differences in translation.
5. British Standards Institute, 'BS EN 13017-1:2001 Solid wood panels. Classification by surface appearance', BSI, London, 2001, Table 1.
6. Uwe Müller et al., 'Yellowing and IR-changes of spruce wood as result of UV-irradiation', *Journal of Photochemistry and Photobiology B: Biology*, vol 69, issue 2, pp 97–105, <https://www.sciencedirect.com/science/article/pii/S1011134402004128?via%3Dihub>, 2003, (accessed 23 April 2019).
7. By Australian architect Jonathan Evans in relation to Tzannes' International House in Sydney, from a presentation at Forum Holzbau International, 24th International Wood Construction Conference (IHF), Garmisch, Germany, 5-7 December 2018.
8. At present a number of manufacturers are building new lines or extending existing lines to also include additional capacity for adding materials (such as insulation or lining boards) or applying finishes.
9. Products and effects will vary – these samples were prepared using an Osmo wax/oil product.
10. Such details may only need to be considered once before being incorporated into visualisation routines or model material libraries.

Chapter 6

1. From Ann Bentley, 'Procuring for Value', Construction Leadership Council, July 2018, http://www.constructionleadershipcouncil.co.uk/wp-content/uploads/2018/07/RLB-Procuring-for-Value-18-July-.pdf, (accessed 26 August 2020).
2. Mark Farmer, 'The Farmer Review of the UK Construction Labour Mode: Modernise or Die', Construction Leadership Council, 2016, https://www.constructionleadershipcouncil.co.uk/wp-content/uploads/2016/10/Farmer-Review.pdf, (accessed 26 August 2020).
3. The guide devoted to CLT is due for publication in early 2021. Refer also to TRADA, *Procuring Engineered Timber Buildings: A client's guide*, BM TRADA, High Wycombe, 2019.
4. From Ann Bentley, 'Procuring for Value', Construction Leadership Council, July 2018, http://www.constructionleadershipcouncil.

co.uk/wp-content/uploads/2018/07/RLB-Procuring-for-Value-18-July-.pdf, (accessed 26 August 2020).

Chapter 7

1. For a comprehensive summary, see Scott Milestone and Paul Kremer, 'Encouraging Councils and Governments Around the World to Adopt Timber-First Policies: A Systematic Literature Review', *Mass Timber Construction Journal*, vol 1, 2019, pp 8–14 <http://www.masstimberconstructionjournal.com/>, (accessed 27 August 2020).
2. For a comprehensive review of Hackney's policy, the cultural and local context and key resultant buildings, refer to: Oliver Lowenstein, 'Hackney, improbable world centre of urban CLT', *Unstructured 9 extra*, *Fourth Door Review*, Lewes, Sussex, UK, 2019, <http://www.fourthdoor.co.uk/unstructured/unstructured_09/extra/hackney_clt.php>, (accessed 27 August 2020).
3. *Wood First Act 2009* (Victoria, British Columbia, Canada), 29 October 2009, https://www.bclaws.ca/civix/document/id/consol31/consol31/00_09018_01, (accessed 27 August 2020).
4. Aggregates (including sand) being the most commonly mined materials in the world.

Chapter 8

1. Few teams have experience working with CLT. At the time of writing, there are fewer than 1,000 CLT buildings in the UK, of around 27.6 million existing homes (households) and a further 2 million commercial buildings.
2. With thanks to Eckersley O'Callaghan Engineers for these project insights.
3. Project insights provided by Foster Structures.
4. A number of products claim to be able to encapsulate CLT use for balconies or even bridges but there is no way of knowing if any waterproofing for these products is compromised.
5. Beyond these practical values (from the National Structural Concrete Specification), tighter concrete tolerances may be available at a premium for fit.

Chapter 9

1. For a broad ranging overview of application for a range of engineered timber products, including CLT, refer to J. Norman, *Structural Timber Elements: A Pre-Scheme Guide*. High Wycombe, Exova BM TRADA, 2016.
2. British Standards Institution, *BS EN 1995-1-1:2004+A2:2014, Eurocode 5: Design of timber structures. General. Common rules and rules for buildings*, British Standards Institution, London, <https://shop.bsigroup.com/ProductDetail?pid=000000000030286965>, 2014, (accessed 1 September 2020).
3. Manufacturers' literature and web resources are of great value to designers when considering appearance, interfaces, accessories and coordination e.g. Rothoblaas (www.rothoblaas.com).

Chapter 11

1. As HSE, 'Construction statistics in Great Britain, 2018', Health and Safety Executive, 30 October 2019, www.hse.gov.uk/statistics/industry/construction.pdf, (accessed 3 September 2020).
2. Last available figures from http://www.hse.gov.uk/construction/healthrisks/cancer-and-construction/silica-dust.htm, (accessed 9 September 2019).
3. Figures for 2016/17 as HSE, 'Cancer and construction: Silica', Health and Safety Executive, http://www.hse.gov.uk/statistics/tables/index.htm#cost-to-britain, (accessed 9 September 2019).
4. As HSE 'Construction statistics in Great Britain, 2018', Health and Safety Executive, 30 October 2019, www.hse.gov.uk/statistics/industry/construction.pdf, (accessed 3 September 2020).
5. Fidelis Emuze and John Smallwood (eds.), *Valuing People in Construction*, Routledge, London, 2018, p 8.
6. Resulting in traditionally high rates of mesotheliomas attributed to carpentry work as HSE, 'Wood dust', Health and Safety Executive, no date, http://www.hse.gov.uk/woodworking/wooddust.htm, (accessed 10 September 2019).
7. Eurban, 'Highpoint Terrace – Elephant & Castle, London', Eurban, no date, www.eurban.co.uk/industry-insights/highpoint-terrace-elephant-castle-london, (accessed 10 September 2019).
8. Including Eurocode 5 (pending for 2022), and International Building Code revisions (due 2021) which address CLT specifically for the first time. England/Wales Building Regulations are being significantly reworked as the general fire safety regulatory framework is reconsidered.
9. Refer to the following paper for a more in-depth discussion of design approaches: J. Schmid, N. Werther, M. Klippel and A. Frangi, 'Structural Fire Design – Statement on the Design of Cross-Laminated Timber (CLT)', *Civil Engineering Research Journal*, vol. 7. no. 5, DOI: 10.19080/CERJ.2019.07.555721.
10. The prominent author of a report used to argue for limitations to timber use rebutted such interpretation, stating instead that there are opportunities to develop better ways of increasing fire safety for the continued use of engineered timber at all scales: Barbara Lane, 'Let's make timber safer', *Building Magazine*, 25 February 2019, https://www.building.co.uk/communities/lets-make-timber-safer/5098040.article, (accessed 10 September 2019).
11. For CLT such risks may be reduced: what is designed is typically what arrives on site – tolerances are extremely tight, minimising gaps and fire paths around apertures for example resulting in reduced opportunities for related errors on site and fire break-out in use.
12. Reaction to fire performance is defined in Europe by tests according to European Standard EN 13501-1.
13. Fire resistance testing in Europe is undertaken as defined by 'EN 1363-1 Fire resistance tests – Part 1: General Requirements'.
14. STA, '16 steps to fire safety: Promoting good practice on construction sites', Structural Timber Association, 2017, https://www.thenbs.com/

PublicationIndex/documents/details?Pub=STAS&DocID=319774, (accessed 10 September 2019).

Chapter 12

1. Such products may require liberal localised washing with water that should be well planned to avoid further marking to adjacent areas.
2. Contractors for several case studies featured noted this issue – wind impacts can be underestimated and not all sites were in obviously windy locations.

Chapter 14

1. British Standards Institute, 'BS EN 15978:2011. Sustainability of construction works. Assessment of environmental performance of buildings. Calculation method', BSI, London, 2011.
2. Ditto when considerations may be published or further scrutinised at a project or corporate level.
3. Such as Bionova's One Click software (that informs BREEAM calculations).
4. Floor slabs for taller and larger multi-storey buildings may contain a disproportionate volume of total material used. Recent work considering a mid-rise, large floor plate in new commercial building suggests that floor slabs may account for 85–95% of all superstructure material.
5. A. Moncaster et al., 'Why method matters: Temporal, spatial and physical variations in LCA and their impact on choice of structural system', *Energy in Buildings*, vol. 173, 2018, pp 389–98.
6. For example: a team considering floor plates to a new commercial building may adopt a reinforced concrete flat slab on a 9 x 9m structural grid as a baseline for comparison.
7. A simple example of initial comparisons in visual form is included within Chapter 15.
8. See Georgina Davis, 'Complex Nature: Implications for Forests with the Rise of Mass Timber Construction', Blog post, Terrapin Bright Green, 28 February 2018, https://www.terrapinbrightgreen.com/blog/2018/02/mtc/, 2018 (accessed 4 September 2020).
9. This is also a contributing reason why no UK timber is used for CLT production – few facilities exist to dry the timber sufficiently for CLT manufacturing.
10. Typically between 0.6%–1% by volume.
11. For potential scope of general efficiency improvements, refer to British Standards Institution, 'BS 8895-1:2013, Designing for material efficiency in building projects. Code of practice for strategic definition and preparation and brief', BSI, 2013 (plus subsequent parts addressing later work stages).
12. Austrian plants to UK (1431km) = 26.90 $kgCO_2e/m^3$, Stora Enso EPD data.
13. Further information is available from the excellent project website, 'Building Carbon12', Kaiser+Path & USDA Forest Service, https://buildingcarbon12.com/, 2019 (accessed 4 September 2020).
14. Ed Suttie, *Trada Briefing: The Role of Timber in Healthy Buildings*, BM TRADA, High Wycombe, UK, 2019. This thorough document contains many references exploring a host of health and wellbeing issues and includes specification considerations.
15. William Browning et al., '14 Patterns of Biophilic Design, Improving health and wellbeing in the built environment', Terrapin Bright Green – Reports, 2014, https://www.terrapinbrightgreen.com/reports/14-patterns/, (accessed 4 September 2020).
16. Suttie, *Trada Briefing: The Role of Timber in Healthy Buildings*.
17. In a recent residential development, CLT concealed above a soffit and boarded to provide the required period of fire protection was conspicuously marked to highlight to future occupants, if they removed the ceiling/protection, that slabs should not be left exposed.
18. Wood Recyclers Association (WRA), 'Exports of waste wood products decrease as UK markets grow', WRA, 25 June 2018, https://woodrecyclers.org/exports-waste-wood-products-decrease-uk-markets-grow/, (accessed 4 September 2020). A quarter of the total was not accounted for and presumably this was disposed of in landfill – such figures will shift as more material is recycled and less burnt.

Chapter 15

1. German-speaking nations typically have greater experience of the materials use, while many residential CLT milestones have been achieved by British projects and Australian timber hybrid workplaces are the leading exemplars, at the time of writing at least.
2. A recent client, for a very large scheme, pointed out that anticipated contract preliminaries, before other overheads and finance costs, were expected to be in excess of £100,000 a week, suggesting that any opportunity to reduce construction programme may have very significant value.
3. Christine Murray, 'Capital is at risk and people in finance do not like that', The Developer Podcast, released 27 January 2020, https://www.thedeveloper.live/podcasts/podcasts/capital-is-at-risk-and-people-in-finance-do-not-like-that, (accessed 4 September 2020).

Case Study: Haus Gables

1. By Susan Jones of Atelier Jones, described in her subsequent book *Mass Timber: Design and Research*, Oro Editions, Novato, 2018.

Case Study: Triodos Bank Office Building

1. Madaster, 'Vision, Mission, Aims', no date, https://www.madaster.com/en/about-us/vision-mission-aims (accessed 5 September 2020).

Case Study: 6 Orsman Road

1. Current project experience (in London) indicates that such a steel frame/CLT slab hybrid arrangement is by some margin, the most cost-effective means of introducing significant volumes of CLT into commercial buildings (the floor

slabs of commercial buildings typically represent well in excess of 75% of superstructure material use).

Appendix: CLT panel characteristics

1. Binderholz (manufacturer) data, unless noted otherwise, from 'Binderholz CLT BBS', *Binderholz.com*, no date, https://www.binderholz.com/en/basic-products/binderholz-clt-bbs/, (accessed 18 April 2019).
2. KLH (manufacturer) stated figure, from KLH UK, 'Frequently Asked Questions', web document, 2011, http://www.klhuk.com/media/11553/frequently%20asked%20questions_05042011_1.pdf, (accessed 23 April 2019).
3. Defined as: 'Medium contribution to fire: combustible if untreated, medium intensity smoke emissions, no flaming droplets', British Standards Institute (BSI), *BS EN 13501-1:2018 Fire classification of construction products and building elements*, BSI, 2019, https://shop.bsigroup.com/ProductDetail?pid=000000000030348263, (accessed 6 September 2020).
4. Randall McMullan, *Environmental Science in Building* (7th Ed), Palgrave Macmillan, Basingstoke, 2012, p 235.
5. Eurocode 5 is British Standards Institute (BSI), *BS EN 1995-1-1:2004+A1:2008 UK National Annex to Eurocode 5: Design of timber structures. General. Common rules and rules for buildings*, British Standards Institute, 2006, https://shop.bsigroup.com/ProductDetail?pid=000000000030259050, (accessed 21 April 2019).

Appendix: CLT panel surface quality

1. Stora Enso data/table reformatted, from: Stora Enso, 'CLT Surface Qualities', *www.clt.info*, 2015, www.clt.info/wp-content/uploads/2015/10/CLT-Surface-qualities-EN.pdf, (accessed 30 April 2019).

INDEX

Page numbers in **bold** indicate figures and tables.

6 Orsman Road, London, UK 22, **184**, 185-189, **187-189**
25 King Street, Brisbane, Australia 125
26BS, Edinburgh, UK 67, **67**

acoustics 78, 90, 99
Acton Ostry Architects 21
adhesives 11, **11**, 105-106, 123, 192
aging and yellowing 46-47, **48**
Allford Hall Monaghan Morris (AHMM) 39, 44, 160, 174
American Hardwood Export Council **139**
appearance *see* visual aspects
applications 17-26
    building elements 23, **24**, **26**
    cellular forms 18
    crosswall forms 18
    future developments 193-194
    hybrid forms 18-22, 193
    modular 22, **22**
    planar forms 22, **23**, 193
    pure forms 18
    sculptural forms 23, **25**
    shell forms 22, **23**
    tall buildings 27, **27**, 31, 122, 194
Architype 57, 77
Arup Associates 20, **139**
Australian market 124-126
Australian National University, Canberra, Australia 127, **127**, 144
Axis Architects 103

Bates Smart Architects 125
Believe in Better Building, London, UK 20, **20**
BIM 38-39, 71, 74, 138
biophilic design 134
Blackwood, Wiltshire, UK 115, **115**
Bonner, Jennifer 150
Brock Commons Tallwood House, Vancouver, Canada 21, **21**, 105, **123**, 144
buckling 88
building control 74-76, 104

Burwood House 72, **72**
BVN Architects 126, 127, 168

Cambridge Mosque, UK 47, **47**, 75, **75**, 79, **79**
carbon accounting 131, 146, 194
carbon emissions 33, 130
carbon footprint 130-131
carbon storage 33, 131
Carbon12, Portland, Oregon, USA 133, **133**
Catja de Haas Architects 72
cellular forms 18
charring 84, 98, 105, **106**
client issues 36, 141-147
CNC cutting 13-15, **13**, **14**
coatings *see* surface finishes and coatings
collaborative working 73-74
concept design 70
concrete
    hybrid forms 20-21
    reinforced concrete (RC) frames 94, **142**
connections
    to existing structures 97-98
    see also interfaces; panel connections and joints
construction industry issues 32
construction stage 111-118
    cranes 58, 117, **117**
    environmental impacts **130**, 132-133
    fire safety 108
    follow-on trades 58, 66, 103, 114-116
    health and safety 58, 61, 102-103, 118, **119**
    metrics 118
    moisture control 113-114, **113**, **114**, 122-123
    programme benefits 37, 57-58, 61, 144
    surface protection 117
    tolerances 118
    typical site 118, **119**
    working environment 61, 66, 103, 114-115
cost 36, 53, 55-56, 59
cracks and splits 48, **48**, **49**
cranes 58, 117, **117**
crosswall forms 18

Daramu House, Sydney, Australia 125, **193**
de Rijke Marsh Morgan Architects 20
decarbonisation 33
decision-making process 36, 142-144, **142**
deconstruction 137
deflection and stiffness 87-88, **87**, **89**
delamination 50, 105-106, 114, 192
demand and supply issues 30, 80
design and procurement 69-80
    accessories 79
    acoustics 78
    appropriate design 71-73
    BIM 71, 74
    collaborative working 73-74
    concept design 70
    concerns and risks 74-76
    fire safety 106-108
    interfaces 78, 97-98, 123
    manufacturer's technical data 80, **81**, 107
    moisture control 76-78
    panel connections and joints 49-50, 78
    procurement integration 54-55, **55**, 61
    roles and responsibilities 74
    spatial coordination 71
    supply issues 80
    technical design 71
    tolerances 78, 123
    see also engineering aspects; refurbishment
Design for Manufacture and Assembly (DfMA) principles 30, 37
Dietrich Untertrifaller Architekten **25**
disposal 137, **137**
disproportionate collapse 99
Drayton Green Church, London, UK 54, **54**
durability *see* moisture control
Dyson Institute of Engineering and Technology, Wiltshire, UK 45, **45**, 112, **112**

edge protection 103, 118, **119**
Elephant House, Zurich Zoo, Switzerland **23**

embodied carbon 33, 65, 124, 126, **130**, 145, 146
emotional response to timber 147
end of life stage **130**, 137, **137**
Energy Performance Certificates (EPCs) 59
energy use 33, 59, 132, 136, 137, 145
engineering aspects 83-91
    acoustics 90, 99
    buckling checks 88
    building layout 84-85
    disproportionate collapse 99
    element design 87-88, **87**, 89
    floor spans 85, **85**
    movement behaviour 86-87, **86**, **87**
    off-site production 85
    panel connections 91, **91**
    properties of timber 8-9, 83-84
    stiffness and deflection 87-88, **87**, 89
    structural openings 85-86, **85**
    structural watchpoints 84
    see also refurbishment
environmental impacts
    carbon accounting 131, 146, 194
    carbon footprint 130-131
    carbon storage 33, 131
    client issues 36, 145-146
    construction stage **130**, 132-133
    embodied carbon 33, 65, 124, 126, **130**, 145, 146
    end of life stage **130**, 137, **137**
    energy use 33, 59, 132, 136, 137, 145
    environmental value 58-59, 61
    green status and ratings 58-59, 124
    materials use 33
    product stage **130**, 132
    reuse, recycling and recovery **130**, 137, **137**, 138
    'timber-first' policies 64
    tree planting 33
    use stage **130**, 133-134, 136
Environmental Product Declarations (EPDs) 131
Ermine Street Church Academy, Huntingdon, UK **172**, 173-177, **175-177**
Eurban 103
extensions *see* refurbishment

facades
    fixed 87
    stacked 87
feasibility stage 35-40, **39**, **40**, 41
Fenner Hall Student Residences, Canberra, Australia 105, **166**, 167-171, **168**, **169**, **171**
finishes *see* surface finishes and coatings
fire safety 104-109

adhesives 11, 105-106, 123, 192
charring 84, 98, 105, **106**
CLT behaviour in fires 105-107, **106**, 123
connections 98, 107
construction stage issues 108
design stage issues 106-108
fire resistance 107-108
fire-retardant coatings 49, 107
handover/in-use issues 108-109
manufacturer's data **81**, 107
refurbishment projects 98
regulations and standards 31, 104-105
First Tech Federal Credit Union, Hillsboro, Oregon, USA 116, **116**
fitzpatrick + partners **26**, 73, 135
The Fitzroy, Falmouth, Cornwall, UK **158**, 159-165, **161-164**
floor spans 85, **85**
follow-on trades 58, 66, 103, 114-116
forestry 7-8, **8**, 65, 192
Forte, Sydney, Australia 124

Gamma method 88
global warming potential (GWP) 130
glue-laminated timber (glulam) 18, 19, **40**, 142
greenhouse gas emissions 33, 130
Greenwich Peninsula Design District, London, UK 136, **136**

Hacker Architects 116
Hale Brown Architects 95
Hands Building, Mansfield College, Oxford, UK 70, **70**
Harris Academy Sutton, Surrey, UK 57, **57**, 77
Haus Gables, Atlanta, Georgia, USA **148**, 149-156, **151-157**
health and safety
    construction sites 58, 61, 102-103, 118, **119**
    see also fire safety
The Hedberg, Hobart, Tasmania, Australia **24**
Heyne Tillett Steel Engineers 95, 96, 97, **99**
Highpoint Terrace, Southwark, London, UK 103, **103**
HoHo Wien, Austria 27, **27**, 31
honeycomb forms 18
housing crises 32
hybrid forms 18-22, 193

insurance companies 74-76, 107-108, 123, 144
interfaces 78, 97-98, 123
International House, Sydney, Australia 125, **125**

John Kinsley Architects 67
joints *see* panel connections and joints

Kaufmann, Hermann 4

labelling 15, **15**, 138
Lendlease **124**, 125, 168
life cycle issues 129-138, **130**
    carbon footprint 130-131
    construction stage **130**, 132-133
    end of life stage **130**, 137, **137**
    product stage **130**, 132
    refurbishment 135
    reuse, recycling and recovery **130**, 137, **137**, 138
    use stage **130**, 133-136
lift shafts 86-87
Liminal Studio **24**
lintel support **85**, 86
London Borough of Hackney, UK 64
Lower James Street, Piccadilly, London, UK 95, **95**

manufacturer's technical data 80, **81**, 107
manufacturing and processing 7-15, **10**, 85
    adhesives 11, **11**, 105-106, 123, 192
    CNC cutting 13-15, **13**, **14**
    drying timber 8-9, **9**, 132
    environmental impacts **130**, 132
    future developments 192-193
    labelling 15, **15**, 138
    layup 9-12, **10**, **11**
    pressing and curing 12, **12**
    quality assurance 15, **15**, 138
    raw materials 7-9, **8**, 132, 192
    transport 15, 132
Marie Reay Teaching Centre, Canberra, Australia 127, **127**
Marks Barfield Architects 47, 75, 79
Markus Schietsch Architekten **23**
masonry structures 94
Massachusetts Institute of Technology (MIT), USA 3, **3**
material passports 138
MEC Store, Vancouver, Canada **123**
melamine urea fode (MUF) 11
Messe Wels, Austria 3, **4**
Mica Architects 70
Michael Green Architects **122**
moisture content 8, 113, 114, 196
moisture control
    construction stage 113-114, **113**, **114**, 122-123
    design stage 76-78
    refurbishment projects 98

INDEX

use stage 134
weather exposure 50, **50**
Mole Architects 136
movement behaviour 86-87, **86**, **87**
Multiply pavilion **139**
Murray Grove, Hackney, London, UK 19, **19**, 64

North American market 122-123

Omicron campus building, Klaus, Austria **25**
Our Lady of Assumption Catholic School, North Strathfield, Australia 126, **126**

panel characteristics 12, 196
panel connections and joints 49-50, 78, 91, **91**, 107
panel edge sealants 76, 114
Piercy & Company 54
planar forms 22, **23**, 193
planning policies 63-64
platform construction 18
polyurethane (PUR) adhesive 11
pool Architekten 49
procurement 54-55, **55**, 61
  see also design and procurement
programme benefits 37, 57-58, 61, 144
punched openings **85**, 86

quality assurance 15, **15**, 138

RAU Architects 180
refurbishment 32, 93-99, **95**, **96**, **97**, 135
  acoustics 99
  advantages 94
  connections and interfaces 97-98
  disproportionate collapse 99
  existing structure types 94-95
  fire safety 98
  moisture control 98
  slab positions 98, **99**
  surveys 96
regulations and standards 31, 104-105, 122, 194
reinforced concrete (RC) frames 94, **142**
Republic Masterplan, Tower Hamlets, London, UK 96, **96**, 97, **97**, 99, **99**
reuse, recycling and recovery 130, 137, **137**, 138
RIBA Plan of Works 70-71
Rider Levett Bucknall (RLB) 56
risk managers 74-76, 144
Rogers Stirk Harbour and Partners 103

rolling shear forces **87**, 88
Rüdiger Lainer + Partner Architekten 27

safety see fire safety; health and safety
screws 91, **91**
sculptural forms 23, **25**
sealants, panel edge 76, 114
Seed House, Castlecrag, New South Wales, Australia **26**, 73, **73**, 135, **135**
Seymour-Smith Architects 115
shear forces **87**, 88
shell forms 22, **23**
Sky Health & Fitness Centre, London, UK 20
social issues 63-66
social value and wellbeing 60, **60**, 61, 66, 134, 147
sound insulation **81**, 90
spatial coordination 71
stacked facades 87
Stapferhaus exhibition hall, Lenzburg, Switzerland 49, **49**
steel elements 20-21, 22
steel frames 94, **142**
stiffness and deflection 87-88, **87**, 89
strategic brief 36
structural openings 85-86, **85**
Structural Timber Association 78, 108
Structurlam 133
Studio RHE 96, 97, **99**
supply and demand issues 30, 80
surface finishes and coatings 47-49, **48**, **49**, 56-57
  fire-retardant 49, 107
  water repellent 114
surface quality 45-46, **46**, 197
sustainability 36, 64, 145
  see also environmental impacts

tall buildings 27, **27**, 31, 122, 194
technical design 71
timber
  emotional response to 147
  glue-laminated (glulam) 18, 19, **40**, **142**
  properties of 8-9, 83-84
  raw materials 7-9, **8**, 132, 192
'timber-first' policies 63-64
Todaiji temple, Nara, Japan 2, **2**
tolerances 78, 118, 123
transport 15, 65, 132, 137
tree planting 33
Triodos Bank Office Building, Driebergen-Rijsenburg, Netherlands **178**, 179-182, **180-183**
two-way spanning slabs **85**, 86

Tzannes 125, **193**

ultraviolet (UV) light 47, 117
University of British Columbia, Vancouver, Canada 21, **21**
use stage **130**, 133-136
  benefits to occupants 60, **60**, 61, 66, 134, 147
  environmental impacts **130**, 133-134, 136
  fire safety 108-109
  moisture control 134

value 36-37, 53-61, 144
  construction site 58, 61
  cost 36, 53, 55-56, 59
  environmental 58-59, 61
  finish 56-57, 61
  health and safety impacts 58, 61
  procurement integration 54-55, **55**, 61
  programme benefits 37, 57-58, 61, 144
  social and wellbeing 60, **60**, 61, 66, 134, 147
  waste minimisation 56
  whole life 56, 59
Virtuoso apartments, British Columbia, Canada 123
visual aspects 43-50, **44**, **45**, **47**
  aging and yellowing 46-47, **48**
  cracks and splits 48, **48**, **49**
  effective viewing distance 46, **46**
  finishes and coatings 47-49, **48**, **49**, 56-57
  managing expectations 44, 50, **51**
  panel connections and joints 49-50
  renders and visualisations 50, **50**, **51**
  surface quality 45-46, **46**, 197
  weather exposure 50, **50**

warranty providers 74-76, 107-108, 144
waste minimisation 56
waste processing 137
water repellent coatings 114
waterproofing 76-78, 98
  see also moisture control
Waugh Thistleton Architects 19, 22, 64, **139**, 186
weather exposure 50, **50**
wellbeing 60, **60**, 61, 66, 134, 147
wetting 50, **50**
whole life value 56, 59
WilkinsonEyre Architects 45, 112
Wood Innovation and Design Centre, Prince George, British Columbia, Canada 122, **122**

IMAGE CREDITS

Figure number	Copyright owner
Endpapers	AHMM
Figure 0.0	Peter Landers
Figure 0.1	Nic Crawley
Figure 0.2	Center for Land Use Interpretation photo. Image reproduced by permission of The Center for Land Use Interpretation.
Figure 0.3	PAUAT / Luttenberger
Figure 1.0	Ledinek
Figure 1.1	Chris Harrod / Creative Commons Attribution 2.0: https://www.flickr.com/photos/9098437@N04/
Figure 1.2	AHMM
Figure 1.3	AHMM
Figure 1.4	Mühlböck Holztrocknungsanlagen GmbH
Figure 1.5	Ledinek
Figure 1.6	Ledinek
Figure 1.7	Ledinek
Figure 1.8	Ledinek
Figure 1.9	Ledinek
Figure 1.10	Ledinek
Figure 1.11	Ledinek
Figure 1.12	AHMM
Figure 1.13	Images reproduced by permission of Hans Hundegger AG
Figure 1.14	Images reproduced by permission of Hans Hundegger AG
Figure 1.15	Images reproduced by permission of Hans Hundegger AG
Figure 1.16	Images reproduced by permission of Hans Hundegger AG
Figure 1.17	AHMM
Figure 2.0	Rob Parrish
Figure 2.1	Waugh Thistleton Architects / Will Price
Figure 2.2	Waugh Thistleton Architects / Will Price
Figure 2.3	B&K Structures
Figure 2.4	www.naturallywood.com
Figure 2.5	www.naturallywood.com
Figure 2.6	Agnese Sanvito
Figure 2.7	Markus Schietsch Architekten / Jean-Luc Grossman
Figure 2.8	Liminal Studio
Figure 2.9	Dietrich	Untertrifaller / Bruno Klomfar
Figure 2.10	Fitzpatrick+Partners / John Gollings
Figure 2.11	cetus Baudevelopment / KiTO.photography
Figure 3.0	Rob Parrish
Figure 3.1	cetus.at / Thomas Lerch
Figure 4.0	AHMM

IMAGE CREDITS

Figure 4.1	AHMM / Hayes Davidson
Figure 4.2	AHMM
Figure 4.3	AHMM
Figure 5.0	Morley von Sternberg
Figure 5.1	Rob Parrish
Figure 5.2	Peter Landers
Figure 5.3	Piveteaubois
Figure 5.4	AHMM
Figure 5.5	Morley von Sternberg
Figure 5.6	AHMM
Figure 5.7	AHMM
Figure 5.8	AHMM
Figure 5.9	AHMM
Figure 5.10	AHMM
Figure 5.11	AHMM
Figure 5.12	Ralph Feiner / pool Architekten
Figure 5.13	AHMM
Figure 5.14	Uniform / Urban Splash
Figure 6.0	Jack Hobhouse / Architype
Figure 6.1	Simone Bossi / Piercy&Company
Figure 6.2	Simone Bossi / Piercy&Company
Figure 6.3	Construction Leadership Council
Figure 6.4	KLH UK
Figure 6.5	Construction Leadership Council
Figure 7.0	Mole Architects/ David Butler
Figure 7.1	John Kinsley Architects / John Reiach
Figure 7.2	John Kinsley Architects / John Reiach
Figure 8.0	Tzannes Associates / Ben Guthrie
Figure 8.1	Eckersley O'Callaghan Engineers
Figure 8.2	Catja de Haas Architects / Tom Rothery
Figure 8.3	Catja de Haas Architects / Tom Rothery
Figure 8.4	Fitzpatrick+Partners / John Gollings
Figure 8.5	Fitzpatrick+Partners / John Gollings
Figure 8.6	Morley von Sternberg
Figure 8.7	KLH UK
Figure 8.8	KLH UK
Figure 8.9	Morley von Sternberg
Figure 8.10	Courtesy of Binderholz
Figure 9.0	Jack Hobhouse
Figure 9.1	AHMM / Ramboll
Figure 9.2	AHMM / Ramboll
Figure 9.3	AHMM / Ramboll
Figure 9.4	Ramboll
Figure 9.5	AHMM
Figure 9.6	AHMM
Figure 10.0	Heyne Tillett Steel
Figure 10.1	Heyne Tillett Steel
Figure 10.2	Galliford Try

Figure 10.3	Heyne Tillett Steel
Figure 10.4	Heyne Tillett Steel
Figure 10.5	Heyne Tillett Steel
Figure 11.0	Tzannes Associates / Ben Guthrie
Figure 11.1	Eurban
Figure 11.2	Mace
Figure 11.3	AHMM
Figure 12.0	Rob Parrish
Figure 12.1	Peter Landers
Figure 12.2	WilkinsonEyre
Figure 12.3	Eckersley O'Callaghan Engineers
Figure 12.4	Mole Architects
Figure 12.5	Neil Speakman / Maple Photo
Figure 12.6	Hacker / Jeremy Bittermann / JBSA
Figure 12.7	AHMM
Figure 12.8	Rob Parrish
Figure 13.0	Andrew Pogue
Figure 13.1	Courtesy of MGA	Michael Green Architecture
Figure 13.2	Nicholas Sills
Figure 13.3	www.naturallywood.com, Ralph Austin and Seagate Mass Timber
Figure 13.4	Rositch Hemphill Architects
Figure 13.5	2020 Google
Figure 13.6	Tzannes Associates / Ben Guthrie
Figure 13.7	Tzannes Associates / Ben Guthrie
Figure 13.8	Brett Boardman Photography
Figure 13.9	Joseph Moser / CWC
Figure 13.10	BVN
Figure 13.11	John Gollings
Figure 14.0	Hacker Architects / Jeremy Bittermann
Figure 14.1	Based upon graphic by Stora Enso
Figure 14.2	Andrew Pogue
Figure 14.3	Fitzpatrick+Partners / John Gollings
Figure 14.4	Mole Architects
Figure 14.5	AHMM
Figure 14.6	Dearbhla Mac Fadden Islington / Creative Commons Attribution 2.0: https://commons.m.wikimedia.org/wiki/File:Multiply-3.jpg
Figure 15.0.	B&K Structures
Figure 15.1	AHMM
Figure 16.0	Courtesy of MALL; Photograph by NAARO
Figure 16.1	Courtesy of MALL; Photograph by NAARO
Figure 16.2	Courtesy of MALL
Figure 16.3	Courtesy of MALL
Figure 16.4	Courtesy of MALL; Photograph by NAARO
Figure 16.5	Courtesy of MALL; Photograph by NAARO
Figure 16.6	Courtesy of MALL; Photograph by NAARO
Figure 16.7	Courtesy of MALL; Photograph by NAARO
Figure 16.8	Patrick Heagney

IMAGE CREDITS

Figure 17.0	AHMM
Figure 17.1	AHMM
Figure 17.2	AHMM
Figure 17.3	B&K Structures
Figure 17.4	AHMM
Figure 17.5	Hugh Hastings
Figure 17.6	Rob Parrish
Figure 18.0	CSR Inclose
Figure 18.1	Brett Boardman Photography
Figure 18.2	Lendlease
Figure 18.3	BVN
Figure 19.0	Rob Parrish
Figure 19.1	Rob Parrish
Figure 19.2a	Rob Parrish
Figure 19.2b	Rob Parrish
Figure 19.3	Rob Parrish
Figure 19.4	Rob Parrish
Figure 19.5	AHMM
Figure 20.0	Ossip van Duivenbode
Figure 20.1	J.P. van Eesteren B.V.
Figure 20.2	Ossip van Duivenbode
Figure 20.3	Carel van Hees
Figure 20.4	Carel van Hees
Figure 20.5	Carel van Hees
Figure 20.6	Carel van Hees
Figure 20.7	J.P. van Eesteren B.V.
Figure 21.0	Waugh Thistleton Architects / Tim Crocker
Figure 21.1	Waugh Thistleton Architects
Figure 21.2	Waugh Thistleton Architects / Tim Crocker
Figure 21.3	Waugh Thistleton Architects
Figure 21.4	Waugh Thistleton Architects / Tim Crocker
Figure 21.5	Waugh Thistleton Architects
Figure 21.6	Waugh Thistleton Architects / Picture Plane
Figure 21.7	Waugh Thistleton Architects / Picture Plane
Figure 22.0	Image courtesy of SHoP / BVN
Figure 22.1	Lendlease Australia